ADVANCING ONLINE TEACHING

The Excellent Teacher Series

Series Editor: Todd Zakrajsek

This series offers fresh approaches to teaching and learning by reviewing traditional methods in light of evidence-based strategies to promote practices that best facilitate student learning. Each volume of the series is written to provide early career faculty with specific strategies that can be quickly implemented, midcareer faculty with the opportunity to adapt and expand on what is currently used, and experienced faculty with new perspectives to augment thinking on foundational aspects of teaching and student learning.

Completed titles:

Dynamic Lecturing: Research-Based Strategies to Enhance Lecture Effectiveness
By Christine Harrington and Todd Zakrajsek

Designing a Motivational Syllabus: Creating a Learning Path for Student Engagement
By Christine Harrington and Melissa Thomas

Advancing Online Teaching: Creating Equity-Based Digital Learning Environments
By Kevin Kelly and Todd Zakrajsek

Forthcoming titles:

Understanding How We Learn: Applying Key Educational Psychology Concepts in the Classroom
By Todd Zakrajsek

Off to a Great Start: Proven Strategies for Faculty Members New to Higher Education
By Todd Zakrajsek and Marina Smitherman

ADVANCING ONLINE TEACHING

Creating Equity-Based Digital Learning Environments

Kevin Kelly and Todd Zakrajsek

Foreword by Michelle Pacansky-Brock

Series Preface by Todd Zakrajsek

Sty/us

STERLING, VIRGINIA

COPYRIGHT © 2021
BY STYLUS PUBLISHING, LLC.

Published by Stylus Publishing, LLC.
22883 Quicksilver Drive
Sterling, Virginia 20166-2019

Library of Congress Cataloging-in-Publication Data
The CIP data for this title have been applied for

13-digit ISBN: 978-1-62036-721-6 (cloth)
13-digit ISBN: 978-1-62036-722-3 (paperback)
13-digit ISBN: 978-1-62036-723-0 (library networkable e-edition) ·
13-digit ISBN: 978-1-62036-724-7 (consumer e-edition)

Printed in the United States of America

All first editions printed on acid-free paper
that meets the American National Standards Institute
Z39-48 Standard.

Bulk Purchases
Quantity discounts are available for use in workshops and for staff development.
Call 1-800-232-0223

First Edition, 2021

CONTENTS

PART THREE: MAKING ADJUSTMENTS TO YOUR ONLINE COURSE

FOREWORD

I STARTED TEACHING ONLINE AROUND 2003. I was working at a large community college that served a diverse student population. When I say *diverse*, I mean diverse in every sense of the word— culturally, racially, linguistically, physically, cognitively, affectively, and more. Access-oriented institutions, like public community colleges and universities, are no strangers to serving diverse students. But that doesn't mean that they effectively prepare faculty to support the differences that the "open door" brings.

At that time, online courses were growing at a very rapid pace, driven by the demand of students. And in the years that followed, that growth would only accelerate. Those of us who taught online at my institution did so by choice. My choice was driven by my interest for technology, my curiosity about what teaching online would be like, and my interest in having more time at home with my toddler and infant. That last interest was quickly realized to be a misstep, as teaching online would require more time than I had imagined.

I took a 6-week preparation course offered by my college, which introduced me to some basic principles like how and why to use discussion forums and set up my syllabus. But, when it came down to it, that course did not prepare me for the road ahead. I remember sitting in front of my blank course shell with fear and trepidation. I was very dedicated to doing my best for my students, but I had no real sense of what that should look like online in a learning management system. Oh, and I was teaching art appreciation, by the way. An image-centric curriculum. Yet, I had no access to digital image repositories in those days, and I didn't even know what it meant to "embed" media in my course.

I did my best. Looking back, the best thing I did was ask my students for feedback. When I saw themes emerge, I took that as a nudge to make a change or smile about doing something well. In the years that followed, I also committed myself to experimenting with the new, free technologies that began to surface—blogs, wikis, podcasts, and this new strange social video repository called YouTube. These were the web 2.0 years, when the internet transformed from a static content resource into a social environment that invited people around the world to connect through sharing ideas and media.

While I made a lot of changes in the early years of my online teaching, there are two that stand out most as I look back. First, I began to record my announcements in an audio file (at the time, made with Audacity and uploaded as an MP3 file), giving students the choice to read or listen. It was fascinating to see how that change influenced the quality of my student interactions. I remember recording an announcement while I had a stuffy nose from a cold. I had multiple students who emailed me just to say, "I hope you feel better soon!" My human presence in my course strengthened my connections with my students and motivated me. Establishing relationships with my students was important to me in my physical classroom, and I knew they were important to my students, too, particularly those with doubt about their academic abilities. That takeaway still plays a role in my faculty development and scholarly work today.

The second significant change came about through my experimentation with VoiceThread, an external tool that fosters asynchronous conversations in voice, video, or text around media. Bingo! I could now engage with my students in conversations around works of art, giving students the opportunity to "doodle" on an image using their mouse (stepping into the role of a teacher and showing their knowledge) and reflect about what they want to say and then record it (removing some of the social pressure of speaking in a classroom), and it granted me the opportunity to hear emotion (excitement, confusion, wonder) in their voices. This was a turning point for my online teaching and when I began to recognize that online courses *could be* better than face-to-face courses for some students.

I embraced the role of a learner and reflected deeply on what unfolded in my multimodal digital learning environment. I remember one student who shared with me that she had dyslexia. She chose to leave video comments in our VoiceThreads. I listened and watched those videos, feeling impressed with her efforts and the knowledge she demonstrated through her spoken words. Then I read her fragmented written responses in our discussion forums. The contrast was stunning. That student taught me more than any other professional development workshop or program about teaching and learning. While my peers around me scrutinized my use of VoiceThread because, at the time, it did not meet accessibility standards, I began to see that text-based learning was far from accessible for many students. That was my foray into equity-minded teaching and universal design for learning (UDL). I realized that when we design courses that provide students with one way to learn and one way to demonstrate their learning, it's like giving every person a size 8 shoe and expecting them to complete a marathon.

Six years after I began teaching online, I resigned from my full-time faculty position in quest of a career in supporting faculty to design and teach humanized, equitable online learning environments to support all students. That is when I met Kevin Kelly, the lead author of this book. Kelly and I worked at different universities and met one day while his team was touring my institution's online and hybrid support center, where I worked. Our shared interests in serving the diverse needs of students through online teaching and learning has kept us connected for more than 10 years.

Kevin Kelly and Todd Zakrajsek have developed a tremendous resource in the pages of this book. I wish I had this book when I started teaching online. Keep it near your workspace. Mark it up. Chew on the reflection and discussion questions. Revisit it frequently. It will be invaluable to you as you move forward with your efforts to develop equity-based digital learning environments. Just remember, improving your online course is a continuous, iterative process. It takes hard work and dedication to your students. Keep looking back at where you've been to recognize evidence of your efforts and look to your students' feedback and learning to relish in the impact. Enjoy the journey.

Michelle Pacansky-Brock
Online Educator, Faculty Developer, and Thought Leader

SERIES PREFACE

A FUNDAMENTAL CHALLENGE IN HIGHER education is rooted in an assumption that most of us faculty recognize all too well: If one has content knowledge, then the ability to effectively teach that information is a given. Essentially, the assumption purports that if you know it you should be able to teach it. This is believed by many, and it is simply not true.

Many of us realized the invalidity of the assumption when we faced our first classroom full of learners. For over 30 years I have watched this assumption that knowledge comes automatically with the ability to teach play out time and again, frequently in very subtle ways. For example, in acquiring an advanced disciplinary degree, content and research methods are carefully taught throughout the graduate program, while scant attention is given to the growing body of research findings that addresses how to teach any of that content to undergraduate students. How does it make sense that it takes more credentials to teach a first-grade class than it does an undergraduate college course?

The good news is that a shift toward recognizing the need to develop instructional skills and then continuing to work at being an effective teacher is occurring more and more frequently. Graduate teaching seminars, workshops on teaching strategies specifically designed for graduate students, and better designed graduate teaching assistantships are increasingly prevalent. Centers for teaching and learning continue to be founded and developed to support faculty of all ranks and across all disciplines. That said, there continues to be insufficient funding and resources to help faculty to establish, maintain, and refine strategies to enhance teaching effectiveness throughout their career as a faculty member.

The Excellent Teacher Series is designed to help address instructional resource issues for faculty members throughout higher education. The topics and content in this series are based on over 20 years of my experience assisting faculty members with enhancing student learning through better teaching strategies. Often, when working with faculty groups, I have asked the question, "What do you find most difficult or challenging in creating effective learning environments for your students?" I have now collected and read literally thousands of responses to this question from faculty throughout the United States and abroad. The faculty responses to this question, along with more than 3 decades of experience teaching in a variety of educational settings, have given me a solid understanding of what faculty struggle with, and serve as the foundation for this series. For each title, I select authors or coauthors who are experts in the topic area, who share my deep vision of what faculty are looking for, and who desire to help faculty members become better educators.

Our collective objective is to provide you with a strong introductory foundation to each topic in the series. We have written these books with three specific goals in mind: (a) to maintain accessible language for faculty in all disciplines and with varying levels of teaching experience, (b) to provide you with evidence-based suggestions and strategies, and (c) to provide sufficient background and prompts to give you the confidence to experiment in your own courses. For example, the first book in the series, *Dynamic Lecturing*, came at a time when lecturing began being attacked as ineffective. The book argues that lecturing itself is not a bad teaching strategy and that not all lecturing is ineffective. Research shows that lecturing can be extremely effective when used appropriately and also when paired with engaged learning strategies. *Dynamic Lecturing* provides the rationale and examples of both lectures and engaged learning strategies you can easily adopt. The second book in the series, *Designing a Motivational Syllabus*, provides evidence-based strategies to help you to think critically about what to include in your syllabus and how it can help students to be successful in your course. We argue in this book that the syllabus can be a foundation for the design of the course, a way to build and then share your enthusiasm for the content with your students and a mechanism to help students to see a learning path that builds their motivation and engagement. The third book in this series, *Advancing Online Teaching*, focuses on the general principles of universal design, design for equity, and human connections as foundational aspects of creating an effective online educational experience for undergraduate students. Operating from these three pillars, this book frames a multitude of evidence-based strategies, concepts, and tips that may be put to immediate use.

The titles in the series are intended to be interrelated, yet each is self-contained. None presupposes reading of prior volumes. What connects them is a common feel and voice. Jump into whichever topic addresses an area you feel has most relevance to your concerns as a teacher or that appeals to your curiosity as you explore effective ways to engage your students and facilitate their learning of your disciplinary concepts and applications. The concepts and strategies in this series are applicable across all disciplines, as well as to all types of courses, from undergraduate to graduate levels, at all types of institutions. The authors draw on workshops given with solid success at research extensive universities, comprehensive undergraduate institutions, private colleges, community and technical colleges, highly selective institutions, and those with open access. There are certainly many differences throughout higher education, but it turns out that there are also some striking similarities when it comes to providing good learning opportunities for our students. Those similarities serve as the foundational themes for these volumes.

The Excellent Teacher Series is authored by experienced faculty members who have framed issues and then drawn from the extensive body of research conducted by exceptional individuals from throughout higher education. Our hope is that this series offers fresh approaches to teaching and learning by reviewing traditional methods in light of evidence-based strategies to promote practices that best facilitate student learning. Each volume of the series is written to provide early career faculty with specific strategies that can be quickly implemented, midcareer faculty with the opportunity to adapt and expand on what is currently used, and experienced faculty with new perspectives to augment thinking on foundational aspects of teaching and student learning.

Teaching is important beyond imagination, anything but easy, and provides us glimpses of the best of humanity, which is why I suspect we all engage in this noblest and most challenging of professions. I do sincerely hope you find this series helpful and wish you well in your teaching endeavors.

Warm regards,
Todd Zakrajsek,
University of North Carolina at Chapel Hill

INTRODUCTION

*F*OR A VARIETY OF reasons, situations exist in which students who desire to learn cannot attend the traditional classroom-based courses in higher education. Correspondence courses have existed for hundreds of years and were quite popular even 30 years ago. Learners engaged in distance learning, in which an educational institution mailed instructional materials and exams for them to complete specific work and then mail it back. At a point early in his career, Todd Zakrajsek, one of the authors of this book, wrote a correspondence course for introductory statistics.

Correspondence courses gave way to distance education courses, in which faculty members would travel to a remote location and teach students in the vicinity of their homes. The efficiency of the internet brought the opportunity for faculty members to teach courses from their home institutions to students in distant and remote locations. All through this time and these various incarnations of education whereby the student does not set foot on a campus, there existed a feeling that it was best for students to come and learn on campus, but if that were not possible, distance learning was considered better than nothing. This "less than" but tolerable perspective is common throughout higher education and has led to many attempts to determine if online education is as good as face-to-face education. Unfortunately, the very core of this question is flawed, due to the many variables involved. The question of late, thanks to organizations such as Quality Matters, has shifted to when, and under what circumstances, distance education courses are valuable learning experiences. This shift from face-to-face courses as the gold standard to learning theory as the standard helped to "legitimize" online learning.

Over the past several years, online education has expanded at a phenomenal rate. Last year, more than one in three students in higher education enrolled in at least one online course per semester. Then in the spring of 2020, the unthinkable happened. Never in the history of U.S. higher education, with tenure, academic freedom, and the fierce independence of faculty members in every discipline, could any of us have imagined that essentially everyone teaching a college or university course would be told they must teach online. In many cases very little warning was given. We have talked to colleagues who were told on Friday that beginning the

1

following Monday all courses would be taught online. No academic council meetings to weigh the merits of such a move. No requests for volunteers or easing in across semesters or even years. No discussions of what support would be provided or what extra compensation would be allotted. The directives came swiftly and, by higher educational standards, unimaginably fast. For the safety of students and faculty alike, the country—and the world—began teaching all higher education courses in an online format and were expected to continue doing so indefinitely.

This pivot to online learning, which some have called *emergency remote teaching (and learning)*, became the new norm in higher education. Faculty developers and faculty members began using the term *emergency remote teaching* to differentiate between thoughtful online teaching and the pressing and immediate need to support course completion without anyone stepping foot into a classroom. At first you do what you must, and when a person must learn the difference between synchronous and asynchronous, one does not fret over details and perfection. You teach the best you can in the environment into which you have been hurled. Very soon, however, new concerns emerge. Ironically, they are the same concerns that have been present since remote learning began. How can we, as faculty members, create learning environments that are fair, equitable, and inviting for students? Further, can we do it in a way that gives each person enrolled in our programs a legitimate opportunity to achieve educational goals through a quality learning experience, and at the same time maintains a strong human connection with each and every student?

This book focuses on those very concepts in an effort to help guide faculty members in advancing where online learning exists today. Part One focuses on course design in creating a distance learning experience. In chapter 1.1 we build a new foundation for online teaching and learning based on inclusion, learning equity, and universal design for learning (UDL), all while keeping a focus on the importance of human connections in a type of learning where it is easy to forget there is a person on the other end of the internet connection. Chapters 1.2, 1.3, and 1.4 present in detail fundamental aspects of writing course outcomes, outlining course structure, and finding or creating course content. Chapters 1.5 and 1.6 give guidance in aligning course activities and assessment strategies with course outcomes and specific strategies to make course content accessible to a variety of learners.

Part Two of the book provides tips and strategies to guide learners from a distance. Chapter 2.1 reminds us all that those teaching online must be even more proactive than face-to-face faculty members and provides common policies that may be adapted for any syllabus. Chapters 2.2 and

2.3 focus on creating and maintaining an "instructor presence" that helps establish a learning community and also describe how to facilitate active learning in the online course. Chapter 2.4 completes this section of the book with suggestions for managing the workload for the intricacies of teaching online.

In Part Three we turn our attention to evidence-based ways to make adjustments to an online course. In order for adjustments to be completed in a meaningful way, they must be informed by data and feedback. Chapter 3.1 shares strategies for assessing and collecting feedback about teaching online, whereas chapter 3.2 guides efforts to assess learning online. This differentiation of assessing teaching versus learning is designed to demonstrate the subtleties of teaching and learning, along with practical ways to make changes.

The overall goal of the book is to provide practical tips, strategies, and concepts related to online teaching and learning that you can use right away. We do this while maintaining a strong grounding in UDL, design for learning equity, and a strong connection with our students. If we are going to advance online learning, we must identify ways to teach in an increasingly inclusive, equitable, and compassionate way.

PART ONE

DESIGNING A DISTANCE LEARNING EXPERIENCE

1.1

EQUITY, CONNECTIONS, AND INCLUSION

*T*EACHING PRESENTS MANY CHALLENGES, whether done face-to-face or in an online environment. Developing learning objectives is challenging, identifying appropriate content is challenging, and assessing student learning in meaningful ways is certainly challenging. In addition to everything else, as faculty members, we must be mindful of the psychological and social needs of the learners. It is challenging for the student to learn course content when stressed, afraid, lonely, or frustrated. All of this would be difficult enough if students were all identical, but vast interpersonal differences exist in any number of dimensions. As a result of this variability we experience in higher education, we face the additional challenge of helping students with a wide range of backgrounds, experiences, skills, and interests. These differences among our students demand that we consider a wide variety of educational experiences that map onto vastly different student characteristics. Some students do well in large courses, others thrive in small classes, some excel in face-to-face class sessions that are carefully structured multiple times per week, and yet others succeed in online environments that are primarily asynchronous. Students also differ in terms of how they desire to interact with the course, with one another, with the teacher, and with the material. With this much complexity within the learning environment, it is no wonder that our profession of teaching is one of the most difficult of professions, but also exceedingly important. John F. Kennedy once said, "Our progress as a nation can be no swifter than our progress in education" (Sorensen, 1965, p. 358).

Given the complexity and importance of teaching, higher education needs a variety of learning systems to meet the needs of diverse learners.

7

For some learners at a given point in time, a digital environment provides the best structure to maximize their educational advancement. For others, the structure of a classroom where they must meet twice a week will best meet their needs. This does not make online or any other form of digital learning less effective, less rigorous, or less anything else than any other kind of learning. For too long, many in higher education have considered online learning to be only a tolerable alternative to face-to-face classrooms. Namely, they agreed with the concept that online courses are the best one can do if it is not possible to get to campus. Online courses are often compared to face-to-face classes as if those brick-and-mortar classes are the gold standard. Just as any online course may be a good or bad learning experience, the same is certainly true of face-to-face courses. That said, teaching online is not the same as teaching face-to-face. There are unique challenges and opportunities for both. This book addresses the challenges and maximizes the opportunities for students who desire to take an online course by providing resources and suggestions for faculty members who desire to teach online. In recent times, events beyond our control, like hurricanes, wildfires, or a global pandemic, force instructors and students to undertake an emergency remote teaching and learning experience. This book will also attempt to address the needs of teachers who are new to teaching and guiding student learning in digital environments.

We designed this book to provide practical, evidence-based techniques for teachers at any level of experience. Whether you are developing an entire course or creating just one learning activity, you can use this book to design, implement, and evaluate your work. Moreover, we designed this book to address some of the most pressing and emerging learner needs, many of which expand beyond online courses to hybrid and even traditional face-to-face environments.

The increasing demand for online courses shows no signs of slowing. Nationally, the percentage of undergraduates taking distance education classes doubled in 8 years, from 16% in 2003–2004 to 32% in 2011–2012 (U.S. Department of Education, 2015). In fall 2014 alone, there were over 5.5 million students enrolled in online courses at U.S. colleges and universities (U.S. Department of Education, 2016). By 2017, that number increased to an estimated 6.5 million students taking at least one online course (Ginder et al., 2019).

This growth trend has increased competition among higher education institutions and distance education providers, requiring schools to focus on meeting students' and regional workforce needs and establishing higher standards of quality. The competition for students and growing demand for distance education have made it easier to identify large-scale issues related to teaching students in a digital environment. For example, studies show that students often enroll in online courses for flexibility and convenience (Allen & Seaman, 2011; Shay & Rees, 2004), but they often underestimate how much work it takes to succeed (Bawa, 2016). Historically, this and other factors have contributed to lower retention and pass rates for online students at national, state, and local levels. Large-scale studies at the state level found online completion and success rates to be lower than face-to-face courses, even for the same student taking courses in different formats (Jaggars, 2014; Xu & Jaggars, 2011). More recently, the California Community Colleges Chancellor's Office (CCCCO) reported that the difference in success rates between distance education and traditional courses decreased dramatically over an 11-year span (see Table 1.1.1). In 2016–2017, 70% of students passed their traditional classes, while 66% of students passed their distance classes (CCCCO, 2018). As an interesting aside, student success rates in distance classes improved by 13%, while student success rates in face-to-face classes did not change over those 11 years.

Although the difference in success rates in California has decreased overall, successful completion in online courses was not equally distributed. When broken down by age, the distance education success rate for students under 18 years old was 10% to 15% higher than any other age group (CCCCO, 2018). When broken down by ethnicity, significant achievement gaps in distance education success rates existed in 2016–2017 among different ethnic groups. Even though every ethnic group improved over that 11-year period, Black/African American and Hispanic/Latinx students still faced the largest gaps—staying roughly 20% and 12% behind the most successful ethnic groups, respectively. When reviewing success rates of students with disabilities, these learners made some of the largest improvements over the 11-year period, but still have room to grow. The

TABLE 1.1.1

Comparison of Success Rates in Traditional Face-to-Face and Distance Education Courses Across All California Community Colleges

	Success Rate for California Community College Students in Traditional Face-to-Face Classes (%)	Success Rate for California Community College Students in Distance Classes (%)	Difference in Success Rates (%)
2006–2007	70	53	17
2016–2017	70	66	4

data for other demographic distinctions, such as students from the first generation in their family to attend college, were not included in the report.

What do these large-scale statistics mean for those teaching online courses? First, the presence of online courses is now ubiquitous in higher education. In the spring of 2020, as a result of the COVID-19 pandemic, nearly every course in higher education around the world moved online to a remote experience due to campus closures. In addition, as with face-to-face courses, students are not universally successful in online environments. Therefore, as a group we regularly must consider how students define *success*, how well online course design sets up every student for success, and how well online students are supported as they progress through the course. With an increasing focus on retention, success, and bridging achievement gaps for online students, it is also increasingly important to avoid outdated and ineffective approaches to teaching online courses. Two examples of ineffective approaches to online teaching are creating a course that (a) does not provide students with any opportunities for human interaction—"set it and forget it"—and/or (b) provides only one path for students to achieve success—"one size fits all." To help online teachers improve their courses, several organizations across the United States have created rubrics that focus on improving the quality and accessibility of online course design (K. Kelly, 2019b). If your institution has not adopted a rubric, select one that you feel best meets your needs and use it as a guide as you work on each course.

So, what makes this book both unique and invaluable? Throughout this book, we will strive to take a humanistic perspective. Overall, the individual components of any course are certainly important, but to be an exceptional course, one must also take into consideration the interests and welfare of the students in that course and treat them like the valuable human beings they are. For this book, we will focus specifically on universal design for learning (UDL), design for learning equity, and keeping a focus on human connectedness. We will share extensive evidence-based tips and strategies for delivering an effective online course. What makes this book unique is that those resources build upon a combined foundation of universal design, learning equity, and human connectedness.

Think back on your own educational experiences. Who was your favorite teacher, and why? As you think about that special person who made a difference in your educational journey, note "why" you selected that person. We have done this at several workshops with faculty members and students, and the items listed almost universally pertained to human interaction and equity. Items recalled frequently include: "She believed in me." "He pushed me to accomplish things I didn't know I could do." "She treated us all with respect." At times, actions remembered fondly were as simple as, "She learned how to pronounce my name the right way." That is why this book is grounded in the principles of UDL, human connectedness, and design for learning equity. We will include many suggestions and examples based on evidence of good teaching, both online and face-to-face. But through it all, we will focus on the student in the digital learning environment not as an unknown entity who logs in from time to time, but rather a student as a human who cares very much about the learning experience and making connections with other humans who desire to learn.

UDL

As the name suggests, *universal design* means designing something that anyone and everyone can use. This is not about giving some individuals more chances or advantages over others, but rather designing in a way that differences no longer matter. It is helpful to you as a faculty member because you won't have to make major changes when someone with different needs comes along. It is helpful to students because it allows a wider variety of people to gain a formal education.

Universal design got its start in urban planning and industry. For example, all urban planners now ensure there are curb cuts where sidewalks meet crosswalks. This helps everyone without disadvantaging anyone. Before curb cuts were the standard, crossing the street was difficult for individuals using wheelchairs, walkers, baby strollers, and skateboards, and for those with mobility challenges. Curbs at intersections are dangerous for many people, and that means individuals need help navigating those curbs. Removing the curbs also keeps otherwise very mobile people from tripping and stumbling at an intersection. Curb cuts help everyone cross the street, even those in wheelchairs and with strollers. The same could be said of automatic doors at grocery stores. There was a time when there used to be large rubber mats over the glass doors, and those leaving the grocery store would bang the cart into the rubber mats to open the doors. With the installation of automatic doors, everyone benefitted, even those in wheelchairs and with baby strollers. Universal design helps everyone, even those with challenges.

UDL is a framework that makes learning experiences more inclusive by helping more students to be successful without disadvantaging other students. When the Center for Applied Special Technology first came up with the idea for UDL, they summed it up with a mantra—Teach every student (Rose & Meyer, 2002). Although some people associate UDL with accommodating students with disabilities, it really does mean *every* student—students with and without disabilities, with varying access to technology and connectivity, who are nonnative English speakers, with crazy schedules, and with different learning needs. The UDL approach is based on *equifinality*—that is, we're allowing people to select different paths to achieve the same goal. Online learning is an ideal environment to support creating those pathways and guiding students to reach their goals.

The UDL framework consists of three core principles, providing students with multiple means of (a) representation, or the "what" of learning; (b) engagement, or the "why" of learning; and (c) action and expression, or the "how" of learning. To build more inclusive learning opportunities for all students, to the greatest extent possible, instructors might consider (a) providing different ways to engage with and comprehend course content and resources, (b) using multiple strategies to engage learners and motivate participation, and (c) giving learners different ways to demonstrate what they have learned. Table 1.1.2 shows the categories from the UDL Guidelines matrix. The full version of the UDL Guidelines (CAST, 2018a) prescribes specific strategies for you to support your students, several of which we will explore more deeply and/or adapt for distance education in the following chapters. See udlguidelines.cast.org to download the matrix and to find more information.

To create more inclusive learning for your students, you do not have to apply UDL to everything you do and certainly not all at once. The goal is to start thinking about how you can support greater numbers of students. One way to work toward this goal while maintaining a reasonable workload is to build up a lesson or course over time. For example, each time you teach the class, introduce additional ways to present content, engage students, or assess learning. Throughout this book, we will give a broad-strokes overview of ways to apply UDL to your online teaching and provide specific strategies regarding how to provide these multiple pathways to online learners.

TABLE 1.1.2
UDL Categories

	Engagement	Representation	Action and Expression
Access	Recruiting Interest	Perception	Physical Action
Build	Sustaining Effort and Persistence	Language and Symbols	Expression and Communication
Internalize	Self-Regulation	Comprehension	Executive Functions

APPLYING UDL TO ONLINE TEACHING AND LEARNING

Following the UDL principles helps accommodate learners with different strengths and interests, including students with specific learning needs. The UDL principles align with the core aspects of online instruction—content presentation, student interaction or engagement, and assessment—that you would find in commonly used online course design rubrics (see Table 1.1.3) and online course design checklists, such as the UDL Quick-Start Guide adapted by Samuel Merritt University (2009). The full document is available at https://docs.google.com/document/d/1TzLR4uwfUAx ssK1Elx2ggD6yrS2we9SPpmHkTTybcyk. UDL principles also align well with being a more humanistically oriented faculty member dedicated to as much inclusivity in teaching as is possible.

When it comes to content presentation, you might provide options to students in any number of ways, including providing content in multiple formats, providing relevant background information, or scaffolding the process of making connections. Providing content in multiple formats means sharing or creating content through different types of media, such as text, graphics, audio, video, or multimedia. This does not mean you have to create six versions of every piece of course content; even just two options can make a difference. For example, a community college instructor conducted a small-scale study of her class and found that when given a choice between watching a recorded lecture as an enhanced podcast video or reading the text transcript, "40% chose to read the lecture, 15% listened to the lecture, 30% did both, and 15% toggled between reading and listening throughout the semester" (Pacansky-Brock, 2013b, para. 12). Providing relevant background information may be as simple as linking to related course concepts.

Another example is providing captioning on any instructional videos you produce. There are many options to do this quickly and easily. Providing captions helps those who are learning while babies are sleeping, studying in a library without headphones, or watching the videos in loud open areas; those who find a particular dialect difficult to understand; and those who are hard of hearing or deaf. Again, universal design helps everyone without disadvantaging anyone.

Providing options related to student interaction and engagement can be done through a variety of actions, such as relating course activities to learning objectives, choosing authentic and relevant activities, offering different levels of challenge, and giving students opportunities for self-assessment. Incorporating these engagement techniques can be done at different stages, such as when you draft the activity instructions, set up the

TABLE 1.1.3
Online Course Design Rubrics

Rubric	Rubric Link	Rubric Last Revised	Rubric License	Rubric Provider	Rubric Provider Type
Online Education Initiative – Course Design Rubric	https://onlinenetworkofeducators.org/wp-content/uploads/2020/06/CVC_OEI_Course_Design_Rubric_rev_April_2020.pdf	2020	CC BY	California Virtual Campus – On-line Education Initiative	Higher ed institution
Blackboard Exemplary Course Program Rubric	https://www.blackboard.com/sites/default/files/2020-02/2020_BlackboardExemplaryRubric_Vert5.pdf	2020	CC BY-NC-SA	Blackboard	Commercial
Open SUNY Course Quality Review (OSCQR) Rubric	https://oscqr.suny.edu/get-oscqr/	2016	CC BY	State University of New York	Higher ed institution
California State University – Quality Learning and Teaching (QLT) Rubric	http://courseredesign.csuprojects.org/wp/qualityassurance/qlt-informal-review/	2019	CC BY-NC-SA	California State University system	Higher ed institution
Quality Matters (QM) Higher Ed Course Design Rubric	https://www.qualitymatters.org/qa-resources/rubric-standards/higher-ed-rubric	2018	Copy-righted	QM	Nonprofit organization
Illinois Online Network – Quality Online Course Initiative Rubric	https://www.uis.edu/ion/resources/qoci/	2019	CC BY-NC-SA	Illinois Online Network	Higher ed institution
University of Wisconsin-La Crosse Online Course Evaluation Guidelines	https://www.uwlax.edu/globalassets/offices-services/catl/guidelines.pdf	2014	License not stated	University of Wisconsin-La Crosse	Higher ed institution

Note. Abbreviations are as follows: Creative Commons Attribution (CC BY) and Creative Commons Attribution-Noncommercial-Share Alike (CC BY-NC-SA) activities in the online environment, facilitate the activity, and give feedback to students. Again, you don't have to go overboard. Select one or two strategies to maintain students' interest, sustain their efforts, and support self-control.

Just as researchers use triangulation to validate their initial findings, an effective assessment approach is to give students multiple opportunities to show what they know. Methods for doing this include giving students choices in how they demonstrate achievement, guiding them in goal setting and planning, encouraging reflection, and letting them track their progress. Options for demonstrating achievement can be as simple as letting students select one of two or three essay questions related to the same class concept or as complex as letting students submit their work in different formats, such as an essay, an online presentation, a video, or an infographic. Providing nontraditional methods to allow students to demonstrate learning often shows amazing results and reduces boredom for faculty members.

These UDL principles work for online, hybrid, and face-to-face courses. As you rethink the online course environment and activities for any of these delivery methods, use the strategies in the following chapters to apply those principles and support online students. We will provide examples throughout this book so you can see what it looks like in practice.

Fostering Human Connectedness

A consistent finding in higher education is that making a meaningful connection with either a faculty member or fellow students is a powerful predictor of student success in higher education (Light, 2004; Robert, 2018). This connection is essential, regardless of the methodology of teaching employed. Connectedness on campus has become a highly studied area (e.g., Jorgenson et al., 2018). Unfortunately, online education has been associated with students who work independently, and often without human connection to faculty members or colleagues. This happens regularly when students choose to take online courses and is even more true when students must take all courses in an online format, such as when a pandemic, wildfire, or hurricane requires that the entire campus pivot to all online teaching. When campuses close, students must become more self-directed—even those who need more support. This independent learning approach results in additional challenges for students. It is times such as these that human connection is more important than ever.

The first step in connecting with students is to determine their learning preferences and needs. These learning preferences are not collected in order to customize or individualize teaching approaches—a practice that has failed to prove that teaching to a given learning style helps students to learn (Pashler et al., 2008). However, when considering a UDL approach that offers multiple pathways to reach learning outcomes, it is possible to enhance student learning by identifying preferences and learning needs. So how do you move from becoming aware of which students may need support to doing something about it? Start by getting to know more about your students. A common netiquette guideline or principle for online courses asks us to remember that there is a person on the other end of each internet connection and, therefore, behave like we were talking to them in person. Taking that rule a step beyond simply monitoring our online behavior, online teachers must think about students as humans in a more holistic sense. That is, we must keep in mind that online students bring a diverse set of personal goals and needs to our classes. These personal goals and needs form an often-hidden layer beneath all of the institutionally driven goals and expectations. Just as our psychological and safety needs can affect our ability to reach self-actualization (Maslow, 1943), that hidden layer of students' unique goals and needs affects their motivation and drives their actions. It also means that you need to keep students' diverse needs in mind as you redesign and facilitate your courses and course activities, especially in an online environment.

One way to increase your focus on students is to ask them to define success. Student success is often defined in the research literature and administrative practice as completion of a course with a passing grade (e.g., A, B, C, or pass). However, faculty and students also feel success includes students gaining the ability to acquire and use knowledge, skills, or attitudes outside of the course where the student learned them. For example, career and technical education students sometimes take a class to prepare for an external certification exam and stop participating in the class after taking the exam even if it means failing that class. In those students' minds, they have achieved success, even if their transcripts say otherwise. Therefore, if we stick with the more administrative definition of success (i.e., completion with a passing grade), then we have to communicate that goal to our students and encourage them to reach it.

Defining Equity

Before you start reading this next section, grab your smartphone, your laptop, or a pen and paper. Take just a minute to note three words or phrases that you associate with the term *equity* (Merriam-Webster, n.d.). Ready? Go!

Have you got three? When we ask faculty and educational technology leaders to complete this task, they typically come up with words and phrases like "fairness," "needs," and "lowering barriers." Routinely, some-one will note that "equity is not the same as equality." Equity and equality are both strategies used to strive for fairness, but they are very different from one another. Equality is giving everyone the same; equity is giving each person what is needed to be successful. In our society, there is a com-mon belief that "everyone should be treated the same," which, for many individuals, means giving everyone the same (Sun, 2014).

The challenge with equality is that although it appears on the surface to be fair, often it is not. Within a school district, the board may decide that computer labs will all be open from 3:00 p.m.–5:00 p.m. Every lab is open at the same time, which is equality and appears fair. The challenge may well be that in lower-income areas, students may not have computers and printers. If those students work between 3:00 p.m. and 5:00 p.m., then they cannot access the lab. If an analysis of computer lab usage shows computers in an affluent area of town are rarely used as students tend to have their own lap-tops, whereas computers in more impoverished areas of town have waiting lines, it would be more equitable to have some labs with longer hours and more staff than other labs. That would be "fair" in that an equitable approach would provide each student with a similar opportunity to use a computer.

In the context of distance education, in Oakland, California, Peralta Community College District (2019)—an organization leading the charge to increase online equity—uses the word *equity* to mean "freedom from biases, assumptions or institutional barriers that negatively impact learn-ers' motivation, opportunities, or achievements" (p. 1). Note that in this working definition, accessible at https://web.peralta.edu/de/files/2019/08/Describing-the-Peralta-Equity-Rubric-Aug-2019.pdf, the Peralta Colleges are going beyond the concept that everyone receives the same treatment, to freedom from biases, assumptions, or barriers that negatively impact learners. Throughout this book, when we discuss fairness, we will use the term *equity* in line with the work of the Peralta Colleges rather than incor-rectly defining it as equality.

Unfortunately (as you saw in the previous California Community Col-leges data), there are equity-based achievement gaps for certain student populations in online courses. This means every online teacher has to be proactive in addressing challenges and barriers that affect the success of those student groups. Those challenges can be as fundamental as providing access—making sure all students have access to the technology required to complete online courses, as well as access to all support services without requiring students to visit your campus. Conversely, the challenges can be as complex as helping students combat stereotype threat or increasing their feelings of social belonging in an online course environment.

Students Facing Equity Challenges in Online Courses

Studies have begun to identify student populations facing the most signifi-cant achievement gaps, characterized by Gloria Ladson-Billings (2006) as "education debt," to recognize our institutions' responsibilities in creat-ing and maintaining those gaps. Student populations who perform less well in online courses include students who are male, first-generation (i.e., the first generation in a family to attend college), low-income, from select underrepresented minority groups (African American/Black and His-panic/Latinx), and/or academically underprepared (Jaggars, 2014). Many higher education institutions also include foster youth, students with dis-abilities, and military veterans in their student equity plans to address equity in all classes—not just online classes. Other student groups that have not yet been studied in detail, but may also face challenges in online courses, include working adults and the lesbian, gay, bisexual, transgen-der, and queer (LGBTQ) community. For many of the previously listed groups, it is difficult to get data about their enrollment, retention, and suc-cess rates, but we will keep their needs in mind as we go.

What Factors Affect Student Success?

There are different factors we need to consider when we redesign and facilitate online courses (see Table 1.1.4). First, students need both access

TABLE 1.1.4

Factors That Affect Online Student Success and Persistence

Category	Factors That Affect Online Student Success and Persistence, Positively (+), Negatively (–), or Both (+/–)
Academic	• online learner readiness (+) • online instructor preparedness (+)
Pedagogical	• course organization and design (+) • interaction opportunities (+) • timely and effective feedback (+)
Psychological	• value relevance (+) • instructor compassion (+) • social belonging (+) • stereotype threat (–)
Social	• alienation/isolation (–) • belonging (+) • learning community (+)
Technological	• no access to technology (–) • ability to use technology (+/–) • accessibility accommodations (+)

to and the ability to use any technology required to complete an online course and its activities. Next, research literature and common online course design rubrics outline some of the most prominent pedagogical factors that affect success, like course structure, interaction, and timely feedback. Further, readiness is a factor for everyone—that is, students benefit from online learning readiness surveys and tutorials, while teachers benefit from proactive training and support. Last, online teachers need to know about the psychological and social factors that affect online student success, like social belonging and community. As it can be daunting to think about addressing all of these factors at once, a practical approach is to adopt and apply learning design principles—UDL and design for learning equity—as you design or redesign your online course.

How Can You Increase Equity in Your Online Course?
We will introduce a few concepts related to increasing equity now and will cover them in more detail later throughout the book, so you may begin to think about how to address these issues in your own course. The following are just a few ways you can increase equity in your online and hybrid course:

- *Identify and manage unconscious bias*: Whether we are aware of it or not, our behavior as teachers is affected by unconscious attitudes, stereotypes, assumptions, and biases. For example, "instructors may assume that students know to seek help when they are struggling" (Yale CTL, n.d., para. 2). You can manage this bias by actively encouraging individual students and the entire class to contact you for help.
- *Identify and manage image and representation bias*: Students' perceptions are influenced by the images they see. As teachers, we rarely think about how the images in our textbooks, presentations, course materials, and other web resources might show unequal representation (e.g., gender, ethnicity, age) and promote stereotypes (Kay et al., 2015). For example, textbooks may underrepresent women and certain ethnicities in images of people in prestigious professions or leadership positions.
- *Create inclusive course environments and activities*: If we're not careful, online and hybrid courses have the potential to exclude different types of learners from participating. Learners with disabilities are one of the most notable groups, but not the only one by any means! There is a wide range of inclusion strategies to change this dynamic.
- *Increase personal connection with students*: Increasing your personal connection with students is critical in an online or a hybrid course.

Alienation and isolation are real factors that drive students to drop out of or stop participating in online courses. Conversely, a higher sense of connection—with the instructor and with other students—leads to higher retention and success (CCCCO, 2013).

- *Use clear language, goals, and measures*: It's easy to think we're clear, but first-generation college students don't work from the same set of assumptions about completing work for college courses—especially online courses. USC's Center for Urban Education (n.d.) shared five principles to achieve equity (visit https://cue.usc.edu/equity-by-design-five-principles/ for all principles). The first principle outlines the need to use clear language, goals, and measures.

- *Refer students to support and resources*: Student success is a team effort—it goes beyond any one course or teacher. In addition to setting up your course to foster success, point students to resources that (a) are relevant to them and (b) do not require an in-person visit to campus.

- *Follow UDL principles*: UDL, described earlier in this chapter, is a framework to support every student in your online courses.

Design for Learning Equity Framework

After reviewing the literature about equity in online courses and helping the Peralta Colleges create their Equity Rubric (described in more detail later), Kevin Kelly (2020) created a design for learning equity framework that aggregates different ways to increase equity in your courses. Table 1.1.5 shows the categories from that framework, explained further (with examples, of course) throughout the book. See learningequity.org to download the matrix and to find more information.

TABLE 1.1.5
Design for Learning Equity Categories

	Interactions	**Content Presentation**	**Assessment**
Access	Humanized Environment	Content Representation and Format	Achievement Pathways
Connection	Social and Human Connection	Content Diversity and Meaning	Feedback Methods
Belonging	Social Belonging	Content and Personal Context	Persistence Beyond Course

NEXT STEPS

- Read through UDL principles in more depth. The Center for Applied Special Technology, or CAST, website udlguidelines.cast .org—has excellent information that is easy to read and understand. Through this website, you can download simple resources, like a one-page flyer with guidelines, or access more robust resources, like entire online books, including *Teaching Every Student in the Digital Age* (Rose & Meyer, 2002) and *Universal Design for Learning: Theory and Practice* (Meyer et al., 2014). For those of you who are K–12 teachers, the CAST site even has lesson plan ideas and tools to build lessons.
- For those of you who are college or university instructors, also check out *UDL Universe* (http://www.udluniverse.com), a UDL resource site created to support higher education faculty.
- Consider purchasing a copy of *Reach Everyone, Teach Everyone: Universal Design for Learning in Higher Education* (Tobin & Behling, 2018). It is an outstanding book focused on UDL for higher education.

CHAPTER SUMMARY

It's easy to fall into the "one size fits all" trap when we build online courses and online course activities. It is challenging to make an online course experience equitable and inclusive. Students bring different needs to the online environment, may require different approaches to distance education, and may face issues like limited technology access or culturally biased content. Overall, the ultimate goal is to design learning in a way that makes learning challenges and differences irrelevant. Adopting learning design principles such as UDL and design for learning equity, along with being mindful of human connections in the course, are ways to start tackling those issues.

Reflection and Discussion Questions

1. This chapter begins by noting the many ways in which teaching is challenging. Think of the best teacher you have ever had. Why was the person you selected your favorite teacher? What do you think that person found most challenging about teaching?

2. Every campus has an office to assist students with learning challenges such as attention deficit disorder, bipolar disorder, cognitive processing delays, and social anxiety. Why might we, in the name of equity, strive to see that all such offices are no longer the only source of support for students with learning challenges? What would be the positive outcome of not needing such offices?

3. Think back to the courses you have taken in college and high school. What different types of assessments did faculty members require for you in those courses? That is, aside from the traditional examinations? What kinds of assignments did you like least? What alternatives might have been implemented in those courses?

4. Read and think reflectively about the categories in the design for learning equity framework in Table 1.1.5. Describe inequity you have seen or experienced that corresponds to one cell within the framework. How might the issue be addressed by the faculty member such that more equity would have been experienced?

1.2

(RE)WRITING LEARNING OUTCOMES FOR YOUR ONLINE COURSE

You ARE LIKELY EXCITED to begin using this book's online teaching strategies as quickly as possible. We will share many practical strategies in this book, but before discussing those strategies, it is essential to identify intended outcomes. Before deciding how to get somewhere, you need to have an idea as to where you would like to go. To do this we will use backward design, the concept of starting with the end in mind, popularized by Wiggins and McTighe (2005).

There are three primary steps to backward design. The first step is to establish learning outcomes. What is it that you anticipate the students will know or be able to do at the end of a learning experience? The second step is to establish acceptable evidence to determine whether the outcome has been reached. The third and final step in backward design is to determine the best teaching and learning strategies to help all students reach the anticipated outcome. For many faculty members, leaving the teaching strategy until the end seems backward. It is common to decide to use active learning strategies such as an asynchronous discussion or to lecture without thinking about the intended outcome and acceptable assessment strategies. In other words, when designing a course, many faculty members start by deciding on teaching strategies or activities, such as lectures, small groups, or clickers. That is why this approach is called "backward design." We begin with the end in mind and finish with what many consider the beginning.

STARTING WITH OUTCOMES

Learning outcomes form the nucleus of any course. Whether you are required to teach to specific student learning outcomes or you create them yourself, the course design process for any course delivery format revolves around the question, "What should the students know or be able to do by the end of the course?" Morrison et al. (2001) note that in designing courses and course units of material, outcomes serve three functions: Outcomes (a) let students know what is expected of them, (b) guide you as you design your course, and (c) provide you with a framework for evaluating student performance. In addition, outcomes help you to select the teaching strategies that you will use in your online course. For online, hybrid, or temporary remote courses, making sure the learning outcomes are clear takes on an increased significance. Online, hybrid, and remote courses often require students to work more independently than they do in traditional, face-to-face courses. Therefore, students need a clear road map for what is expected of them and ways to know whether or not they are making progress at an acceptable level.

There are many reasons that outcomes are critical to any course, whether face-to-face or online. Outcomes will help you to focus your course. Nearly every course suffers from having too much content to teach in the time given. As you gather instructional materials and resources to share with students, outcomes will help ensure that you do not head off in too many directions. Outcomes will also help you prioritize the material that you are going to teach. Once you have identified what you expect students to know and be able to do at the end of the course or unit of material, you will have a better idea of what information they will need to be successful.

Outcomes will also help you teach the course at the appropriate level and make adjustments as needed. In writing outcome statements, you will identify not only what students will be able to do but also at what level. This will help you know the extent to which students are reaching the goals you have set for them and, if not, what changes you might need to make in the course.

Outcomes will guide your instructional strategies. Once you identify the destination for your students, you will be able to determine the best instructional strategy to get there. When you go on vacation, you must decide where you want to go before you decide how you will get there, right? If you are visiting relatives that live within a few hundred miles, then either a car or train would seem to be the most appropriate mode of transportation, depending on where you live. If you decide to spend a week in Europe, then air travel really is your only option. As with vacations, determining the anticipated outcome will often strongly suggest the best methods to realize that outcome.

The extent to which you will have the freedom to write your outcomes depends on the institution at which you teach. Some colleges and universities will give you nearly complete freedom to teach whatever you feel is appropriate. At other institutions, you may be given the text and exams that will be used to assess students. In still other institutions, the course will be completely determined for you, including the specific outcomes that have already been written. Regardless of where you fall on this continuum from complete freedom to develop outcomes to having everything determined for you, outcomes will be the driving force, and the first step, to the teaching process.

OBJECTIVES VERSUS OUTCOMES

You may have heard about outcomes and objectives previously and may be uncertain about the difference between the two. You are not alone. Over the past 50 years, there has been rather intense debate regarding the definitions of *outcomes* and *objectives*. The use of objectives in education dates back to the 1800s, when philosopher Herbert Spencer classified objectives of human activities related to education (McAvoy, 1985). Many years later, Bloom (1956) and his colleagues developed taxonomies for educational objectives in the cognitive, psychomotor, and affective domains—that is, objectives to attain knowledge, skills, and attitudes—that quickly became popular. Adaptations of the original work by Bloom are still important in education today. The concept of learning objectives was also widely disseminated by way of a 62-page book by Robert Mager (1962), which went through numerous editions until 1997. Working with industry and the military, Mager argued that the result of learning should be objectively stated. These learning objectives, he explained, had three parts: (a) something a person is able to do or to perform; (b) the conditions under which the performance is to take place; and (c) the criteria demonstrating an acceptable level of performance under a given condition (Mager, 1997).

Although competency-based education was introduced toward the end of the 1960s, it did not become popular until the late 1990s. The controversy between outcomes and objectives seems to have been around from the beginnings of outcome-based education. At that time, guidelines explaining how to write outcome statements very closely matched Mager's descriptions of how to write learning objectives: expected resulting behavior or performance, conditions under which performance is completed, and the criteria for success (Malan, 2000). The confusion likely started at that time, as outcomes were defined based on descriptions of how to write objectives.

At present, the confusion over learning objectives and learning outcomes continues. There are several perspectives as to how to differentiate between these two terms: objectives being the process (how something is done) versus outcomes being the results of the process (Rosenberg, 2018); objectives being the intentions of the student and outcomes being the product (Barkley & Major, 2016); objectives being the goals of the professor and the outcomes being what the student has accomplished (Rensselaer Polytechnic Institute, n.d.); and any number of publications that discuss the specificity of a stated anticipatory result as the defining factor (UCLA Health, 2016). There are many who argue that the level of work done by most faculty members does not require differentiation between objectives and outcomes (e.g., "Objectives, Goals, and Outcomes," 1999; Renton Technical College, n.d.).

In writing this book, we will take the position that learning objectives and learning outcomes still do not have a commonly accepted differentiation within the field of education. Although many highly respected scholars in the area of educational assessment and curriculum design certainly have strongly held positions on this issue, the distinction between these terms is overly specific for faculty looking to write lesson plans and basic curriculum programs. For us it is more important that everyone who teaches has a strong understanding of what the student should be able to do at the end of the instructional time, the conditions under which they should be able to perform, and the criteria for success. To maintain consistency of terminology in this book, we will use *learning outcome* to refer to this process, and we hold no ill feelings toward those who feel *objective* is the term that best defines this concept.

FOUNDATIONS OF LEARNING OUTCOMES

As outcomes refer to the knowledge, skills, or attitudes that students should showcase at the end of an educational experience, they should be specific and measurable. Measurable outcomes define a specific action (do what?) that will be realized after a student has learned something new. In addition to the action, outcomes often include conditions (with what?) or criteria (how well?). Table 1.2.1 offers some example learning outcomes (K. Kelly, 2008b).

In addition to making your outcomes measurable, action verbs define the level of achievement you want students to reach. To support these

TABLE 1.2.1
Example Learning Outcomes

Conditions		Action	Criteria
Without the use of any aids		arrange the 24 steps of isolating DNA from yeast cells	in the proper order
Given a list of equations		use the appropriate equation to calculate the yield of a reaction	accurate to the nearest 0.1%
Given a liquid, an analytical balance, and a graduated cylinder	the student will be able to	calculate the density of the liquid substance	accurate to the nearest 0.01g/ml
Given two drafts of peer essays and a rubric		provide constructive feedback to student peers	within 1 week
When prompted by a lab assistant		describe why wearing safety glasses in the lab is important	for each type of lab work completed

efforts, the educators mentioned previously, such as Benjamin Bloom, David Krathwohl, and Anita Harrow, have led or conducted efforts to create and publish taxonomies to classify and describe the three domains of learning—cognitive (knowledge), psychomotor (skills), and affective (attitudes). More recently, educators like Leslie Owen Wilson (n.d.) and Don Clark (2015) have done the work of summarizing the original works and their later revisions, outlining the levels of achievement in each domain and even providing sample action verbs for each level. For example, when it comes to working with knowledge, remembering facts is a low-level activity characterized by verbs like *identify, list*, or *recall*. Applying concepts is a midlevel activity characterized by verbs like *calculate* or *demonstrate*. Creating new knowledge is a high-level activity, characterized by verbs like *generate, plan*, or *produce*.

Although Bloom and his colleagues arranged the taxonomies as hierarchies, this does not mean that a lower-level achievement (remember) is any less important than a higher-level achievement (analyze). For example, comprehending and being able to quickly recall information (both lower-level outcomes) are critical to understanding a concept well enough to be able to think critically about it. Do not think of this hierarchy as a "race to the top," but rather as a reminder that it is important to be able to demonstrate outcomes of learning at many different levels, depending on the goal of the educational experience. Experts must be able to remember foundational attributes of the work they are doing.

Similarly, with respect to attitudes, the affective taxonomy ranges from becoming aware (low level) to internalizing values and modifying behaviors as a result (high level). With respect to skills, you will find more than one taxonomy. These taxonomies start with low-level activities like observing or imitating someone who performs a physical skill and work up to high-level activities such as adapting a skill to new situations, creating new variations of skills, and using nuanced movements like body language. It is important to note that students can achieve outcomes in all three domains—at any level—and demonstrate that achievement through online activities and assessment.

As you develop your online course, you will write hundreds of outcome statements. Keep in mind that as you work with student learning outcomes more and more, they will become easier and easier to write. Later in the chapter, we will provide for you specific guidelines on how to write effective outcome statements for each aspect of your course.

TAKING OUTCOMES TO ANOTHER LEVEL

Now that you've looked at outcomes in terms of levels of achievement let's look at the difference between course-level outcomes and module-level outcomes. Most instructors have course-level outcomes, as they are usually required as part of a course syllabus. However, it is also important to create and share module-level outcomes with your students.

Are you wondering why you would put time into writing module-level outcomes? Writing outcome statements for each module will take a bit of time. As noted previously in this chapter, outcomes serve four primary functions in teaching an online course, and this is true at the module level as well as the course level. First, outcomes let your students know what is expected of them in that module. This will help students determine the amount of work needed to be successful and the amount of time it will take to complete that work. Outcomes at this level will also help students become better metacognitive thinkers by better understanding when they are being successful at each step of the way. Second, outcomes at the module level will help guide you in designing your course. These outcomes will help you decide when to have asynchronous activities, or where to provide video tutorials or links to additional materials. Well-developed module-level outcomes will help you think more critically about what you will need to provide for your students to help them to be successful in your course. Third, module-level outcomes also help you determine appropriate assessment measures. Because one component of any outcome is how the learned behavior will be demonstrated, outcomes have built-in suggestions for assessments. Fourth, outcomes help you select the teaching strategies for each module.

In addition to these four reasons to have module-level outcomes, there is another that might be most important for students: It will impact their motivation to learn. We can take a lesson from the psychology of the progress bar, that little bar that tells you what percent of a file has downloaded or how many pages of an online survey you still have to complete. If you think only user experience (UX) and web designers should care about progress bar research, think again. This research is directly tied to cognitive, behavioral, and emotional aspects of learning, such as task completion, motivation, and focus. As we get close to completing a task, our brain releases neurotransmitters like dopamine, which makes us feel good (Lee, 2013; Salisbury, 2016). However, if we perceive slow progress, we are more likely to abandon a task completely, have a negative experience, or both (Conrad et al., 2010). This is especially true at the beginning of a given process.

Now imagine a progress bar that takes 16 weeks to complete. For online students, that could be the plot of a horror movie. More to the point, imagine tracking 10 to 20 progress bars—that is, the achievement of your learning outcomes for multiple classes—over an entire semester. If it's true that we're happiest after the progress bar reaches the 75% complete mark, then our online students won't feel like they are making progress until week 12 of the semester! And that's assuming they have a valid and consistent way to track their progress for each outcome.

In chapter 1.1, we shared that students complete online classes less often than their face-to-face counterparts, and the lack of module-level outcomes may be one reason why. You can help your students maintain their motivation to complete your online class by (a) creating and sharing module-level outcomes so they know what they need to accomplish each week (see Figure 1.2.1 for examples), (b) encouraging students to focus on one learning task at a time, and (c) giving students a way to track their progress, which will involve providing timely feedback.

Figure 1.2.1. Examples of learning outcomes at the course and module levels.

- Course-level outcome: You will explore using different technologies, specifically for learning.
  - Module-level outcome (low level): After reviewing each mini-lecture, complete a quiz to show what you know about how we learn with mobile technologies.
  - Module-level outcome (midlevel): Participate in discussions about how you learn with mobile technologies, with specific, personal examples from your experiences as a student.
  - Module-level outcome (high level): Using a rubric and a template, write a 500-word plan that outlines how you will research using mobile technologies for learning in another course, for a workplace training, or to teach yourself a new skill.

WRITING AND SHARING OUTCOMES

There are many ways to think about writing outcome statements. George Doran (1981) published the mnemonic SMART for writing effective student learning outcomes. It was later adapted and popularized by Peter Drucker. The components of this mnemonic are the essential elements to all outcomes statements: specific, measurable, assignable, realistic, and time-related. Each of the components is explained in the following sections, relative to the following outcome statement:

> At the end of the first module, students will be able to describe in writing the five important behaviors of a successful online student, as presented in module 1. The success of this outcome will be determined by scoring at least 90% on a rubric developed by three online instructors.

Specific

A well-written outcome will state specifically what will happen at the end of the educational experience, whether at the course or module level. Making outcomes specific includes streamlining them so students do only one thing. If you see a "double-barreled" learning outcome (i.e., "you will be able to X and Y"), turn it into two outcomes or decide which of the two results is more important.

The sample outcome is specific in that it pertains to describing the five behaviors presented in the course. It does not say, "list behaviors associated with," or even "list any five behaviors." Those alternatives would be less specific. The final level of specificity is up to you as the instructor. The important consideration is that there is a degree of specificity that removes a preponderance of doubt for both the student and the instructor as to what is expected.

Measurable

The outcome must be measurable so that it is possible to determine if the expected learning has been realized. Ideally, a criterion is included, so the level of performance to be considered successful is clear. In the previous example, the outcome states, "scoring at least 90% on a rubric." The level set is totally up to you as the instructor, unless predetermined by the institution for which you are teaching the course.

Achievable

Outcome statements always state who is demonstrating the learned behavior and the time by which the outcome will be met. Achievable outcomes also consider if it is reasonable for the learner to be successful in the time allotted. The most common convention is "By the end of some period of time, [the person for whom the outcomes statement is written] will be able to . . . In the example provided, "At the end of the first module, students will be able to . . . ." An outcome for a teaching conference might be, "By the end of the plenary session, participants will be able to . . . ."

Realistic

Keeping in mind the resources, abilities of the learner, and the time provided for instruction, realistic means that it is reasonable for the target learner to achieve the performance at the level expected. In the previously provided example, the outcome notes students will be able to "describe five behaviors." It would be decidedly less realistic to say that students will be able to "develop and publish a new model of student behaviors to bring about success in online courses." Often, to determine realistic levels, it is helpful to show outcomes to another faculty member who teaches a similar course.

Time-Related

Outcomes also note by what time the results will be realized. The example outcome clearly states, "By the end of the first module . . . ." The time-related component helps with course design and laying out what students will be expected to learn and how long you have to provide the instruction for that learning to take place.

In addition to being SMART, outcomes for online courses must be clearly written, aligned well, and placed where they will best support learners within the course shell.

Many common rubrics to guide and evaluate online course design have several criteria related to learning outcomes (or objectives). This is true for national organizations like QM and the Illinois Online Network's Quality Online Course Initiative (QOCI); statewide initiatives like the California Community Colleges' Online Education Initiative (OEI) and the California State University system's Quality Learning and Teaching (QLT) project; and even individual campuses like University of Wisconsin-La Crosse and New Mexico State University, each of which created rubrics to help faculty design and facilitate online courses (see Table 1.1.3 in the previous chapter). In the following paragraphs we describe some of these course design rubrics' criteria for outcomes.

Clarity

It's easy to say that outcomes should be written clearly, but what does that mean? First, avoid jargon and terms the students will not have learned yet. For example, in one of his education courses, Kevin had to change an outcome that used the term *metacognitive*, since most students did not know what that meant when they started the class. The old outcome was, "Write at least one reflection essay on using metacognitive strategies." The revised outcome is now "Write at least one reflection essay on using strategies designed to improve your learning." Second, several of the course design rubrics require outcomes to be written from the learner's perspective. Third, the Center for Urban Education (n.d.) asks instructors to use clear language as one of its five principles to increase equity and student success. As one way to check the clarity of your outcomes, ask a colleague or student who is not familiar with your course to review them.

Alignment

Backward design sets you up to align outcomes with assessments, learning activities, and course content. However, courses change over time, and sometimes you might inherit a course that someone else developed. As you prepare for each semester or as you transform a face-to-face course into a hybrid or online course format, make sure your outcomes align across the module and course level. This alignment can be as granular as going through questions from a publisher's test bank. Rather than create a test that randomly draws questions from a giant test bank, go through and choose a smaller set of questions that relate to your outcomes, content you have assigned, and activities students will complete.

Placement

It is not enough to share your outcomes only in the syllabus, as you cannot count on students referring back to the syllabus regularly. We discussed the importance of sharing module-level outcomes earlier in this chapter, and that includes listing those outcomes at the beginning of each module. If you use a learning management system (LMS) for your online or hybrid course, there are two ways to do this. LMS solutions like Moodle allow you to show all of the course modules on one page, so you can list the outcomes for each module at the top of each topic area or "section," or create a separate page called "Outcomes for Module X." For LMS solutions like Canvas, list the outcomes for each module on content pages. In the next chapter on outlining your course structure, we'll go into more detail and provide examples.

To help students understand the relationship between your outcomes and course activities and assessments, refer to the relevant outcomes in the instructions for each activity and assessment. For example, Mary-Ann Winkelmes (2014) from the University of Nevada, Las Vegas, created "Transparent Assignments" that include the learning outcomes for the purpose of the assignment, right at the beginning of the instructions. If you're interested in this approach, Winkelmes (2013) shares a Transparent Assignment Template as a Creative Commons document that anyone may use (https://tilthighered.com/assets/pdffiles/Transparent%20 Assignment%20Template.pdf). Please go to Appendix C for links to the online resources mentioned in this chapter.

WRITING OUTCOMES WITH HUMAN CONNECTEDNESS, UDL, AND DESIGN FOR LEARNING EQUITY IN MIND

Throughout this book we propose that online learning is best served by having the three components of human connectedness, UDL, and designing for learning equity. Bringing these concepts together while writing outcomes will ensure a course designed for inclusion by keeping individuals in mind while providing for a variety of ways for those individuals to be successful in the course. The following sections provide a few ideas to consider.

Outcomes and Human Connections

As you develop outcomes, keep in mind that how you write course- and module-level outcomes will clearly indicate the extent to which you see students as individuals in your course. The outcomes you develop will also guide their behaviors. For example, create outcomes that require students to interact with you and other students such as, "By the end of the second module, students will have completed the information worksheet with input from at least two other students." Another possible student learning outcome could be, "By the end of one of the three synchronous chats in the second week of the semester, each student will be able to state one similarity between how they can be the best student possible and how the instructor typically studied when she was in school."

There are many ways to humanize the course, and student learning outcome statements are an ideal place both to demonstrate to the students that you care about them and to push them to interact with others in the course.

Outcomes and UDL

Although the UDL Guidelines focus primarily on the course itself, course activities, and course materials, the UDL principles do relate to outcomes as well. According to UDL Universe, a "[UDL-based] strategy for making [student learning outcomes] a more prominent focus, while adding to understanding of how the individual parts of a class constitute the whole (i.e., the purpose), is to graphically represent them" (Christie, 2019). One way to depict your outcomes in a graphic format is to create a graphic organizer or outcomes map (Nilson, 2007) that shows the connections to course activities and assessments. See Figure 1.2.2 for an example outcomes map for Kevin's course, ITEC 299 – How 2 Lrn w ur Mobile Device.

Outcomes and Design for Learning Equity

Last but not least, check your outcomes using the design for learning equity framework. Look for things like assumptions you may be making about what students know or what technologies students have and are able to use or cultural biases that may make it difficult for some students to understand what the course will prepare them to do. Consider adding module-level outcomes that ask students to connect course content to their sociocultural backgrounds or the backgrounds of others and to interact with each other in ways that deepen learning. Also, if it is appropriate, let students know that you will provide alternative technology pathways to demonstrate achievement of the course outcomes.

NEXT STEPS

Conduct an outcome audit. Reviewing a course you have taught or a course you have taken, read through the outcomes and determine the extent to which each of the following prompts are achieved:

- Are your outcomes measurable?
- Do you have weekly or module-level outcomes for your online or hybrid course?

Figure 1.2.2. Learning outcomes map.

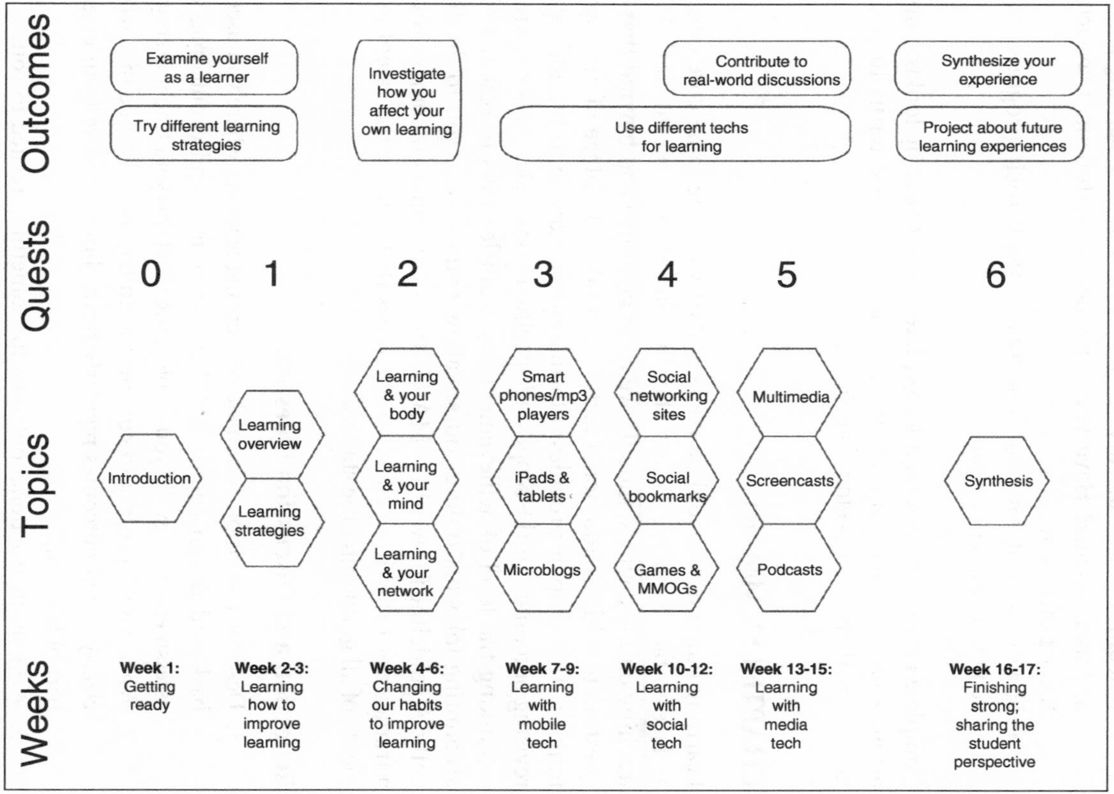

- Have you asked someone who is not familiar with your course to review your outcomes for clarity? Do the outcomes use student-centered language?
- Are the outcomes aligned with, and have you referred to the outcomes in the instructions for, related course learning activities and assessments? Have you explained how students may achieve those outcomes?
- How easy is it for your students to track their progress toward achieving each outcome?

Complete an inquiry-oriented lesson like a *WebQuest* by looking up the terms *goals, outcomes*, and *objectives*. These are good terms to become familiar with as you develop your instructional skills.

CHAPTER SUMMARY

Learning outcomes for online courses start with the same core question as face-to-face courses: "What should students be able to do?" When teaching online courses, though, we must go above and beyond that core question to address additional factors and take advantage of new opportunities. This chapter provides information pertaining to (a) adding and revising outcomes for the scope and specificity online learners require, (b) rethinking the level of achievement you want learners to reach, and (c) accounting for what online courses allow you or force you to do differently. A guideline for writing SMART student learning outcomes provides a framework for writing effective outcomes that contain the essential elements of all good outcome statements.

Reflection and Discussion Questions

1. Describe a decision you made concerning teaching where you used the backward design approach. What was your intended outcome, what assessment strategy did you employ, and what was your teaching strategy?
2. What would you say to convince a student or colleague that writing clearly stated outcomes regularly throughout a course is an essential part of learning?
3. Write an instructional outcome for something related to your course (either a course you are taking or one you are teaching). Identify each of the components for your outcome to show that it is SMART.
4. Write an outcome related to human connectedness that is also equitable. Describe why the specific outcome for human connectedness is important to you and your thinking to ensure it is an equitable outcome.

DEVELOPING YOUR ONLINE COURSE STRUCTURE

O*NE CONSTANT ACROSS HIGHER* education is that there is always too much content. It is impossible to include everything related to the course topic. Across all disciplines, new information is becoming available at an alarming rate. Making decisions about what the course will "look" like in terms of structure, content, and organization is critical to online learner persistence and success.

THE ORGANIZING FORCE BEHIND YOUR COURSE

If this is the first iteration of an online, a hybrid, or a temporarily remote course, a detailed outline of the course structure is essential in developing that course. If you have taught a course in an online or hybrid format previously, you likely have a structure in place for that course. It is worthwhile to review the existing course structure and organization to determine if the course uses optimal design to help online students succeed. As you teach any online course or any course with online elements, make notes about the structure of the course as the semester proceeds. Regardless of how well things go, a course can always be improved.

Setting Up an Organizational Framework

There are several different ways to break up a course into manageable chunks. Consider segmenting a course using any of the following strategies:

- *weeks* in the semester (e.g., week 1, week 2, etc.)
- *topics* in the course (e.g., for anatomy, you might break up the course by systems of the body; for history, you might use specific periods or events)
- *chapters* of the course textbook(s), in the order you will explore them (e.g., chapters 1, 3, and 4; chapters 6–8; chapter 10)

Kevin regularly organizes online courses according to course topics and frames them as questions that he and the students will answer together, such as "Quest 1: How do we learn?" or "Quest 2: How do we affect our own learning?" (Note that Kevin uses gamification principles—calling each module a "Quest"—to increase student motivation.)

Students taking online courses must be more independent than those taking face-to-face courses, making it important for you to provide as much information as possible in the title of each module or topic area in the LMS. Information typically includes the name of the module, a date range during which the module will be open, the main topic(s) covered, and so on. For example, module titles might look like this:

- Week 1 – Musculoskeletal System – August 28 to September 3
- Unit 9 – February 21–February 27 – *American History* textbook – Chapters 11–13 – American Revolution

Considering one of Kevin's courses, each module or "Quest" lasts 3 weeks, so he includes both the weeks of the semester and the start and end dates—for example, "Quest 4 – How do we learn with social technologies? – Weeks 10–12 (October 28–November 18)."

Most LMS providers will allow you to create and edit your own module titles. If your LMS does not do it automatically, or if it does not include the information you feel is helpful, create a list of "Quick Links" at the top of the course home page to make it easy for students to navigate to each module or week (see Figures 1.3.1 and 1.3.2 for examples of Quick Links in Moodle and Canvas).

Remember that students are novices with respect to your course content and, as such, frequently find the vast amount of information on the LMS overwhelming. This challenge is compounded for students who are new to online learning, and it is exponentially compounded when traditional, face-to-face classes are converted to emergency remote classes. Your students will need to determine where to focus their attention when looking at LMS pages and focus on that material for long periods of time. Students' ability to maintain this selective attention over time is affected by

Figure 1.3.1. Moodle Quick Links with module titles.

Course information - How 2 Lrn w ur Mobile Device

Expand all | Collapse all

Course quick-links menu

Quest 0 - Getting Started	Quest 1 - How do we learn?	Quest 2 - How do we affect our own learning?	Quest 3 - How do we learn with mobile technologies?	Quest 4 - How do we learn with social technologies?	Quest 5 - How do we learn with media technologies?	Synthesis Quest - Putting it all together
QUEST 0 — Getting ready	QUEST 1 — How do we learn?	QUEST 2 — How do we affect our own learning?	QUEST 3 — How do we learn with mobile technologies?	QUEST 4 — How do we learn with social technologies?	QUEST 5 — How do we learn with media technologies?	SYNTHESIS QUEST — Putting it all together
Start here (due Feb 10)	Weeks 01–03 (Jan 27–Feb 17)	Weeks 04–06 (Feb 17–Mar 9)	Weeks 07–09 (Mar 9–Mar 30)	Weeks 10–12 (Mar 30–Apr 20)	Weeks 13–15 (Apr 20–May 11)	Finish strong (due May 20)

Figure 1.3.2. Canvas Quick Links with workshop titles.

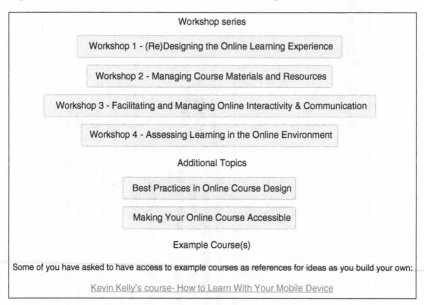

Workshop series

Workshop 1 - (Re)Designing the Online Learning Experience

Workshop 2 - Managing Course Materials and Resources

Workshop 3 - Facilitating and Managing Online Interactivity & Communication

Workshop 4 - Assessing Learning in the Online Environment

Additional Topics

Best Practices in Online Course Design

Making Your Online Course Accessible

Example Course(s)

Some of you have asked to have access to example courses as references for ideas as you build your own:

Kevin Kelly's course- How to Learn With Your Mobile Device

many factors: cognitive load, working memory load, value relevance, their own motivation, and the presence of competing distractors. Students will be attempting to process the information on the course LMS along with many environmental competitions for their attention. The goal is to set up an LMS course shell that makes it as easy as possible for students to attend to and process the information they need.

As you set up your material on the LMS, keep in mind that physiological factors like fatigue, hunger, and dehydration also play a role in attention. For example, in *The New Science of Learning*, Doyle and Zakrajsek (2018) point out exercise facilitates learning of new course material and that it is very difficult for a sleep-deprived brain to learn. We are not suggesting that you force students to sleep more hours or to exercise regularly. That said, research has shown that when students are made aware of these factors, they do better in the course (Nabours & Koh, 2019). International students and English language learners add language translation to their cognitive load when reading course material, which adds to the effort it takes to learn. If you have international students in your course, it will be helpful to be mindful of the words used and even the structure of the material. For example, students from other cultures may not understand the technical jargon used in the field, as this can be language-dependent. Many face-to-face instructors break lectures into 10- to 15-minute segments to give students time and space to process ideas and clear working memory for the next round of new information. In designing your online course, give careful attention to how much learning material can be placed into well-organized pieces.

The structure created by chunking the course into modules is repeated at a smaller level by chunking large modules into smaller topics, and even chunking large, individual content pages into discrete, bite-sized pieces. The chunking not only organizes the course materials and activities but also helps students manage their cognitive load and time management. If it sounds like a lot of work, it's really not.

- *Topic-level chunking*: LMS tools make it easy to break modules into topics. In Canvas, add Text Headers to organize and chunk a module that has too much information. In Moodle, add Labels to do the same thing. Students find it challenging to navigate long lists of pages, files, and activities and will forget where they left off during their last visit to an online course. If you organize this material for them, it will greatly help them to navigate the information and to learn the material.
- *Page-level chunking*: Although some instructional content pages are short and sweet, others seem to go on forever. Use the styles and headings tool in any HTML editor to organize long pages of instructional content as well as instructions for activities. Using styles and headings also makes your pages more accessible (see chapter 1.6, "Making Your Online Course Accessible", for more on this and other accessibility techniques). In Canvas, this is called the Paragraph drop-down menu—the "Paragraph" menu option is equivalent to the "Normal" style in Microsoft Word, while Header 2, Header 3, and Header 4 are used to denote new topics and subtopics. Canvas reserves Header 1 for the title of the content page itself. In Moodle, use the "Paragraph Styles" menu in the ATTO editor, and select Heading (large), Heading (medium), and Heading (small) to organize your page. Figures 1.3.3 and 1.3.4 show these HTML editor tools in each LMS.

Figure 1.3.3. Screenshot of headings tools in Canvas LMS Rich. Content editor.

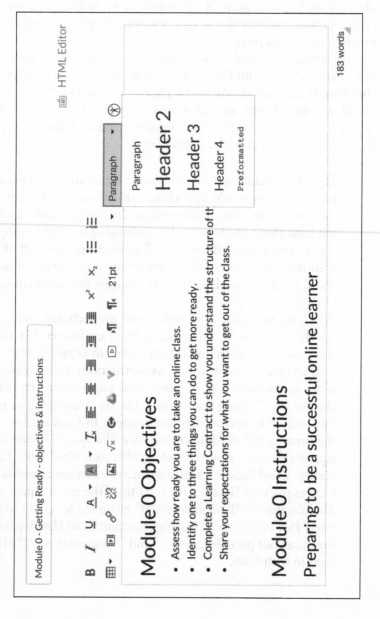

Figure 1.3.4. Screenshot of headings tools in Moodle LMS ATTO editor.

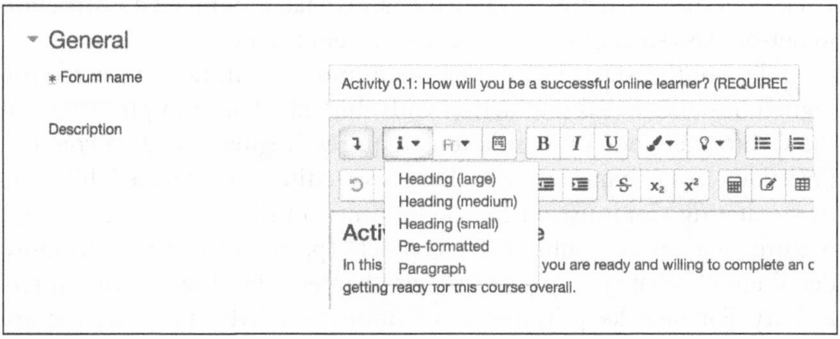

Calculating Instructional Time

Once you have an organizational scheme figured out, you will need to determine how much information to include in each module. Although there is variability as to the amount of information you include in a course, keep in mind that there are also some standard guidelines for the amount of work a student should complete for each unit of credit earned. Most institutions and/or regional accreditation agencies publish methods to measure instructional time. The U.S. Department of Education allows institutions to define distance education credit hours by measuring student progress toward achieving learning outcomes, as long as that institution also uses the federal definition of a credit hour to award student aid (U.S. Department of Education, 2009). Colleges and universities typically require distance education students to complete an amount of instructional content and related instructional activities equivalent to what they would experience in a face-to-face course. In other words, homework does not count toward instructional time totals. Instructional content might be something you create yourself (e.g., lecture capture or screencast videos), something you find (e.g., publisher videos, open educational resource [OER] multimedia, or simulations) or a combination of the two. For instructional activities, you might replicate classroom activities in the online environment (e.g., create an online discussion about the weekly reading assignment, form small groups to review for an upcoming exam).

To start, identify the total number of hours required for students to earn the units associated with your course. For example, for distance education courses—hybrid or 100% online—Southeastern Oklahoma State University (2020) requires "not less than three hours of student time per credit hour for each week for approximately sixteen weeks for one semester, or an equivalent amount of work for a different amount of time" (para. 2).

For a three credit hour course, students would work roughly 9 hours per week, with the instructor deciding the ratio of faculty-directed instruction to out-of-class student work based on the course type.

Like Southeastern Oklahoma State, most institutions also require regular, instructor-led interaction with students. For example, Title 5 of the California Code of Regulations requires "regular effective contact" (Westlaw, 2017, para. 2). Similarly, accreditation agencies like the Accrediting Commission for Community and Junior Colleges (2013) require "regular and substantive contact" (p. 2). We will go into more detail about what this means in later chapters about facilitating inter-activity. For now, keep in mind that online and hybrid courses require faculty–student interaction, and the research literature shows that more interaction of this kind can improve student retention and success (e.g., Hart, 2012; Nash, 2009; Orso & Doolittle, 2012). These requirements discourage using a "set it and forget it" approach of creating self-contained or self-paced course experiences that students complete entirely on their own.

Given the variety of requirements for online classes with respect to both "instructional time" and "student work time," confer with the department chair or another person responsible for the delivery of the course to ensure you build a course that is consistent with the standards at your institution.

COURSE STRUCTURE AND UDL

There are many UDL concepts to help students to navigate your course structure, to set short-term learning goals, and to monitor their progress. After all, you want students to spend their time focused on learning tasks, not searching for files or trying to figure out what to do!

Clarify Structure

To increase consistency, consider clarifying the course structure through the names or titles of your links, pages, files, and activities. If you organize your course by weeks or modules, then you can use the week or module numbers like an outline. For example, a recorded mini-lecture for week 3 of an art history class might be "3A – Mini-lecture screencast – Women artists from every continent." A content page for that same module might be "3B – Annotated web links – Biographies of women artists and galleries of their work." Any naming convention that makes it clear how the information is laid out and then consistently used throughout the course is acceptable (e.g., 3.1, 3.2, 3.3; Chapter 6-01, Chapter 6-02). In this book, chapters are numbered with the first number reflecting the section and then a period, followed by a second number that represents the chapters within the section (i.e., 1.1, 1.2, 1.3, 1.4, 1.5, 1.6, 2.1, 2.2, 2.3, 2.4, 3.1, 3.2). With this numbering system, you know right away that chapter 2.2 is the second chapter in the second section of the book. If we had used conventional chapter numbers, that same material would be in chapter 8. It is less clear in which section of the book the material from chapter 8 belongs. In the online environment, renaming everything to numerical identifiers has an added benefit. LMS solutions like Canvas display pages and files alphabetically on their respective course menu tabs, so students will be able to find learning materials easily when they leave the main course page.

Guide Appropriate Goal Setting

Guiding students to set short-term goals helps them become better, self-directed learners (Nilson, 2013). Just as importantly, it supports all students, including those who have heavy work schedules, students with children, students who have an attention deficit disorder, and students with learning challenges. To support goal setting, the UDL Guidelines suggest that you "provide prompts and scaffolds to estimate effort, resources, and difficulty" and "post goals, objectives (or outcomes), and schedules in an obvious place" (CAST, 2018a, para. 2). Table 1.3.1 shows how you can accomplish both of these tasks by creating columns for module outcomes, module activities (with the level of difficulty), and estimated time to complete activities. With this information, students who ride on public transportation can plan which activities to complete during their commute, and students who work can plan which activities to complete during a lunch break.

Enhance Capacity for Monitoring Progress

Most LMS platforms let students track their progress. For example, Canvas can show checkmarks next to resources that students have reviewed and activities that students have completed. The teacher can decide what constitutes completion—for content, it can be as simple as students visiting a page or clicking a button to self-report that they have reviewed the material; for activities, it can be participation in a discussion, submission of an assignment, and so on. Similarly, Moodle has a course completion feature (that a Moodle administrator must turn on) and, at a smaller level, an activity completion feature; Blackboard uses activity completion as well, and D2L Brightspace has a Class Progress feature based on "indicators" that the teacher sets. All that is to say that the technology supports

TABLE 1.3.1

Outcomes, Activities, and Estimated Time to Complete

Module 2 Outcomes	Module 2 Activities	Estimated Time to Complete Activities
Outcome 2.1a/b/c: Identify different ways we can affect our own learning—through our body, our mind, and our network.	Activity 2.1a/b/c – Challenge level 1: After reviewing each mini-lecture, complete a quiz to show what you know about how our body, mind, and network affect our learning in general.	Outcome 2.1 tasks: 65 minutes–95 minutes • review instructions: 5 minutes • watch three mini-lectures: 10 minutes–15 minutes each • complete three quizzes: 10 minutes–15 minutes each
Outcome 2.2: Describe how you affect your own learning.	Activity 2.2a – Challenge level 2: Participate in small group discussions about how we affect our own learning, with specific, personal examples. Activity 2.2b – Challenge level 2: Participate in a small group discussion about how your personal values create a greater connection to what you learn.	Outcome 2.2 tasks – Activity 2.2a: 40 minutes–45 minutes • review instructions: 10 minutes • create forum post: 15 minutes–20 minutes • reply to two others: 15 minutes Outcome 2.2 tasks – Activity 2.2b: 55 minutes–75 minutes • review instructions: 10 minutes • create forum post: 15 minutes–20 minutes • reply to two others: 15 minutes • contribute to a summary of group discussion: 15 minutes–25 minutes
Outcome 2.3: Complete a personal exploration (individual project) that involves using body, mind, or network-related strategies to improve your learning.	Activity 2.3a – Challenge level 3: Write a plan that outlines how you will use body, mind, or network-related strategies to improve your learning. Activity 2.3b (Bonus points) – Challenge level 3: Keep a journal of your personal exploration activities. Activity 2.3c – Challenge level 3: Write a reflection that describes your use of body, mind, or network-related strategies to improve your learning.	Outcome 2.3 tasks: 80 minutes–100 minutes • review instructions: 10 minutes • write a plan (with or without template): 20 minutes–30 minutes • keep a journal (optional): 30 minutes • write a reflection essay: 20 minutes–30 minutes

enhancing students' ability to check their progress, but as the teacher, you may have to define completion and set up those markers of completion.

COURSE STRUCTURE AND DESIGN FOR LEARNING EQUITY

One intersection on the design for learning equity framework asks us to increase learners' access to course content. Increasing learners' access to course content means more than just making sure students (a) have appropriate access to adequate devices, adequate internet connectivity, and the campus LMS; (b) can view videos; or (c) can download files. For many students—first-generation students especially—increasing access to content also includes helping students place each piece of content in a larger context, find meaning in reviewing the content, and, make sense of what to do with it.

Make Your Course Structure Transparent

For individual assignments, the Transparency in Learning and Teaching project (tilthighered.com) has shown that students succeed when teachers convey the *purpose* for doing something, the *tasks* to complete, and the *criteria* for success. We will look at the "transparent assignment" concept in more depth in chapter 3.2, "Assessing Learning Online." For now, however, you can apply the same concept to your course structure. For each week or module, start by sharing the outcomes (*What* will you do?), an overview or rationale (*Why* will you do it?), and instructions (*How* will you do it?). Figure 1.3.5 outlines an example of how this might look. Writing transparent module overviews consistently trains students to go to this page first each week—to identify expectations and plan their time and work accordingly. You can even name this page something obvious, such as "START Module 3."

Humanize the Course Environment

When Kevin's friend and former colleague, Ruth Cox, reviewed an online teaching Venn diagram Kevin had made to emphasize aspects of pedagogy, technology, and logistics, she quickly (and rightly) told him that he needed a fourth circle for "being human" (R. Cox, personal communication, March 1, 2010). Early studies in online learning showed that learners prefer having a guide they can see as they complete tasks. Even an avatar or pictures of a cartoon cat throughout a course experience are better than text-only instructions on every page. In their community of inquiry framework, Garrison et al. (2000) describe the value of creating a combination of a social presence by creating a sense of community-based

Figure 1.3.5. Example purpose/outcomes/instructions.

PURPOSE

This first Quest is designed to help you meet the first learning outcome for our class: "Describe yourself as a learner in the past, present, and future."

OUTCOMES AND ACTIVITIES FOR QUEST 1 – HOW DO WE LEARN?

To complete this Quest, you'll do the following:

- Outcome 1.1: Demonstrate knowledge of learning about learning, also called "metacognition."
- Outcome 1.2: Describe yourself as a learner.
- Outcome 1.3: Identify learning strategies—such as strategies for note-taking, studying, and retaining information—that you will try this semester.

INSTRUCTIONS FOR QUEST 1 – HOW DO WE LEARN?

First, you'll learn about learning. Learning about learning is also called "metacognition."

- Review Content 1.1 – it's a presentation called "Learning about learning." You can choose from the PowerPoint, the PDF, and mp3 (audio) files.
- Then complete Activity 1.1 – it's a quiz to show that you understand the basic concepts.

Next, . . .

---

interpersonal relationships and a teaching presence by creating and facilitating meaningful learning processes that correlate with students' cognitive presence of constructing meaning through reflection and interaction. Educational developer Michelle Pacansky-Brock (n.d.b) provides practical advice about "humanizing" online learning or "designing human-centered learning experiences" to increase student motivation and success. See her website at https://brocansky.com/humanizing for more information, resources, and examples. (Please go to Appendix C for links to the online resources mentioned in this chapter.)

Finally, in Fink's (2003) course design model, six components are noted in creating a significant learning experience for students. Of the components listed in his taxonomy of significant learning, a full third of the model, the caring and human dimension, pertains to the human aspect of learning. Within caring, Fink (2003) describes the importance of developing new feelings, interests, and values. For the human dimension, he notes the importance of learning about oneself and others, reminding educators that we not forget the humans when it comes to the best way to facilitate human learning.

One way to humanize the course structure is to send an email to students several days before the course begins to let them know how excited you are to meet them. In this email you may also explain briefly how the course is structured. Another way to humanize the course structure involves creating short screencast videos on how to navigate your course and how to get started in each module or unit. Several screencast tools allow you to record both yourself (headshot video) and your actions in a browser—the result is like the "picture-in-picture" feature on television. It doesn't take any more time to record than a screen-only version and does a better job of making students feel welcome and less nervous about taking the course. Likewise, students can create similar screencast videos to share with you and one another regarding what they are looking forward to in the course and anything they may find confusing about the course.

NEXT STEPS

Now you're ready to create a structure for your online or hybrid course. Use the following questions as a guide as you do this:

- How do you organize your course in your syllabus? By weeks, by course topics, by chapters, or by some other unit?
- How do you calculate how much work students can complete in a week? Are you including homework-type activities in that calculation?
- How are you supporting students in knowing where to go and what to do? How do you name your modules? How do you label your content pages, files, links, and activities? Do you chunk large modules with lots of content and activities? Do you chunk long content pages?
- Do you provide your students with outcomes, an overview, and instructions (i.e., the what, the why, and the how) for each course module?

SUMMARY

Research shows that course structure and organization are critical to online learner persistence and success. Using frameworks of UDL, learning equity, and humanizing the course, this chapter guides you through the processes of (a) identifying the organizing "force" behind your course, (b) chunking and connecting your course concepts, and (c) making the course workflow consistent for online delivery.

Reflection and Discussion Questions

1. What is your preference for how a course is organized: time, topic, sync with a book, or some other way? Why do you prefer this organizational framework? Describe which framework you find most challenging and why.
2. On your campus, what is the perception students hold about the workload of online courses versus face-to-face courses? How can faculty demonstrate to students that, according to accreditation standards, work expected for online courses must be similar to work expected for face-to-face courses?
3. What system do you prefer to track student progress? How might this process be used to increase students' self-awareness and tracking of their own work?
4. Describe how you can include human connections in the course structure. In what ways might an instructor make human interaction a required part of the course?

1.4

FINDING, CREATING, AND SHARING COURSE CONTENT

ONLINE TEACHERS HAVE EXTENSIVE choices to make regarding course content. There is a massive amount of existing instructional materials (e.g., OERs), with new information continually emerging. There is also an increasing number of opportunities to create original instructional materials using a variety of emerging technologies (e.g., Vimeo, Captivate, VoiceThread, Zoom). UDL principles recommend presenting your content in multiple formats, scaffolding content review by highlighting relationships among concepts presented, and helping students decode the material. Design for learning equity suggests sharing content from multiple perspectives, managing or preparing to discuss representation bias, and encouraging learners to connect content to their backgrounds and lives. Fostering human connections keeps us mindful of ways to create and maintain relationships with and among our students through creating course content and sharing the resulting work.

MAKING A CHOICE: CREATING CONTENT, FINDING MATERIALS, OR ADAPTING EXISTING MATERIAL

If we consider teaching both a science and an art, then we might describe online faculty members as collage artists who follow scientific principles. That is, when you put together an online course, you have choices. For example, you can create all of the content yourself. You can find, possibly adapt, and use existing materials (as allowed by ethical standards, licenses, and the law) that have been created by other online teachers or that content publishers provide for students to purchase. Or you can combine some of these options. Together we'll explore reasons and techniques for doing each.

When faced with reinventing the wheel, it is always important to ask yourself, "Is this a wheel that needs reinventing?" There are times when creating new material is warranted. Perhaps you cannot find instructional materials that align with your learning outcomes and that are at the quality that you demand. Maybe you want to create a consistent set of resources that makes the content more meaningful to the specific students you serve at your institution. It could be that your pedagogical goals or approach to teaching specific content differ from publisher textbooks and materials currently in existence. Or by following UDL principles, equity principles, and human connection concepts, you feel it is important to make additional versions of your course content in new formats. These and many other reasons all point to creating your own instructional resources. That said, even if you feel the need to create your own content, before you put in a significant amount of work it is advisable to see what is available through vendors, instructional designers, and other teachers who have decided to share their creations.

There are many reasons to search for existing resources before beginning the task of creating your own content. Improving the students' learning experience, meeting a teaching need, or following a peer's suggestion are primary reasons for many faculty to reuse open content (White & Manton, 2011). White and Manton also identify critical questions that may influence your decision to find something rather than make something—do you have the time and/or skills to create the content your students need?

Cost to students is often a reason faculty give for creating their own course content. Many faculty fail to realize that there are many ways to use current educational content that can reduce the cost for students, from OER textbooks to free online tutorials. As faculty members, we must remain vigilant in keeping costs down for our students, which provides much more equitable access to education. Student spending on course materials has decreased consistently over the past few years (McKenzie, 2018; Nemec, 2020). Over half of higher education faculty "believe that cost is the primary reason that not all of their students have access to the required course materials" (Seaman & Seaman, 2018, p. 18). Research by the U.S. Public Interest Research Group has shown as many as 65% of students have skipped buying a textbook due to cost (Senack, 2014). In a more recent survey by Morning Consult for the publisher Cengage, almost 9 in 10 students stated that course materials had a "big impact" (46%) or "somewhat of an impact" (41%) on their financial situation (Whitford,

2018, para. 3). This impact influenced students' choices—at times, they skip meals, take fewer trips home to see family, register for fewer classes, or take a job to pay for books (Whitford, 2018). At San Francisco State University (2017), where Kevin teaches online courses, "79% of students reported that the cost of materials causes them stress" (para. 1). In sum, textbook and course material costs affect students not only financially but also academically and emotionally.

Several recent studies show most faculty care about the students' financial situation. However, not as many choose lower-cost textbook options such as subscription-based or digital versions, and under half even know about using OERs to make sure course materials are more affordable (K. Kelly, 2019a). You can change this dynamic by educating yourself about all of your options as you select course materials for your classes.

There are other reasons for finding and using instructional materials over creating your own. You may have heard about a trusted expert, institution, or organization sharing instructional resources for topics in your discipline. Maybe you will explore how other teachers have approached teaching a particular topic and decide to use high-quality OERs. Or you might prefer using materials that someone else maintains and updates so you can focus on other aspects of teaching.

Another option is to adapt the course content that is already available online. There are several reasons to take this path. Of course, before adapting any resource for use in your own course, ensure it is ethical and legal to do so. If it is permissible, there are many reasons to go this route. You may lack the skill and time to create information from scratch but can adapt it to your needs. Modifications might be adding to, updating, or "fixing" a Wikipedia article. Another option is to have students in a course adapt a Wikipedia page—for example, see Wiki Education's Teach With Wikipedia program (wikiedu.org/teach-with-wikipedia/). (Please go to Appendix C for links to the online resources mentioned in this chapter.) Your decision to adapt existing content might also be a result of finding content that is nearly perfect for your course, but in need of adjustment to make it appropriate. For example, a site might use the word "university" multiple times, and you simply want to change "university" to "college." A final example is that you might want to change the length of a resource. If a posted video is too long or if you plan to annotate it, using EdPuzzle will allow for a custom adaptation to well-developed existing material.

Regardless of your reasoning, there are many options for creating content, using existing content, or adapting existing content. Provided you follow guidelines and rules put into place to give credit where credit is due, you too can be a faculty member content artist.

FINDING EXISTING INSTRUCTIONAL MATERIALS FOR YOUR ONLINE COURSE

Whether it's just one resource about a single topic or many materials that span a quarter or semester, instructional quality is a primary concern. Once you have decided to look for instructional materials, you have to know which sources you can trust. Publisher materials typically go through editing and peer review processes. As a result, if a publisher offers content as part of the textbook purchase, that content is usually of very high quality. Large-scale OER projects are also a good source of quality content for your course. These programs often start with external funding from organizations that require both sharing the OER publicly and vetting the OER quality, either internally or through feedback from early adopters. For example, the Skills Commons project is dedicated to building a library of workforce training materials, with its initial funding provided by the U.S. Department of Labor. To ensure the quality of the materials shared via Skills Commons (n.d.), the project "provides information, evaluation rubrics, and access to experts" (para. 1) who support people designing teaching and learning materials. The Khan Academy's mission is "to provide a free, world-class education to anyone, anywhere" (Khan Academy, 2020, para. 1). One of its first significant and long-standing supporters is the Bill and Melinda Gates Foundation, which brings additional credibility to the quality of the materials posted on the Khan Academy website.

Looking for vetted or curated collections is another way to find quality materials. For instance, OER Commons shares collections curated by digital librarians. Some curated collections also harness the power of the community to check resources for quality. As one example of this approach, MERLOT—Multimedia Educational Resources for Learning and Online Teaching—uses a peer-review process. Let's learn more about these sites and others like them, organized by conventional types of materials you might find for your class—textbooks, instructional materials, and recorded lessons or lectures.

Textbooks

The OER Commons Open Textbooks Hub (n.d.) (www.oercommons.org/hubs/open-textbooks) has a comprehensive list of open or affordable textbooks in many disciplines for community college and lower division university classes.

Run by a nonprofit organization, the site allows you to search for textbooks by subject and provides reviews of each book's content and accessibility. Supported by the Center for Open Education and the Open Textbook Network, the Open Textbook Library (n.d.) (open.umn.edu/

opentextbooks/) also lists textbooks in several disciplines that may be freely used, adapted, and distributed. These texts have been reviewed by faculty from various higher education institutions. Various discipline-specific organizations have open textbook projects as well, such as the Open Textbook Initiative by the American Institute of Mathematics (AIM, n.d.) (aimath.org/textbooks/). An editorial board evaluates textbooks for AIM, based on specific criteria. In addition to nonprofit organizations and discipline associations, you can also search for open textbooks provided by specific higher education institutions, like Oregon State University (open .oregonstate.edu/textbooks/) or the State University of New York (SUNY) system (textbooks.opensuny.org/) or entire states, such as the Rhode Island Open Textbook Initiative (www.innovate.ri.gov/opentextbook).

OERs

As mentioned previously, OER Commons (2020; www.oercommons. org/) shares collections curated by digital librarians. OER Commons allows projects, institutions, districts, and other entities to create Hubs to "create, organize and share OER collections that meet their common goals" (para. 4). Check to see if a group you work with or respect has created a Hub. The Community College Consortium for Open Educational Resources (www.cccoer.org/) promotes open education to "enhance teaching and learning at community and technical colleges" (CCCOER, n.d., para. 4) and to provide students with equal access to high-quality instructional materials.

The aforementioned Skills Commons (n.d.; www.skillscommons.org/) is a free and open digital library of workforce training materials. Browse the Skills Commons site according to specific grant projects, type of learning material or credential, institution, industry, or occupation. One of the oldest and most significant sources of OERs, MERLOT (2020; www .merlot.org) is "a curated collection of free and open online teaching, learning, and faculty development services contributed and used by an international education community" (Pitt Community College Library, n.d., para. 6). With its advanced search function, MERLOT allows you to find materials by keyword, discipline, language, type of learning material, file format, level of review, readiness for mobile platforms, license for use, author information, and date added to the collection.

Recorded Lessons or Lectures

The Khan Academy (n.d.; http://www.khanacademy.org) offers free courses and lessons in several broad categories: science and engineering, computing, arts and humanities, economics and finance, and math.

Some online teachers point to Khan Academy to support students who need additional assistance with foundational concepts required for their courses. Others provide links to specific lessons so students can review a concept presented in a different way than it was explained in the textbook. LinkedIn Learning (n.d., www.linkedin.com/learning), formerly known as Lynda.com, is another collection of learning modules, similar in concept to the Khan Academy, although this service does require a paid subscription. Check with your campus to see if your institution has a site license. LinkedIn Learning uses an online learning platform with videos and courses primarily related to business, software applications, technology, and creative skills. If you require students to perform specific tasks (e.g., creating pivot tables in Excel, databases in MySQL, or animations with Maya) then you can link to the appropriate videos or chapters for students to refresh or relearn those skills. Sites like EdX (www.edx.org/), Coursera (www.coursera.org/), and Open Culture (www.openculture.com/) aggregate free online courses taught by instructors around the world.

Images

You will likely use images throughout your course materials. Keep in mind that most images on search engines are copyright protected. The good news is that there are several websites with images that can be freely used, although giving photographers and artists credit for their work is always suggested. Creative Commons Search (search.creativecommons.org/) has over 300 million reusable images indexed from multiple collections. For amazing photographs and excellent character drawings, check out Unsplash.com and Pixabay.com. Later in this chapter, we will describe image and media galleries that accurately and adequately represent a more diverse population.

Other Materials Found on the Web

There are many content-rich resources throughout the internet. Faculty members and instructional designers often create these materials. A question quickly emerges as to whether you can use these materials in your course. If you wish to download the material and post the actual resource or information in your online course, the best practice is to contact the person who created the materials or resources and ask permission to use what you have found in your course. As long as you are not making money on the resource, most faculty members are happy to permit you to use the material. Keep in mind that if a faculty member has published a resource, the permission must come from the publisher (or person holding the copyright on the material), rather than the faculty member.

Another option is to post the link to the resource. If the link is freely available on the web, you can point individuals to the link without permission. The downside to this approach is that you cannot control when the link might be removed or moved. That said, pointing students to online resources is commonly done and requires no work on your part to secure permissions.

LEGAL USE OF PREEXISTING CONTENT

In this chapter, we have shared quite a few collections and websites to help you find materials that people have agreed to let you use or modify. Even with all of that, you may still want to utilize copyrighted materials, or materials that an author has not shared freely. If you do, check out online guides to copyright and fair use (e.g., *The Educator's Guide to Copyright and Fair Use* [Educator's World, n.d.]) or Tom Tobin's (2017) fun and informative comic book, *The Copyright Ninja*. You also can obtain permission to reproduce copyrighted text via the Copyright Clearance Center (n.d.; www.copyright.com/). The Technology, Education, and Copyright Harmonization (TEACH) Act applies explicitly to distance education, seeking "to balance the needs of distance learners and educators with the rights of copyright holders" (Copyright Clearance Center, 2011, para. 3). If these guides and documents do not provide clarification, check with a librarian or library faculty at your campus who specializes in copyright or your institution's office of legal counsel. For example, The University of San Diego's Office of the General Counsel (2020) has a statement on copyright basics. Although colleagues may seem knowledgeable and helpful, it is best to double-check with someone who specializes in copyright to determine what is permissible.

VETTING INSTRUCTIONAL MATERIALS FOR YOUR ONLINE COURSE

Although the previous sites and others like them do provide high-quality instructional materials, remember that you should review anything that you share with your students. Quality is just one of several criteria you must consider before using instructional materials created by someone else. Ask yourself the following questions as you vet learning resources you have found for your online class:

- *Alignment*: Does each resource align with your course- or module-level learning outcomes? Compared to the existing course materials or your lectures, do the resource author(s) present a conflicting viewpoint about a course concept that could confuse your students?
- *Reliability and bias*: Does the author(s) present a viewpoint or information that is biased and/or unsupported? Is each resource accurate in the information it presents?
- *Accessibility*: Is each resource accessible to students with disabilities, or can it be made accessible easily?
- *Equity*: Does each resource meet simple equity guidelines, such as avoiding stereotypes or, where appropriate, providing equal representation of today's students (e.g., gender, ethnicity, age)?
- *Usability*: Does the resource use specialized vocabulary that your students are unlikely to know? Does the resource support students who are English language learners?
- *Acceptability*: Is the material presented in a way that adheres to your school and/or course policies regarding acceptable language and behavior? Do they raise any controversial issues or present content inappropriately?
- *Human Connection*: Does the material encourage or support a connection between you and students and also among students? In addition, does the resource allow students to either select something that aligns with themselves or to express their individuality?

MODIFYING INSTRUCTIONAL MATERIALS FOR YOUR ONLINE COURSE

After scouring the entire internet, you still may not find resources that fit your needs or the previous review criteria. Even if you do find resources that could work, you may have an excellent reason why they cannot be used in your course as currently available. However, before discarding any materials completely, check to see if any are OERs that allow you to make modifications. Building on the work of someone else can save you time and effort as you create your own course materials.

Many works that are published with a Creative Commons license can be modified. Review the various Creative Commons (2020; creativecommons .org/share-your-work/licensing-types-examples/) license conditions on their website.

Also, if you find materials developed by individuals, you may be able to adapt their instructional materials or resources with their permission.

Often the faculty member granting permission simply wants the option to use what you have created and to learn from what you have done.

The process of adapting existing material will be identical to developing it from scratch, except that you have the benefit of something from which to work and a framework to guide you. Again, we cannot stress enough the importance of giving credit to those who have created the foundation from which you will work and proceeding in alignment with both ethical standards and the laws in place to protect intellectual property.

DEVELOPING INSTRUCTIONAL MATERIALS FOR THE ONLINE ENVIRONMENT

If you have decided to make your own materials, let's review some of the tools you can use—tools for recording video or hosting video meetings and online authoring tools for rich media.

Tools for Recording Video or Hosting Video Meetings

To create mini-lecture videos for your online or hybrid course, you can record yourself giving a presentation right from your computer or laptop. You can also create narrated how-to videos to show students how to use the technology required for your class, such as how to use Excel for an accounting assignment. To create these videos, you can use a variety of tools, including videoconference tools, lecture capture tools, screencast tools, and interactive presentation tools. Let's take a look at some typical solutions for each type of tool.

If your campus has an LMS, then the chances are good that it also has a license for videoconference tools like Collaborate, Big Blue Button, or Zoom. You can record either synchronous online or hybrid class meetings that your students attend or asynchronous lectures or screencasts by yourself and at your convenience. The Blackboard LMS has a tool called Collaborate (Blackboard, n.d.; www.blackboard.com/online-collaborative-learning/blackboard) that works in your browser. In addition to allowing you to share your screen, Collaborate provides tools to annotate as you go—for example, use the pen tool to circle an important part of a diagram as you describe it. Big Blue Button is the default videoconference tool embedded in the Canvas LMS—use the Conferences tab on the Course menu to access it. Check out the Canvas Guides (n.d.a) to get step-by-step instructions on how to record a Conference (guides.instructure.com/m/4152/l/117864-how-do-i-record-a-conference). Zoom (zoom.us/) is a popular videoconference tool that integrates with almost any LMS. If your campus does not offer any videoconference tools, then create a free Basic account in Zoom (n.d.). The free version allows you to host an unlimited number of meetings up to 40 minutes long with as many as 100 participants. Whether or not you invite your students to join you, you may record each session and save it as both a video file (MP4) and an audio file (M4A).

If your campus has a license for a lecture capture tool like Echo360 or Panopto, ask your information technology or academic technology team to load the necessary software on your desktop or laptop computer. Echo360 (echo360.com/) provides both Mac and Windows versions of its Personal Capture software (Echo360, n.d.). After you make each recording, you may edit it before publishing it for your class. The recordings are stored centrally, and data reports analyze who is watching the videos and for how long. Like Echo360, the screen recording tool by Panopto (www.panopto.com) allows you to record and display a video of you, the presenter, along with what you show on your monitor or laptop screen. It's easy to add bookmarks for your students to jump to specific points in each video, and students can search your videos for particular words that are spoken or shown on your screen (Panopto, n.d.). Solutions like Echo360 and Panopto are usually part of a bigger ecosystem involving LMS integrations, video storage, analytics, and reporting.

If you don't have lecture capture, your campus may still have a license for a more individualized or personal screencast tool, such as Camtasia, TechSmith Relay, or ilos. Camtasia (n.d.) is a sophisticated video editor that allows you to record your screen and voice, add effects, and much more (www.techsmith.com/video-editor.html). TechSmith Relay (n.d.; www .techsmith.com/lecture-capture.html) is a lecture-capture tool that simplifies the screen recording process for you. The screen recording tool called ilos (Ilosvideos, n.d.; www.ilosvideos.com/) has integrated quiz features and allows students to make recordings from their mobile devices.

If your campus has none of the solutions listed, do not fear. There are free screencast tools that you can use on your own, such as Screencast-o-Matic and Loom. Screencast-o-Matic (screencast-o-matic.com/) has a free version of its cloud-based screen recorder service. You can create recordings up to 15 minutes long, then publish to YouTube or save as a video file to upload to your LMS. The Pro version is less than $20 per year—that's only $1.65 per month!—and provides more features like draw and zoom, allows you to make longer recordings without the company's watermark, and lets you edit the videos (Screencast-O-Matic, n.d.; https://screencast-o-matic.com/plans). As with all software solutions, prices change with market demand. Loom is a free screen recorder for the Chrome browser.

On the website's homepage, you just use the "One-Click Install" button to get started. Loom is easy to use and allows you to edit your video before saving. For ideas about how to use Loom (n.d.; www.useloom.com/), check out some of their education use cases (www.useloom.com/use -cases#education), such as explaining homework assignments, recapping lessons, or providing feedback to students.

Last, interactive presentation tools create a path for you and your students to engage around course content. One of the best of these tools is VoiceThread, which allows you to create online presentations with text and voice comments for each slide. By recording your narration in a slide-by-slide fashion, it's easy to rerecord a snippet if you don't like it the first time around, rather than having to start recording a 15-minute mini-lecture again from the beginning. What's even better is that your students can add text and voice comments on each slide as well, turning an asynchronous recording into an interactive experience. VoiceThread (2019; voicethread .com) also offers VoiceThread Universal, a tool that helps people who use screen readers interact with the recordings.

Online Authoring Tools for Rich Media

We've just described quite a few tools to create videos for your class, but we're not finished yet! If the content you want to create is something other than a video, there also are tools you can use to create interactive modules and/or rich media files—for example, infographics and concept maps. Let's look at a few of these tools.

While PowerPoint is usually used for linear presentations, it can be used to create interactive modules as well. For example, you can create case study scenarios for your students to review and make decisions. Use images, shapes, or text to link to separate slides showing what would happen if the student chose the correct course of action or one of the alternatives. Some campuses have licenses for SoftChalk (2020; softchalk.com), a popular tool that higher education faculty and instructional design staff use to make interactive online lessons with games, self-assessment quizzes, and/or annotated text. OER Commons (n.d.; www.oercommons.org/) provides a free Module Builder to develop simple interactive modules for higher education topics. You can work alone or with colleagues to create a web-based sequence of content to review and tasks to complete.

If you want to create rich media files like infographics or concept maps, you can explore a number of free, online tools that specialize in making one or the other. Infographics are diagrams used to present information in a visual format or to make it easier for your students to review complex concepts or data. Some instructors have even made infographic versions of their syllabus—for examples, see the Visually Enhanced Syllabi block at UDL Universe (Christie, 2019; https://enact.sonoma.edu/c.php?g=789377&p=5650618). Free online tools like Canva (2020; www.canva.com/create/infographics/), Venngage (venngage.com/), and Piktochart (piktochart.com/) provide templates, themes, fonts, and icons for you to create infographics and allow you to upload your own images as well. If you have data that you want to use to create graphs, charts, or maps, Infogram (infogram.com) has a built-in tool for entering, editing, and displaying that data in different ways on your infographic. As with all media discussed in this chapter, consider accessibility and check the infographic you create.

Concept maps, or mind maps, are another type of visual learning tool, usually used to show connections between and among course concepts. In separate meta-analyses of research studies on the use of concept maps, Nesbit and Adesope (2006) found that using concept maps increased students' retention, and Cañas (2003) found that concept maps outperformed other methods for learning relationships among course concepts. Bubbl.us (bubbl.us/), Mindmup (www.mindmup.com/), and MindMeister (www.mindmeister.com/) are all free, online tools to create concept maps for or with your students. The online presentation tool Prezi can also be used for concept maps. Prezi's Zoom Reveal feature and nearly infinite capacity to zoom in further allow you to share more details when students click on any part of the overall diagram. Prezi has a free Basic account that allows you to make unlimited presentations (2020; https://prezi.com/pricing). The for-fee Plus account provides additional features such as voice-over for narration, video upload storage to enrich your concept maps, and the ability to export your map as a PDF file.

CONSIDERATIONS WHEN CREATING INSTRUCTIONAL MATERIALS FOR YOUR ONLINE COURSE

As you start thinking seriously about creating your original content and instructional materials for your online course, there are a few things to consider. Regardless of what tool you use or in what format you save your resource, it has to be usable, accessible, mobile friendly, and more. Ask yourself the following questions as you create course content and learning materials for your online class:

- *Video length*: How long should each video be? If you decide to create videos for your class—mini-lectures, how-to instructions, or anything else, then consider what might be a reasonable length for each video. Research on student attention, working memory, and cognitive load point to breaking your video content into chunks no longer than 12 to 15 minutes, followed by some sort of activity designed to help students encode and retain the information. If you want to create longer videos, identify good stopping points for students with a phrase like "Now press pause and complete the following activity before continuing this lecture video."

- *Accessibility*: Will everyone in your class have the same ability to review the content you create? Before you get started, consider the accessibility of the file formats you'll save and share with your students, as well as any video or media players students may have to use to view your content. Videos should be captioned and/or accompanied by a transcript. The latter is relatively easy if you read a script when you record your mini-lectures. To get information on captioning your videos, check with your disability programs and resource center to see if your campus uses a captioning service. If you must do it yourself, adding caption files is easier with some tools, like VoiceThread. Or use YouTube to create rough captions that you can then edit (see YouTube's [n.d.] instructions for automatic captioning at support.google.com/youtube/answer/6373554).

- *File size*: How big are your instructional materials? Videos and rich media files can get very big, very fast, and students may not have access to high speed internet, particularly if they are accessing material off campus. If students will watch the video or review the rich media file online, then the file size may only affect how fast it streams or displays in a browser. However, if students need to download the file, then do your best to compress it before sharing.

- *Mobile friendly*: Can the instructional materials you create be viewed easily on a mobile device?

- *Equity*: Have you checked your materials for image and representation bias? Images influence our students' perceptions. Building on what we mentioned about this in Chapter 1.1, it's worth taking time to review the imagery in our textbooks, lecture slides, and class materials for how adequately and accurately those images represent the students in your class and at your institution. Better yet, ask your students to share the extent to which they feel the textbook images represent them. For example, textbooks may underrepresent women and certain ethnicities in images of people in prestigious professions or leadership positions. Several sites offer images that better represent traditionally underrepresented populations. For example, Lean In has worked with Getty Images to close the gender gap in how women are portrayed in stock photos (leanin.org/getty/). Similarly, Representation Matters has created a royalty-free, commercial stock photo library focused on inclusion, ethnic and social diversity, and healthy body image (representationmatters.me/), and Blend Images provides a variety of multicultural and ethnically diverse commercial images (www.blendimages.com/).

- *Human connection*: Have you developed material that is presented in a voice whereby you are talking directly to your student? The images used are best when they create human connections with our learners. It is easy to get overly focused on the content and the delivery of that content. Always remember there is a person processing and responding to the material you assign. Help students connect course content to their lives. Beyond seeing themselves in the content through diverse perspectives, guiding students to make personal connections to the content increases their motivation and retention. Author and community college music instructor Elizabeth Barkley does this in a simple way. She finds pictures of famous classical composers as young people so students can relate to them more than they do to more familiar images of those same musicians at the ends of their lives (E. Barkley, personal communication, February 28, 2012).

SHARING COURSE CONTENT AND UDL

Whether you create or find your course content, UDL principles recommend presenting that content in multiple formats, aiding learners' comprehension in different ways, and helping students decode the material. Here are just a few UDL strategies related to course content:

- *Provide materials in alternate formats*: One of the UDL principles— provide multiple means of representation—recommends providing alternatives to information presented exclusively in either auditory or visual formats, as well as illustrating key points through multiple media. Visit udlguidelines.cast.org/representation for more details on the UDL Guidelines (CAST, 2020) and the UDL principle.
- *Connect the content with the course-level or module-level learning objectives*: For example, "This content will prepare you to demonstrate your knowledge of learning about learning, also called 'metacognition.' It also will help you to achieve the first learning outcome in the course, to 'describe yourself as a learner in the past, present, and future.'"

- *Provide prompts to support students as they review the content*: For example, when using a mini-lecture video, provide skeletal notes—in other words, a simple document listing key points and providing room for students to write or type their notes (Kiewra, 2008). Alternatively, create a set of questions for students to answer as they review the mini-lecture recording.
- *Activate prior knowledge*: Let students know when any content or resource requires or builds on prior knowledge. Provide links to summary versions of that prior knowledge so that students can review foundational concepts. Activating prior knowledge is especially meaningful for students who may be underprepared to complete your course successfully.

SHARING COURSE CONTENT AND DESIGN FOR LEARNING EQUITY

In addition to some of the equity suggestions previously given (e.g., managing image and representation bias), design for learning equity suggests sharing content from multiple perspectives and preparing to discuss with students any stereotypes or representation bias if you cannot change the content itself. It is particularly important to encourage learners to connect content to their backgrounds and lives, as it provides a strong context to which learners can relate. Here is a short list of ideas to address learning equity as you share content:

- *Ensure equitable access to the content itself*: Inform students if they need special software to review an instructional material or resource. In the instructions for each piece of content, add links to the required software along with the UDL-inspired prompts listed previously. For example, share a link to get Adobe Reader (get.adobe.com/reader/) if you ask students to review Adobe PDF files.
- *Use discussions to help students analyze and address stereotypes and misrepresentations*: After you have selected the very best content to help students learn your course topics, you may find that the concepts are well represented. However, some demographics may not be portrayed accurately or may not be represented at all. Stock photography in textbooks may underrepresent certain demographics (e.g., women, minorities, people with disabilities) in leadership positions or in the workforce sector that your career and technical education course prepares students to enter. If you choose

to use that textbook, then engage your students in a discussion that asks them to analyze the potential impact of inaccurate representation or to suggest (or create) alternative media that improve representation. A sociology instructor at Laney College in Oakland, California, goes even further. She encourages her students to write a letter to the publisher explaining how inaccurate representations affect them and suggesting how to improve them.

- *Showcase diverse perspectives on course topics*: In addition to offering content in multiple formats—text, graphic, audio, video, multimedia—it is also important to provide your course content from multiple perspectives. This may involve providing culturally relevant examples, applications of concepts in various contexts, alternate presentations or interpretations of concepts from different perspectives, or recognition of relevant contributions to the field. For example, a history teacher might pair Howard Zinn's *A People's History of the United States* and/or narratives written by former slaves to complement a traditional history textbook chapter about the Civil War. Or a teacher may ask students to play the interactive game *Bury Me, My Love* to present real-life refugee experiences as part of a unit about international crises. This concept is especially important for particular fields such as the science, technology, engineering, and math (STEM) disciplines, in which women and some minoritized groups have a harder time seeing themselves as professionals within those fields. Kimberly Tanner cites Ladson-Billings (1995) and applies her culturally responsive teaching ideas to biology:

    Although it is not possible to represent aspects of all students' lives or the cultural background of each student in your course, careful attention to integrating culturally diverse and personally relevant connections to biology can demonstrate for students that diverse perspectives are valued in your biology classroom. (Tanner, 2013, para. 20)

NEXT STEPS

- Take the time to read the TEACH Act. Faculty members often mention that it is okay to use preexisting information because of "fair use." Adopt a model of reading policy papers and laws pertaining to this subject to get the most accurate information (Copyright Clearance Center, 2011; www.copyright.com/wp-content/uploads/2015/04/CR-Teach-Act.pdf).

Now that you have explored finding, creating, and sharing instructional materials for your course, ask yourselves these questions as you prepare to act on what you learned:

- What course materials best help students reach the desired learning outcomes? Do those materials exist as publisher-created media, OERs, or anything in between?
- If adequate materials do not exist, do you have the skills and time to create what your students need? Do you have an idea of the tools you need to produce the materials in different formats?
- Have you paid attention to how different groups are represented within the content itself—through the actual text, images, and/or media? Will the students see accurate and equitable depictions of different people? Do students have a chance to explore multiple, diverse perspectives related to course topics, through examples, additional presentations, or contextual references?
- When sharing course content with your students, do you do more than create a link? Do you outline expectations, connect the content to the learning outcomes and prior knowledge, provide prompts to guide them as they review material, and provide links to any software they need to access?

CHAPTER SUMMARY

Creating course content will be one of the most challenging aspects of developing your online course. It can also be one of the most fulfilling. Whether you use existing material, adapt existing material, or build your own course content, always be sure to keep the outcomes of the course in mind. It is of little value to produce elaborate content for something unrelated to the course. Also, it is exceedingly important to give credit to any work previously developed that you wish to use in your course. Through the process of gathering course content, keep in mind the need to give full credit to anyone who has done work on any resource or information used. Finally, strive to develop content to make the course an exceptional learning opportunity for your students by following UDL principles, applying equity principles, and building strong human connections throughout the course.

Reflection and Discussion Questions

1. Is your overall preference to create online content, use content already developed, or adapt existing content? Explain the rationale behind your preference.

2. Look back at the course outcome you wrote for Reflection and Discussion Question 3 in chapter 1.2. For that outcome, find three existing sources to meet that instructional outcome. Explain why you chose these resources and what legal implications there might be in using those resources.

3. Identify one method of creating your own content as described in this chapter to support the outcome listed in the previous question. The content should be related to one of the three existing sources you found in Question 2. Discuss the extent to which the process of creating your own content was easier or more challenging than you had expected.

4. Describe how the material you either found or created addressed learning equity. Was it challenging to keep equity in mind when developing or selecting material? Describe how following the design for learning equity framework might change your course in the future.

1.5

ALIGNING ACTIVITIES AND ASSESSMENT STRATEGIES WITH COURSE OUTCOMES

THERE ARE THREE CRITICAL elements in designing your online course: the outcomes you expect your students to achieve, the methods you will use to determine if success has been realized, and the activities in which students will engage to bring about the outcomes desired. As noted in chapter 1.2, the very popular approach of backward design (Wiggins & McTighe, 2005) outlines this process thoroughly. When activities and assessments are not aligned with anticipated outcomes, students are frequently frustrated, and it may be difficult for you, as the instructor, to justify your designed curriculum and grades assigned in the course. For an online course, this takes on additional significance as you "light up the runway" for the learners. In this chapter, you will choose methods to make sure your activities and assessments map to the outcomes for your online course.

ALIGNING ASSESSMENT STRATEGIES WITH YOUR OUTCOMES

In chapter 1.2, you reviewed the learning outcomes for one of your classes and created some module-level outcomes. Maybe you even rewrote one or two to make them stronger or to raise the expectations for what students will do. Students can frequently achieve levels they themselves did not realize they could reach if you develop a robust curricular program, provide support for them to proceed, and then give them the chance to succeed!

To help students meet those higher levels of challenge, let's look at how well the different parts of the course align with the outcomes. Although this alignment is critical for all teaching, we will look specifically at how this applies to your online instruction. In the process, we're also going to challenge you to streamline your course.

When you think about aligning parts of a class with outcomes, picture the process as designing or mapping a path (see Figure 1.5.1). If we guide students in the correct direction, each checkpoint helps to increase the probability they will reach the desired outcome. Conversely, if we include course elements that are not well aligned, we can hinder students' ability to succeed by distracting students from the learning path. In chapter 1.4, you explored how to align course content that you create or find. However, even the best textbook, screencast lecture video, or learning material may not prepare every student to reach an outcome on its own. Now you'll review assessments and activities with a focus on aligning them with your outcomes.

To get a fresh perspective, put yourself in your students' shoes. Imagine yourself learning something new, such as beekeeping, starting a nonprofit organization, learning to teach online, or studying the psychology of learning. From all the possibilities, let's pick something you've likely never done before, like surfing. Yes, some of you reading this book may know how to surf, but in the general population of the United States, this outdoor activity is relatively rare. For your first half-day surfing lesson, the overall outcome is simple—you want to ride a wave. For our assessment, let's use observation and select the criteria of 5 seconds. Therefore, if the instructor sees you stand up on the board and stay upright for at least 5 seconds, you will have successfully met the desired outcome. Now that we have an outcome and an assessment, the next consideration is to determine the best instructional strategy to help you to score well enough on the assessment to meet your desired outcome.

The instructor might select an instructional strategy of giving demonstrations or mini-lectures (content presentation), then asking you

Figure 1.5.1. Learning outcomes alignment (generic).

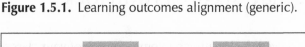
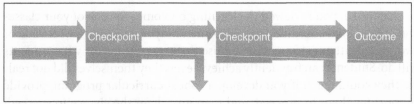

to practice the fundamental elements of standing on the board (activity). The fundamental elements may well be paddling, popping up onto the board, and standing on the board. The instructor may first explain or model these elements to you for about 10 to 15 minutes and give you some things to consider as you start your new career as a professional surfer. Once those have been explained, you get into the water for the engaged learning part of the lesson. The instructor will watch you try each skill and give you additional, individual feedback and advice as you practice. You need to try paddling in a calm place before you get between the waves or try to catch a wave. You will need to practice how to pop up onto the board in calm water, keeping in mind elements taught during the lecture, such as speed, fluency, and balance. For standing on the surfboard, you'll need the instructor to give you some additional basic information, such as how to pick which foot goes in front. Are you natural footed (right foot forward) or goofy footed (left foot forward)?

With a bit of practice and feedback, you will make progress. To determine if your first lesson was successful, you need only to consider the curriculum elements of outcomes, assessment, and teaching strategies. At the end of the lesson, if you were able to get up on the board and ride a wave for at least 5 seconds, then the session can be deemed a success. At some point in your surfing career, you'll want to learn more about wave group velocity, but that's not relevant information that you need for your first half-day lesson. If you don't know how to stand on the surfboard and ride a wave for at least 5 seconds, you're going to wipe out with respect to your newly acquired outdoor sport.

Let's look at some more concrete online teaching and learning examples, using a tool that will help you to align your own assessments, activities, and content with your outcomes. In Table 1.5.1, the first column shows three possible learning outcomes related to cell division for a biology class. The outcomes ask students to reach three different levels of thinking or achievement. The second column identifies potential assessment strategies for each outcome. For the outcome designed to promote lower-level thinking, the instructor has chosen a quiz and a discussion to assess achievement. For the outcome designed to promote midlevel thinking, the instructor has chosen two pathways—an essay or a diagram—for students to show they can explain abnormal cell growth. For the outcome designed to promote higher-level thinking, the instructor selected a case study for students to demonstrate what they can do. In each case, the assessment strategy is aligned with not only the outcome but also the level of thinking students should reach.

TABLE 1.5.1

Backward Design: Three Examples of Mapping Assessment Strategies to Learning Outcomes Requiring Different Levels of Thinking

Outcomes	Assessment Strategies	Activities	Resources or Learning Objects
Students will distinguish between two different types of cell division: meiosis and mitosis.	• Discussion: Evaluate the quantity and quality of items in a compare-and contrast-table • Quiz: matching, short answer, or multiple-choice answer		
Students will explain how abnormal cell division occurs during the two types of cell division.	• Assignment with diagram rubric or essay rubric (includes key differences from normal cell division, possible causes, etc.)		
Students will recommend a cancer drug therapy to prevent specific types of abnormal cell division.	• Assignment with case study rubric		

ALIGNING ACTIVITIES WITH YOUR OUTCOMES

Now that you have chosen and aligned your assessment strategies, we'll continue to work backward and align activities that allow students to practice working with concepts and prepare to show what they know. You can also use these activities as a bridge, asking students to make connections between prior knowledge and new concepts. The practice they get through course activities should be at the same level of thinking or achievement that you'll assess later. Remember that online learning can and should include activities that take place offline, which students can document during and analyze after the process. For example, English-as-a-second-language students can use mobile devices to take pictures of billboards with grammar errors and post them later with their corrections to solicit feedback from classmates or you, the instructor.

Let's revisit our biology examples, aligning different learning activities with outcomes, as well as with the assessment strategies. In Table 1.5.2, the third column shows possible learning activities that would give students appropriate practice with different aspects of cell division. As the outcomes and the assessment strategies ask students to reach three different levels of thinking or achievement, the activities should do the same. If students will be discussing tables that compare and contrast different types of cell division, then it makes sense to ask the students to prepare in advance by creating compare-and-contrast tables. If you would like to evaluate your students' ability to explain abnormal cell division, then perhaps have students practice by describing cell division or cell division that is abnormal in a different way. If you are using a case study to solicit treatment recommendations from students, then ask them to work in small groups to review a similarly structured case study and to practice drawing conclusions from the facts presented. In each case, the learning activity is aligned with not only the outcome but also the assessment strategy.

We can round out the mapping exercise by reviewing what resources students may need to demonstrate achievement of the outcomes. Table 1.5.3 shows possible resources that would adequately prepare students to practice with different aspects of cell division and then demonstrate the achievement of the outcomes. As the required level of thinking increases, the instructor has added relevant resources rather than substituting them. This both-and approach supports learners who may need additional support with foundation-level concepts before attempting higher-level thinking activities.

At each previously outlined stage, we described how to prepare students to show that they have reached a specific level of achievement. Even though you may not see them in a physical classroom setting, your students can demonstrate knowledge (cognitive), skills (psychomotor), and attitudes (affective). Table 1.5.4 provides example activities that students can perform to show achievement of low-, mid-, and high-level outcomes, based on the taxonomies described in chapter 1.2. Review the table and identify what levels of achievement you're asking your students to reach.

TABLE 1.5.2

Backward Design: Three Examples of Mapping Activities to Learning
Outcomes Requiring Different Levels of Thinking

Outcomes	Assessment Strategies	Activities	Resources or Learning Objects
Students will distinguish between two types of cell division: meiosis and mitosis.	• Discussion: Evaluate the quantity and quality of items in a compare-and-contrast table • Quiz: matching, short answer, or multiple-choice answers	• In-class: Students create a compare-and-contrast table. • Online: Students debate which cell division terms go with meiosis or mitosis.	
Students will explain how abnormal cell division occurs during the two types of cell division.	• Assignment with diagram rubric or essay rubric (includes key differences from normal cell division, possible causes, etc.)	• In-class: Students draw annotated diagrams of normal and abnormal cell division and compare with a classmate. • Online: Students explain different forms of abnormal cell division (essay/screencast).	
Students will recommend a cancer drug therapy to prevent specific types of abnormal cell division.	• Assignment with case study rubric	• In-class or online: In a small group discussion, students complete a case study analysis of a patient with a specific type of cancer, including recommendation.	

TABLE 1.5.3

Backward Design: Three Examples of Mapping Resources to Learning Outcomes Requiring Different Levels of Thinking

Outcomes	Assessment Strategies	Activities	Resources or Learning Objects
Students will distinguish between two types of cell division: meiosis and mitosis.	• Discussion: Evaluate the quantity and quality of items in a compare-and-contrast table • Quiz: matching, short answer, or multiple-choice answer	• In-class: Students create a compare-and-contrast table. • Online: Students debate which cell division terms go with meiosis or mitosis.	• Textbook: *Intro to Biology*, Chapter 3: Cell Division • Handouts: Detailed charts of each type of cell division • Media: Video clips of cell division
Students will explain how abnormal cell division occurs during the two types of cell division.	• Assignment with diagram rubric or essay rubric (includes key differences from normal cell division, possible causes, etc.)	• Students draw annotated diagrams of normal and abnormal cell division. • Assignment: Students explain different forms of abnormal cell division (essay/screencast).	• Same as previous resources • Web article: "Abnormal Cell Division Explained," by News-Medical, www.news-medical.net/?id=9615
Students will recommend a cancer drug therapy to prevent specific types of abnormal cell division.	• Assignment with case study rubric	• Small group discussion: Students complete a case study analysis of a patient with a specific type of cancer, including recommendation.	• Same as all previous resources • Excerpt from *Dimensions of Cancer*, by C. E. Kupchella • Web article: "Cell Cycle Regulation and Anticancer Drug Discovery," www.ncbi.nlm.nih.gov /pmc/articles/PMC5785171/

TABLE 1.5.4
Online Course Activities to Help Students Reach Different Levels of
Thinking and Achievement

	Knowledge (cognitive domain)	Skills (psychomotor domain)	Attitudes (affective domain)
Achievement of low-level outcomes	*Remembering*: Students use virtual flashcards you create to review definitions or facts. *Understanding*: Students review images or charts you post on a content page and interpret or summarize in a forum.	*Imitating*: Students watch a video or an animation showing specific movements and copy them. *Manipulating*: Students set up a lab experiment using written or video instructions.	*Receiving*: Students acknowledge different beliefs with respect in a VoiceThread activity. *Responding*: Students participate in class discussions about their most important values.
Achievement of midlevel outcomes	*Applying*: Students use a curated set of links to try out class concepts. *Analyzing*: Students review a case study and provide analysis and recommenda-tions in a forum.	*Refining*: Students record themselves demonstrating a task for beginners. *Articulating*: Students use images or a video to showcase an end product that combines a series of skills (e.g., welding, dance).	*Valuing*: Students work in small groups to generate a plan that applies course concepts for social improvement and reports on what happened after.
Achievement of high-level outcomes	*Evaluating*: Students review three budgets and appraise which one would best meet an organization's goals, defending their position in a video conference meeting. *Creating*: Students create original work and share as eportfolio artifacts.	*Naturalizing*: Students show mastery of high-level performance during a video conference.	*Organizing*: Students create a plan or schedule that shows how they have organized values into priorities. *Internalizing*: Students describe how their values have changed based on participation in an internship.

COMBINING UDL, DESIGN FOR LEARNING EQUITY, AND HUMAN CONNECTEDNESS TO BRING ABOUT MEANINGFUL ALIGNMENT

As you apply the alignment process to your course, ask yourself the following questions:

- Will your assessment strategies show that students have reached the actual learning outcomes? Do you ask students to do things in ways that parallel performance expectations in the real world?
- Do you have activities related to each outcome? Do your students practice thinking critically or performing skills before they're tested?
- What content are you assigning for each learning outcome? What's required? What's optional? In what formats are you providing the course materials?

As you generate ideas, you will likely come up with more assessment strategies or activities than you need. That's a good problem to have, but it is still a problem. If you have too many assessment strategies, students will tire of being assessed, and you will tire of grading those assessments. If you have too many activities and strategies, your course will be confusing and likely demand more time from students than it should. When it comes to selecting assessment strategies and activities, the challenge is to pick the *best* ones. Combining UDL and design for learning equity principles in the context of human connectedness provides other factors to consider when choosing which assessment strategies and activities to use:

- Is the assessment or activity *aligned* with the outcomes?
- Is the assessment or activity *authentic,* and does it recognize the individuality of the learner? (increased meaning and ownership)
- Is the assessment or activity *frequent*? (increased opportunities)
- Is the assessment or activity *supportive*? (increased feedback)

Some course design rubrics provide criteria to check for one or more of these factors, but we recommend using them all.

Aligned

Clear alignment with your outcomes is the most critical factor when choosing how students will demonstrate learning in any educational setting, but it is particularly important in your online class. In Table 1.5.1, you can see that the first outcome asks students to distinguish between two types of cell division. The assessment strategies include a focus on human connectedness by having learners create a compare-and-contrast table and then discuss it with classmates, as well as having them answer quiz questions about each type of cell division. Conversely, avoid assessing skills or knowledge that you don't cover or that aren't connected to the outcomes. For example, if you use a publisher's pool of test questions, handpick the questions your students will see and answer. If you randomly draw questions from a pool containing hundreds of questions, then you will likely end up with questions that are not aligned with the outcomes from your course. Looking at outcomes when examination questions are developed or purposefully selected ensures they are aligned. Using the base of an outcome as a writing prompt results in alignment. Having students discuss their own ideas for methods to show they have learned a concept should start with a discussion of the outcome desired.

Showing students how each assessment aligns with outcomes helps students to develop metacognitive strategies they will be able to use later in their academic programs and even later in life. As we saw in chapter 1.2, Mary-Ann Winkelmes (2013) lists the purpose of the assignment first in the instructions from her Transparent Assignment Template. Her research showed that using simple techniques like this increased success rates for underserved college students, including first-generation, low-income, and/or underrepresented students (Winkelmes et al., 2016). When it comes to online courses, these same groups have larger achievement gaps to hurdle than other student populations, so taking small steps like this makes a big difference.

Authentic

It is also critically important for assessment strategies and practice assignments to be as authentic as possible. An authentic assessment places the learned material and outcomes in a real-world context, perhaps even asking students to complete real-world tasks. UDL guidelines suggest maintaining high goal salience to help students persist. The design for learning equity framework prescribes connecting course elements to students' goals or backgrounds to increase belonging. Authentic learning ensures that we do not forget our learners have unique lives and are learning in ways that will benefit themselves and others. Making assessments and activities more authentic can do all of these things.

Authenticity increases meaning for the students and facilitates the transfer of knowledge, skills, and attitudes to analogous scenarios. For example, taking another look at Table 1.5.1, the third outcome—"Students will recommend a cancer drug therapy to prevent specific types of abnormal cell division"—asks students to apply and work with the concepts of cell division at a higher level. The assessment strategy includes the use of a case study for which students might synthesize information about cancer drug therapy options.

With 54% of American families reporting that they or someone in their immediate family has been diagnosed with cancer (CBS News, 2017), this assessment activity will be meaningful personally to many students. You could also use the COVID-19 pandemic in the same way. Although at the writing of this book the total number of cases in the COVID-19 pandemic was not known, it is highly likely that every student in your course has been impacted in some way by this virus. If you teach a class that serves students with health-care career goals, then you have made the concept of cell division more meaningful to them as they prepare for the workforce. Multiple-choice tests can play an essential role in evaluating whether or not students understand core concepts before working at higher levels of thinking, and there are ways to make those questions meaningful, too. If possible, throughout each semester, provide opportunities for students to do something they might be asked to do when they enter the workforce.

Want another perspective? Perhaps one from the learner's point of view? At the end of the term, list your course level learning outcomes, and ask your students to identify the content and activities that they found most helpful to achieve each. Have your students work in small discussion groups to identify at least one piece of content and one activity that could be included to benefit the next cohort of students in that class! Ask them how well the multiple assessment strategies you developed allowed them to show what they know and then give them a chance to tell you what other strategies they would have liked to use.

Frequent

Frequency is another factor to consider when choosing the best assessment strategies for your class. Perhaps you'll use low-stakes (worth only a few points) or no-stakes (ungraded) quizzes to let students practice with concepts before taking a high-stakes exam like a midterm or final, or completing a higher-level activity like a presentation, essay, or group project. Kevin does both for his online class, using a scaffolded approach for each module with a consistent practice and assessment process over 3 weeks. In essence, each module starts with a quiz about the basic concepts, moves to a discussion to solidify thinking, and ends with a reflection essay.

Whichever process you use, ask students to show what they know throughout the course. UDL encourages you to offer self-assessment opportunities to support students' self-regulation, but this technique also increases the number of opportunities for students to practice or check their progress. They should get feedback as quickly as possible and regularly throughout your course timeline, which leads us to our last factor for choosing optimal assessment strategies.

It is also helpful to explain to students why you have them complete assessments frequently. Practicing recall is one of the best ways to learn (Dunlosky et al., 2013; Roediger & Butler, 2011). Explaining this to students helps them to see the importance of quizzes, practice tests, discussions, and even exams.

Supportive

Hopefully, you can use every assessment strategy to monitor student progress and identify problem areas, both for individual students and across the entire class. Whenever possible, use the assessment process to support both student learning and the students themselves. You can use different types of feedback loops to offer this support. For quizzes, take the time to add automated feedback that students see after they complete each attempt. If they get a question wrong, you don't have to give them the answer, but you can point them to the materials they should review to answer that question (or one like it) correctly next time. The design for learning equity framework suggests providing opportunities for peer review feedback and creating meaningful prompts for students to give each other feedback that respects diversity. Using rubrics and providing timely feedback through written comments or videos also allows students to learn from their mistakes and make adjustments for improvement. To drive home this point about support, a comprehensive literature review (Lister, 2014) showed that timely and effective feedback is critical to online learner success.

Helping students to adopt a growth mindset (Dweck et al., 2014) and letting them know you believe they can succeed (Wood, 2015) will help them to see that assessments, when properly aligned with outcomes, can be constructive in the learning process. When a student looks at assessment results from a growth mindset perspective, they feel more supported as they see those results as information to help them get better at achieving the desired outcome. Fixed mindset students, in contrast, perceive any deficiencies as criticisms or personal limits. We'll cover more about activities in Part Two and assessment in Part Three, but as you select the best strategies for your class, consider those that help students gain awareness of gaps in their knowledge or skills and give them ideas about how to bridge those gaps.

NEXT STEPS

Before moving to the next chapter, take a minute to answer the following questions for yourself:

- Are the assessments and activities for your class all related to, and aligned with, the learning outcomes?
- Have you considered other factors such as increasing meaning, authenticity, frequency, and feedback for assessments and activities?
- Can the online environment support streamlining your class in some way? What can be made optional? What can be deleted or removed?

Use Table 1.5.5 to create your own set of assessment strategies, activities, and even content that aligns with the course learning outcomes. When you're done, you'll have a checklist of items to add or create as you construct online or hybrid course modules in the LMS.

TABLE 1.5.5

Activity—Map Your Assessment Strategies, Activities, and Resources to Learning Outcomes

Outcome	Assessment Strategies	Activities	Resources or Learning Objects

CHAPTER SUMMARY

Helping students stay on the path to achieving desired learning outcomes takes careful planning. The methods and activities you choose for the course will be challenging but are extremely important. In addition to selecting activities and equitable instructional practices that are in line with universal design, students find learning processes are best when they connect learners to you as the instructor and to their fellow students. There are a wide variety of teaching methods and learning activities that are available. Learning best occurs best when the activities selected align well with outcomes, are authentic to the learner, occur with regular frequency, and are carried out in a way in which students feel supported.

Reflection and Discussion Questions

1. Referring to Figure 1.5.1, identify a learning outcome that you have used or intend to use in an upcoming course. Describe three learning checks that you could ask your students to complete that would help keep them on the path to this learning outcome.
2. Describe a learning activity that you have used as an instructor or experienced as a student. What was the desired outcome for this activity? If you are uncertain, then describe what you feel would have been a reasonable outcome for the activity.
3. Imagine that you are teaching this chapter in an online format to undergraduate students in an educational psychology course. Using the format of Table 1.5.5, list three intended outcomes, and then complete the table. Keep in mind with your assessment strategies, activities, and resources to include UDL, design for learning equity, and human interaction components.
4. In designing activities for an online course, which of the following do you feel would cause you the most uncertainly or difficulty: alignment, authenticity, frequency, or support? Describe the challenges you have experienced or anticipate that you would experience.

1.6

MAKING YOUR ONLINE
COURSE ACCESSIBLE

THERE IS AN OLD phrase in higher education that we "teach the way we were taught." This phrase is often used to explain why so many faculty members still lecture much of the time. Although it sounds like a good rationale, that phrase as an explanation for the continued use of lecture strategies may not be all that accurate. Almost 40 years ago, Larry Michaelsen, a faculty member at the University of Oklahoma, began promoting team-based learning (Michaelsen et al., 1982). A decade earlier, Johnson and Johnson (1975) were writing books about the value of cooperative learning. A plethora of teaching strategies were regularly used nearly half a century ago, with lecture strategies by far the most prominent. Lecture strategies continue to be frequently used today. As most of us experienced many different teaching strategies as college and university students, we likely noted the ones that worked well for us and those that did not. As a result, when we became educators, without even thinking about it, we each likely relied implicitly on the strategies that worked best for us. Those were the ones that just seemed best. Given this scenario of using the strategies that make sense to our own learning, it seems appropriate to replace the phrase "we teach the way we were taught," with the phrase "we teach the way we prefer to learn." The distinction of this new phrase is that we, as faculty members, are not passive recipients who choose a pedagogical strategy simply because it is what we experienced. It means we select that which works for ourselves, not because we are consciously deciding to ignore the needs of others, but because we noted that it worked well. As a result, we will, at times, fail to consider that other perspectives on learning exist. Not everyone learns the way I, or you, do. Human brains do this naturally. We have the most experience with our own experiences. As a result, those are the things with which we are most familiar because they are the things with which we have the most experience.

Before reading the rest of this paragraph, think about three tasks—the first step in rebuilding a car engine, identifying the key player in building a new defensive strategy in football, and deciding how many presentation slides to include in a typical 50-minute class period. What comes most easily to mind is what you most frequently experience. To understand what others experience takes additional consideration. If you have mobility issues, you likely are always aware of the many challenges in getting into buildings and regularly look to see if there are appropriate ramps or doors that open automatically. If you lost most of your hearing in childhood or while serving in the military, then you are firmly aware of the challenge of hearing only portions of conversations. If you lost your eyesight in an accident, or have difficulty sitting in one place for more than 15 minutes, you are firmly aware of the challenge of learning when a faculty member presents 50 slides in 50 minutes. When we have not had the challenges to perceive the world in a way different from others, we lose the opportunities to perceive the world in those different ways. For example, if you have never been in a wheelchair, you likely never really thought about what the world looks like from 3 feet off the ground or how important flat rest areas are on a long incline. As we cannot perceive the world, and the significant challenges, from the perspective of others, we also inadvertently decrease the probability individuals different from ourselves can be successful. This is true of face-to-face courses and is perhaps even more true in online courses.

There are clear challenges to making your online course accessible to students with specific physical and learning challenges, starting with an awareness of what needs to be done and including preparedness and workload. Planning will result in extra work at times. Still, all students appreciate this extra work, including those who likely cannot be successful without the accessibility accommodations.

WHY ACCESSIBILITY IS IMPORTANT

You control the content you teach, whether you create your own or use content created by someone else. In this chapter, we'll explore techniques for making your course both more technically accessible for students who are differently abled and more usable for all students. The quest for accessibility continues by making interaction and assessment more accessible, often through managing settings in the LMS environment. As you go through this chapter, we will explore accessibility for different types of content (e.g., content pages as web pages in your LMS, downloadable files, and multimedia) as well as for various course activities and assessments. After you have addressed accessibility issues for the individual course elements, it is essential to test the accessibility of the learning environment itself and any other learning technologies you ask students to use.

Remember the underlying goal for UDL is that designing for everyone makes sure everyone is advantaged, even those with learning challenges. Making your course content more accessible helps everyone in one way or another. Students with physical and learning challenges benefit from accessible course content for different reasons, including but not limited to the following:

- *Vision challenges*: Vision challenges are much more common than most faculty realize. Did you know that "among computer users in the United States, approximately 1 in 4 (27%) has a vision impairment" (Microsoft, 2011, p. 9), such as low vision (requiring glasses or contact lenses), colorblindness, or blindness? Globally, that percentage is slightly higher—"at least 2.2 billion [of a total of 7.6 billion] people have a vision impairment" (World Health Organization, 2019, para. 1).
- *Learning challenges*: "According to the International Dyslexia Association and the Learning Disabilities Association of America, about 15% of the population (close to 1 in 7) has a learning disability" (Microsoft, 2011, p. 14). The National Center for Learning Disabilities estimates that 1 in 5 U.S. children are affected by learning and attention issues (Horowitz et al., 2017).
- *Mobility or dexterity challenges*: Whether the cause is temporary or permanent—accidental (e.g., car accident), occupational (e.g., repetitive strain injury), or genetic (e.g., muscular dystrophy)—not everyone can use a mouse or a keyboard.
- *Hearing impairments and deafness*: "It is estimated that 1 in 5 computer users [in the United States] has some form of hearing loss," ranging from slight hearing loss to deafness (Microsoft, 2011, p. 21).
- *Language production and reception challenges*: Ability to perceive aspects of language structure can affect students' ability to communicate; comprehend, process, or remember information; or solve problems.
- *Translation challenges:* Nonnative English speakers are challenged by the extra cognitive load that results from needing to translate learned material and their unfamiliarity with many of the examples, stories, and idioms that educators native to the United States frequently use.

Beyond these identified populations, students who have specific learning preferences or flexibility needs may choose a content or activity format that best fits their current learning circumstances. For example, students who face long commutes via public transportation may prefer reviewing audio or video over reading text in a moving vehicle. The accommodations we share in this chapter support all students equally, regardless of their needs.

Making Accessible Files—Overview

Whether you create web-based content pages in the LMS, downloadable course files, or both, making them accessible helps almost everyone in some way or another. However, files can present a significant challenge, as there are many types of files compared to just one type of content page in your LMS.

Checking Your Files

Many faculty members struggle with the concept of checking files for accessibility. Luckily, there are many tools available to conduct these checks. For example, Blackboard's tool, Ally (ally.ac), works with all major LMS solutions. It identifies any files with accessibility issues and provides suggestions for instructors to correct them. The following are three common file types—documents, presentations, and spreadsheets—along with more accessibility checker tools.

Built-In Tools

- *Document (Word), presentation (PowerPoint), or spreadsheet (Excel)*: If you are an Office 365 user, you have a built-in accessibility checker in Word, PowerPoint, and Excel. To open the checker, use the Check Accessibility button on the Review tab on the Ribbon. For more details, see the Microsoft [2020a] article, "Use the Accessibility Checker on Your Windows Desktop to Find Accessibility Issues"; support.office.com/en-us/article/use-the-accessibility-checker-on-your-windows-desktop-to-find-accessibility-issues-a16f6deo-2f39-4a2b-8bd8-5ad801426c7f
- *Document (PDF)*: If you are an Adobe Acrobat Pro user, you have a built-in accessibility checker. To open the checker, use the Full Check button on the Accessibility tab on the Tools pane. For more details, visit www.adobe.com/content/dam/acom/en/accessibility/products/acrobat/pdfs/acrobat-xi-accessibility-checker.pdf for the Adobe (2012) article, "Using the Acrobat Pro Accessibility Checker."

Third-Party Tools

- *Document (Word)*: If you have an older version of Word (e.g., Word 2010 or earlier), you can use the Section 508 Compliance Test Process for Microsoft Word Documents (Department of Homeland Security, 2015; https://www.dhs.gov/sites/default/files/publications/DHS_Section_508_Compliance_Test_Process_for_Applications_0.pdf). (Please go to Appendix C for links to the online resources mentioned in this chapter.) Although not an automated tool, it gives "How to Test" instructions for each type of content or interactive element.
- *Document (PDF)*: If you do not have Adobe Acrobat Pro, there is a Free PDF Accessibility Checker (PAC 3) (www.access-for-all.ch/en/pdf-lab/pdf-accessibility-checker-pac.html).
- *Document (Google Docs), presentation (Google Slides), or spreadsheet (Google Sheets)*: If you use Google Docs, there is a free Google Suite accessibility checker called Grackle (www.grackledocs.com/) that you can download for Chrome, Google's web browser.

Making Accessible Files and Content Pages—Basic Techniques

If you have taught online, hybrid, face-to-face, or temporarily remote courses, you probably have created web pages, or content pages, in an LMS such as Canvas, Moodle, D2L, or Blackboard. These content pages play different roles, ranging from giving instructions to providing unique course content. Downloadable files serve many functions in our courses as well. In addition to their common purpose, there are a variety of common methods to make your content pages and downloadable files more accessible.

Text Formatting

- *Use heading styles:* Rather than just changing the font size of text headings, use heading styles to provide an organizational structure to help all students navigate your content page. To learn how to use heading styles in Microsoft Word, review the Microsoft (n.d.a) article "Add a Heading" (support.office.com/en-us/article/add-a-heading-3eb8b917-56dc-4a17-891a-a026b2c790f2). In Canvas (2020a), the Rich Content Editor provides a menu to apply a heading style (community.canvaslms.com/docs/DOC-12855-415241511). Similarly, in Moodle, D2L, and Blackboard, the HTML or ATTO editors provide a pull-down menu to apply styles to your text.

- *Use bulleted or numbered lists*: Just putting dashes in front of text will not tell students who use screen readers that you have created a list. Use the bulleted list or numbered list tools to let everyone know when they have reached a list on your content page or in your document. To learn how to make bulleted or numbered lists in Microsoft Word, review the Microsoft (n.d.b) article called "Create a Bulleted or Numbered List" (support.office.com/en-us/article/ Create-a-bulleted-or-numbered-list-9FF81241-58A8-4D88-8D8C-ACAB3006A23E)

Descriptive Text

- *Use descriptive links*: Students with screen readers often jump from link to link, skipping the text before each link. As a result, repetitive links such as "click here" or "more info" can be confusing and do not tell the student anything about what the link does or where it goes. Research by the Nielsen Norman Group (2014) reported that "good links are descriptive, unique, and start with keywords" (para. 11). For example, for your links, use descriptive text such as "Download instructions for the week three assignment" or "Visit OWL, Purdue's Online Writing Lab, and check out their page on APA style (owl.purdue.edu/owl/research_and_citation/apa_style/ apa_formatting_and_style_guide/general_format.html) to learn more about APA citation formats." To get more tips, review the Nielsen Norman Group (2014) page on writing descriptive links (www.nngroup.com/articles/writing-links/).
- *Use alternative descriptive text for images*: If there is no alternative text, screen readers just read the file name for each image. As many images are labeled poorly (e.g., "DSC0409.jpg"), it's important to add alternative text. Alternative text should be 5 to 10 words that describe the image you have embedded on the page. Avoid phrases like "Picture of . . ." or "Image of . . ." to describe the image. The HTML or Rich Content Editor should display a field for alternative text when you insert an image in a content page. To learn how to add alternative text to images in a downloadable file, review the Microsoft (n.d.c) article called "Add Alternative Text to a Shape, Picture, Chart, Table, SmartArt Graphic, or Other Object" (support .office.com/en-us/article/Add-alternative-text-to-a-shape-picture-chart-table-SmartArt-graphic-or-other-object-44989b2a-903c-4d9a-b742-6a75b451c669).
  Note: If a complex image such as a flowchart or diagram requires a long description, it is helpful to include both the alternative text and

a separate document describing the image as if you were describing it over the phone to a friend. Upload that document and create a link to it next to the image.

Color

- *Provide sufficient color contrast between the text on the page and background color*: As a reference point, this page is black text on a white page, which is the highest contrast possible. An example of poor contrast would be a lemon (yellow) on a white page: an insufficient color contrast that is nearly impossible for anyone to read! It is best to use dark text on a light background or vice versa. Use the Color Contrast Checker tool by WebAIM (n.d.a; webaim. org/resources/contrastchecker/) to test your color combinations. Also, note that bounced light can make reading slightly more challenging. White text used on a black or dark background bounces the light, which can make it more difficult to distinguish individual letters. Using black text on a slightly gray background provides excellent contrast, and gray bounces less light than white. There is a plethora of research in the area of optics, and, of course, not everyone agrees on what is the easiest to read. The general rule is to consider the contrast between the text and background (e.g., Caldwell et al., 2008; www.w3.org/TR/2008/REC-WCAG20-20081211/#visual-audio-contrast-contrast).

- *Use more than color to convey meaning*: Sometimes, you might want to use color to add meaning to a word or phrase. For example, some people use red text to tell students they are reading something important or that they have reached a required field on a form. Other teachers may use color coding for calendar events in Canvas. Reports of the prevalence of colorblindness differ by ethnicity and range up to 8% of the population. That means in a class of even 20 students, it is fairly likely at least one student will be colorblind. Therefore, color is not enough to convey the same meaning to everyone. It's okay to keep using color for your text, but use another visual element like **bold**, *italics*, <u>underline</u>, or ALL CAPS to make sure every student gets your point. For required fields on a form, add an asterisk (*). To augment color coding in the LMS calendar, add a text element such as (Q) for quizzes, (D) for discussions, and (A) for assignments, and create a symbol legend to let students know what the letters mean.

Figure 1.6.1. What it's like to review a table with no headers.

Let's get an idea of what it is like to use a screen reader to review a data table without headers. Try to mentally keep track of the aspects of each of the first seven items as you read this entire list: molecular compound, solid state, freezing point, liquid state, melting point, gaseous state, boiling point; H_2O, ice, less than 32°F or 0°C, water, greater than 32°F or 0°C, steam, greater than 212°F or 100°C; CO_2, dry ice, less than −109.3°F or −78.5°C, not applicable—no liquid state, not applicable–carbon dioxide, greater than −109.3°F or −78.5°C; C_2H_5OH, solid ethanol, less than −173.5°F or −114.1°C, liquid ethanol, greater than −173.5°F or −114.1°C, ethanol gas, greater than 173.1°F or 78.37°C; and so on.

Now, can you remember the freezing point for CO_2? Which has a lower boiling point—ethanol or water? Imagine if this table had more than three rows of data! Some students use screen readers, which read the content of each page to them in order. Tables without header rows or header columns just read each item once in order, which means the learners have an extremely difficult task to keep track of information. The irony is that tables are intended to organize information to make it easier to consume!

The following is the same information as a table with headers for table columns and rows, which means it will repeat the header information to provide context for each cell as it is read. For example, in the middle of the second row, the screen reader will now say "melting point—H_2O—greater than 32 degrees F or 0 degrees C." Much nicer!

Molecular Compound	Solid State	Freezing Point	Liquid State	Melting Point	Gaseous State	Boiling Point
H_2O	Ice	Less than 32°F or 0°C	water	Greater than 32°F or 0°C	Steam	Greater than 212°F or 100°C
CO_2	Dry ice	Less than −109.3°F or −78.5°C	Not applicable—no liquid state	Not applicable	Carbon dioxide	Greater than −109.3°F or −78.5°C
C_2H_5OH or EtOH	Solid ethanol	Less than −173.5°F or −114.1°C	Liquid ethanol	Greater than −173.5°F or −114.1° C	Ethanol gas	Greater than 173.1°F or 78.37°C

Table Formatting

- *Use headers for table rows and columns*: If you do not use header rows and columns in your data tables, students who use screen readers have to keep track of everything in the first row as well as what's being read. Want to see what we mean? Try it yourself using Figure 1.6.1! With properly formatted tables, screen readers repeat header information for every cell, making it easier for students to keep track of the data. To learn how to create header table rows and header table columns in Microsoft Word, review The Pennsylvania State University's (n.d.) accessibility article called "Designating Table Headers" (accessibility.psu.edu/microsoftoffice/microsofttableheaders/).

Making Accessible Files—Advanced Techniques

Documents—specifically Word documents—are the most common file type that faculty share with students. If you are creating different file types, such as PDF, Excel spreadsheet, or PowerPoint presentation, the following are some advanced techniques for making more accessible files.

Set the Digital Reading Order for Each File

Sighted people typically review English language files from left to right and from top to bottom, whereas screen readers use the document structure to determine the reading order. With simple, one-column, text-only documents, the reading order is fairly straightforward. However, the reading order may change each time you insert an image or table in a document, save a Word or PowerPoint file as a PDF, or otherwise make the file more complex.

In Adobe Acrobat Pro, the Touch Up Reading Order tool allows you to set or change the reading order. This tool is on the Accessibility tab on the Tools pane. Visit Adobe (2020; helpx.adobe.com/acrobat/using/touch-reading-order-tool-pdfs.html) to learn more about the Touch Up Reading Order tool. Unfortunately, Adobe Acrobat Reader does not have accessibility tools.

In newer versions of Microsoft PowerPoint, the Selection Pane allows you to set or change the reading order on each slide. This tool is found on the Home tab, in the Arrange menu. Note: PowerPoint lists the reading order in reverse, with the slide title last in the list. Visit Microsoft to learn more about using the Selection Pane to set the reading order on each slide (Microsoft, n.d.d; support.office.com/en-us/article/Make-your-PowerPoint-presentations-accessible-6f7772b2-2f33-4bd2-8ca7-dae3b2b3ef25).

Make Presentations Accessible
- *Use slide layout*: One of the easiest ways to make PowerPoint presentations accessible is to use the existing slide layout templates. Regardless of which theme you pick, the different slide layout templates (e.g., title slide, title and content, section header, two content, etc.) are designed with accessibility in mind. These designs automatically structure the presentation, set the reading order, and more. Use the placeholder boxes to enter text and to insert images or media. Creating new textboxes or adding images outside of the placeholder boxes can change the reading order.
- *Use unique slide titles*: A short descriptive title for each slide helps students using screen readers to navigate the presentation. If you use more than one slide to continue the same idea, you can add descriptive text to make each slide title unique (e.g., "equations of motion—1 of 2" and "equations of motion—2 of 2"), or you can refer to the subtopic covered on that particular slide (e.g., "U.S. Civil War—1861—causes" and "U.S. Civil War—1865—surrender & aftermath"; "Parts of speech—nouns" and "Parts of speech—interjections").

Follow the guidelines you reviewed about making accessible files with these adaptations in mind:

- *Add alternative text for images*: Just as you do for content pages and documents, be sure to provide alternative text for images and SmartArt graphics. Use the notes field for long descriptions of complex diagrams or pictures.
- *Text formatting*: Use a larger overall font size (24 point or larger) for the content and leave as much white space as possible.

Make PDFs Accessible
Starting with an accessible Word document or PowerPoint presentation that follows the guidelines we've shared makes it that much easier to create an accessible PDF. First, choose "Save as Adobe PDF" from the File menu in Microsoft Word rather than Print as PDF. Be sure to check your Preferences—"Enable Accessibility and Reflow with tagged Adobe PDF" should be checked. If you have Adobe Acrobat Pro, you can select "Create PDF from file" from the File menu, then select the appropriate Word or PowerPoint file to convert. For more details, review the WebAIM (n.d.b; webaim.org/techniques/acrobat/converting) guide for "PDF Accessibility: Converting Documents to PDFs."

After saving your file as a PDF, you may still need to clean it up to make it more accessible. Primarily, you should check to make sure your document has tags which provide structure, alternative text, and proper reading order. You can also run a Full Check of accessibility. For a complete list of instructions, see the Using a PDF editor portion of San Francisco State's (n.d.; its .sfsu.edu/guides/creating-accessible-pdf-documents-word-2013#use) guide for "Creating Accessible PDF Documents With Word."

Make Spreadsheets Accessible
- *Unique sheet titles*: Give unique names to each spreadsheet tab and remove any blank tabs or sheets.
- *Table formatting*: Avoid merging cells when possible, as merged cells can cause issues with the column headers.

Follow the guidelines you reviewed about making accessible files with these adaptations in mind:

- *Add alternative text for images*: Just as you do for content pages and documents, be sure to provide alternative text for images and SmartArt graphics.
- *Text formatting*: Remove blank rows or columns, as someone with a screen reader might assume there is no more information to review.

For more information, check out these resources on making files accessible:

- "Make Your Word Documents accessible to People With Disabilities" (Microsoft, n.d.e; support.office.com/en-us/article/Make-your-Word-documents-accessible-d9bf3683-87ac-47ea-b91a-78dcacb3 c66d)
- "Create and Verify PDF Accessibility" (Adobe, n.d.; helpx.adobe .com/acrobat/using/create-verify-pdf-accessibility.html)
- "Make Your PowerPoint Presentations Accessible to People With Disabilities" (Microsoft, n.d.d; support.office.com/en-us/article/ Make-your-PowerPoint-presentations-accessible-6f7772b2-2f33-4bd2-8ca7-dae3b2b3ef25)
- "Make Your Excel Spreadsheets Accessible to People With Disabilities" (Microsoft, 2020b; support.office.com/en-us/article/ Make-your-Excel-spreadsheets-accessible-6cc05fc5-1314-48b5-8eb3-683e49b3e593)

Making Multimedia Accessible and Selecting Accessible Multimedia

Whether you create your own multimedia or share someone else's multimedia with your students, there are some accessibility guidelines to follow.

Provide Alternate Formats for Audio and Video

- *Provide an accurate transcript for audio files*: Transcripts support a wide variety of students, aside from those who are deaf or hard-of-hearing. Other students who benefit from a transcript include non-native English speakers; students who have information processing challenges; students who are studying in a library without their headphones; and students who like to stop, process, and then review something just presented.
- *Provide captions for video files*: Captions support students who are deaf or hard-of-hearing, nonnative English speakers, and students who prefer to read.
- *Provide narrative descriptions, if possible, for actions in the video that do not have an audio component*: For example, someone who is blind or who has a vision impairment will not see someone quietly leave a room or wave to a friend in a video clip. A narrative description will describe these actions.

Captioning and transcription services may be available to you through your institution. Contact someone at the office on your campus that serves students with disabilities to find out how to get started.

Provide Alternate Formats for Live Broadcasts

If your online class has synchronous meetings, many videoconferencing platforms have a closed captioning feature. For example, if your class uses Zoom, Skype, or another videoconferencing tool, then that tool should have a way to provide live captioning if a student requires it. Keep in mind that students using screen readers may face challenges during live class events—for example, the screen reader may read text from the chat window simultaneously while a speaker gives a presentation on video. Consider taking breaks to accept comments and questions via chat.

Do Not Set the Media to Auto-Play

Whether you are linking to a YouTube video or a video you have made, avoid having it set to auto-play. Auto-play means the video will start playing as soon as your students visit the page with that video. For students with screen readers, this creates two competing sources of information—the screenreader reads what is on the page, while the video plays with its own audio. It's like trying to pay attention to two conversations at once. To turn off auto-play, add the text "?&autoplay=o" (without quotes) to the end of your YouTube link.

Avoid Flashing Content

You may have found some blinking animated images or multimedia that you feel would make your course pages more interesting. In addition to making it challenging for students with attention deficit disorder to focus on a page with moving images, flashing or blinking images may trigger seizures in susceptible individuals. In general, it is advisable to avoid using any images or media that blink or strobe.

Create an Instructional Materials Inventory

List any course materials or multimedia that are not yet accessible, and work with the Disability Resource Center on your campus to plan how to address each one. If a hurricane, wildfire, or pandemic requires switching to an emergency remote teaching situation, then focus first on any specific accommodations your students require.

Making Online Interaction Accessible

Although most accessibility rubrics focus on making content accessible (content pages, files, and multimedia), your course is more than just content! This section outlines how to make the rest of your online course experience accessible, too. Specifically, you'll look at making course activities (student engagement) and assessments more accessible. The following are some accessibility considerations for common online activities.

Discussions

Discussions are the most common way to engage students in an online course. Here are a few ways to improve the accessibility of the online discussion experience in ways that help all students.

- *Ask students to create brief, unique titles for their posts and replies*: As students with screen readers navigate their classmates' discussion posts and replies, they face the challenge of having to listen to each post without being able to skim them. In large classes, this can equal quite a few posts! In your instructions, have students create a unique title for their posts and replies. As an example, "After you have written your response to the prompt, summarize your post in five to seven words and use that as a title in the subject line of your post."

- *Ask students to create alternative text for images they post*: Students may want to insert images in their discussion posts, and that's great! However, they'll need to use alternative text to describe their images, just like you. At the very least, they should describe the image in the body of their discussion post or reply. If you anticipate students inserting images, you can point them to tutorials like the Canvas (2020b) guide for students titled "How Do I Embed an Image in a Discussion Reply as a Student?" (community.canvaslms.com/docs/DOC-10700-4212190965) or the D2L-related video tutorial, "Adding an Image Into D2L" (The Skeptical Educator, 2015; www.youtube.com/watch?v=jPEUJ4SBWsE). Remind students to insert helpful alternative text.
- *Consider your own language and discussion settings*: Use the following sample text to help structure your language for facilitating accessibility: "The Discussions tool in Canvas is accessible, though usability is enhanced with clear and concise language. The structure of Canvas Discussions can be simplified by turning off threaded replies."

Groups

- *Consider which collaboration tools are accessible*: Although there are a variety of online collaboration tools that support group work, not all of them are accessible. Before you begin using a tool, search for the name of the tool plus the word "accessibility." The tool's creator should provide accessibility information, including a Voluntary Product Accessibility Template (VPAT) and any special instructions required to make the product more accessible. These search results also usually include helpful advice or tutorials from individuals, nonprofits, or higher education campuses that have taken the time to document accessibility considerations. For example, the nonprofit organization Knowbility published a brief article called "Accessible Tools for Online Collaboration and Learning" with links to helpful tutorials and resources (Vasquez, 2020).

Third-Party Interactivity Tools

- *Review interactivity environments for accessibility*: Tools outside your LMS may not be accessible yet. For example, the team at

VoiceThread worked with faculty to make their online presentations and feedback tool (for teachers and students alike) more accessible. If you are not sure about the accessibility of a tool that you already use or are considering, ask someone in your Disability Resource Center to help review each one for accessibility.

- *Use tools that promote accessibility*: Some companies work hard to include accessibility in their tools and make the process nearly seamless. For example, the video-based social learning tool Flipgrid automatically captions videos by teachers and students, allows users to create their own transcripts, and incorporates Microsoft's Immersive Reader (Flipgrid, n.d.; help.flipgrid.com/hc/en-us/articles/115004848574-Flipgrid-and-Accessibility). Find and use tools that make students more aware of accessibility needs and that empower them to help improve the accessibility of the entire course experience—not just the parts you develop.

Making Online Assessments Accessible

In addition to evaluating the work students post in forums, quizzes and assignments are the most common assessment strategies that teachers use online.

Quizzes
The same core accessibility practices for content pages apply to quiz instructions, quiz questions, quiz response options, and automatic feedback for correct and incorrect answers. For example, if you include a video as part of the quiz, it should be captioned. However, one of these core practices has an added twist when it comes to quizzes:

- *Use alternative text to describe images in your quiz*: If you include an image in a quiz question or quiz response option, you must use alternative text to describe it. This is especially important if you use images to show equations that students must solve or music notation that students must identify, or if you ask students to identify something in the picture (e.g., parts of the digestive system in anatomy). Alternative text for images in a quiz can be tricky, though—if you are asking students to identify what's in the picture, the alternative text may hold the answer! You may have to rethink how you describe what's in each image to support students with screen readers without giving them the answers.

In addition to the core accessibility practices, here are some considerations specific to quizzes in the LMS:

- *Show one question at a time*: Students with attention-deficit/ hyperactivity disorder, certain learning disabilities, sleep disorders, and other conditions can have a hard time maintaining attention or focus. When these same students take an online quiz, the challenge with the focus can lead to conflating answers from the previous quiz question with the next question listed on the page. To address this issue, use the Canvas quiz setting, "Show one question at a time." (Note: Do not select "Lock questions after answering," as this prevents students from checking their work and making adjustments.)
- *Provide different lengths of time to specific students*: If (a) you use a time limit on your quizzes and (b) one or more students need more time, you can provide extra time. To learn how, review the Canvas guide, "Once I Publish a Timed Quiz, How Can I Give My Students Extra Time?" (Canvas Doc Team, 2020a; community .canvaslms.com/docs/DOC-13053-4152276279).
- *Particularly for practice tests, provide additional attempts to specific students*: Similarly, if you limit the number of quiz attempts, you can support each student who requires additional attempts. To learn how, review the Canvas guide, "Once I Publish a Quiz, How Can I Give My Students Extra Attempts?" (Canvas Doc Team, 2020b; community.canvaslms.com/docs/DOC-13076-415250753).

Assignments
- *Make accessibility a part of your assignment design*: Effective assignments include accessibility from the start. For a quick set of guidelines, review "Characteristics of Effective Online Assignments" by Brown University (2020; www.brown.edu/sheridan/teaching-learning-resources/teaching-resources/course-design/enhancing-student-learning-technology/effective-online-assignments).
- *Make sure the attached media are accessible*: Ensure your assignments are accessible by making all attached media files accessible, such as rubrics, instructions, or case studies. Do not include inaccessible websites as part of the assignment.

Third-Party Assessment Tools
- *Review learning environments for accessibility*: Tools like Pearson's MyMathLab have used, or still use, Flash to create interactive presentations as well as assessment activities. Flash causes

problems for students who use screen readers, which typically cannot decipher Flash. Ask someone in your academic technology unit or disability resource center to help review online learning tools—new or old—for accessibility.

UDL, Design for Learning Equity, and Humanizing Your Course

Although the UDL Guidelines ask you to consider accessibility as an essential practice, the CAST (n.d.a) team reminds us that "UDL is more than simply providing information in accessible ways" (para. 2). In a brief video about UDL and accessibility, CAST's (n.d.b) senior policy analyst, Skip Stahl, encourages teachers both to use and to go beyond content-focused accessibility accommodations by embracing all three principles of UDL. So, as you consider how to make the course experience more accessible for every learner, use UDL strategies like minimizing potential distractions, optimizing access to assistive technologies, and allowing students to use multiple tools for construction and composition.

Along the same lines, the design for learning equity framework encourages the use of accessible course elements and also offers ideas to address equity needs as you make your course more accessible. As a group, students with disabilities are working to close achievement gaps related to completing and passing online courses. For them, accessibility is a large part of an equity strategy. In addition to using accessible course elements, connect students with disabilities to appropriate (and accessible) resources and services that do not require a visit to campus. By asking all students to caption the videos they produce or to use alternative text for images they share, you are doing the following:

- Managing a type of human interaction bias—in other words, when all students use accessibility accommodations, more learners are included in the entire learning process
- Showing all students that they belong—in other words, you value their participation in all aspects of the course and the course community, not just responding to prompts in isolation

Being mindful of the humans in your course is always a concern in online classes. You may only ever see a photo of a student, and across a semester, it is easy to forget all of the individual challenges students face every day. Remember that our own experiences come to mind most frequently, and we must be mindful of the variety of human experiences in our course to understand the challenges our students face every day. Building a community of learners, being mindful of challenges, and encouraging communication in multiple formats will help learners realize that you are mindful of them as individuals. Keep in mind that a core component of UDL and learning equity frameworks is the desire to teach such that every individual learner has an opportunity to succeed.

NEXT STEPS

In this chapter, we presented a large number of tools and strategies to make your course environment and the elements in that environment more accessible. These tools and strategies are important for everyone—including those who teach face-to-face classes. Now it's time to get to work! Ask your department chair or dean if your campus offers support or provides any tools like Blackboard's Ally. If the project seems daunting, then start with one file, like your syllabus. You can move the mountain one teaspoon at a time. If you are interested in learning more about accessibility accommodations, then take a look at some of these articles, resources, and websites:

- National Center on Accessible Educational Materials (Center for Applied Special Technology): aem.cast.org/
- Access by Design: Accessible Instructional Materials Checklist for Faculty (California Polytechnic State University): accessibility.calpoly.edu/content/instmaterials/fac_checklist
- Accessible Digital Materials (Northern Illinois University): www.niu.edu/ethics-compliance/technology-accessibility/course-materials/index.shtml
- Guidelines for Adopting Publisher Content (Portland Community College): www.pcc.edu/instructional-support/accessibility/publishercontent/
- "30 Tools to Test Higher Education Website Accessibility" (Bradley, 2019) uxdesign.cc/28-tools-to-test-higher-education-website-accessibility-a59be955b398
- ADA Compliance for Online Course Design (Educause Review): er.educause.edu/articles/2017/1/ada-compliance-for-online-course-design

CHAPTER SUMMARY

This chapter focuses on moving from teaching the way we, personally, learn best to teaching in a way that helps a wide variety of learners to be successful. Strategies to aid the learning of a wide variety of students that we support each semester include (a) considering different learning needs, accommodations, and assistive technologies; (b) guidelines associated with accessibility of instructional materials, such as files and multimedia; and (c) practices for making online course environments and activities accessible. This chapter also includes tools for assessing the accessibility of different online course elements and strategies for addressing what needs to be done.

Reflection and Discussion Questions

1. How did you best learn as a student? To what extent has your learning as a student impacted your teaching as a faculty member? Discuss one thing that you could begin doing differently to more effectively include those who learn differently than you do?
2. Reflect on the challenges you have with respect to learning. Keep in mind that there are challenges that are physical (e.g., seeing, hearing, mobility), learning (e.g., dyslexia, attention deficit disorders, or cognitive processing speeds), and environmental (e.g., no internet access, food insecurity, homelessness, no quiet place to study). These also overlap at times, so they may not fall into a clear category. What have faculty members done in courses you have taken that have helped you personally, given any challenges you experience or experienced previously? You will not be asked to discuss unless you are comfortable doing so.
3. If there were no technological or economic restrictions, what might be done to make education much more inclusive?
4. What resources exist on your campus to assist those who struggle as a result of any form of challenge that makes it more difficult for an individual to learn course content or demonstrate learning through an appropriate assessment technique?

PART TWO

GUIDING LEARNERS FROM A DISTANCE

2.1

SUPPORTING ONLINE LEARNERS

*A*DDRESSING LEARNER NEEDS IS a challenging aspect of being a faculty member. Students come to our courses with very different individual life experiences that often put their academic abilities to the test, and even students who are very successful academically and appear to be model students face difficult circumstances from time to time. Unfortunately, as online teachers, there are times we don't realize when our students are struggling. One advantage face-to-face instructors have is the ability to see students regularly, and potentially pick up on subtle cues, such as looking fatigued, appearing lost during class, or even coming late and leaving early. In this situation, faculty members can address learners' needs as they arise and, on occasion, may walk a student to the counseling center or other campus office designed to assist students in need. Online faculty members have fewer interpersonal cues to notice when students struggle and must be proactive in meeting the needs of learners who may live far away or may be unable to get to campus for in-person support. In this chapter, we will consider common policies for an online course syllabus that you may modify and help you to outline student support services—both academic and nonacademic—that are relevant to your courses and your students. We will also outline how to help learners assess their readiness for an online course and prepare to be an online learner. Finally, we will describe how to use discussions to foster community and social belonging to create a more inclusive online environment for your students.

IDENTIFYING AND SHARING RELEVANT POLICIES

Online course design rubrics such as the QM rubric for higher education and the course design rubric by California Virtual Campus—Online

105

Education Initiative (see Table 1.1.3 for a list) typically include multiple criteria related to clearly outlining the course or institutional policies that affect online students (K. Kelly, 2019b). In this chapter you will find examples of online course policies that you may modify and use in your own online course syllabus. It is essential to look up the information for your campus to make sure our examples do not contradict the campus-specific policies at your institution and to note when you have resources at your campus that we have not indicated!

At the end of this chapter (Appendix 2.1) we share a few sample syllabus polices for online courses. We use bold text and square brackets (e.g., [**sample text**]) to show which information you may adapt to include your own campus or course information. If you use any of our policies as templates, remember to change the sample text and remove the brackets. Again, these policies are provided as examples, with the intention that you will adapt them to your specific institution and your preferred instructional approach. Note that we have included policies that might seem unrelated to online courses, like basic needs security. Too many students—as many as 58% during the spring 2020 term (Goldrick-Rab et al., 2020)—face food insecurity, housing insecurity, homelessness, or a combination of these challenges. These challenges affect online learners' success, too.

IDENTIFYING AND SHARING RELEVANT STUDENT SUPPORT SERVICES

Student support is available for anyone taking credit-bearing courses throughout the entire campus community, but getting that support can be challenging for online students who do not, or cannot, attend classes on campus. It is also challenging to point students to campus-based resources for student success when the entire campus must close unexpectedly (e.g., due to earthquakes, hurricanes, wildfires, or a pandemic). If your campus is closed, be sure to contact each appropriate office to identify how student support will be provided remotely. That will give you the information needed to pass on to your students. To help facilitate student success, point students to resources that are (a) relevant to completing your online course or online course activities and (b) valuable to online students. These resources include, but are not limited to, academic services like academic advising or counseling, tutoring, writing support, library services, and accessibility accommodations and services for students with disabilities and nonacademic services like technical support, health and wellness services, psychological counseling, and financial aid. If you do not know which services exist on campus and how an online student might best utilize those resources, start with the office of the dean of students or the student affairs office. There are often many more resources than both on-campus and online faculty realize.

In your course shell or on the syllabus, post course-level instructions to explain how each of the appropriate resources will help students succeed in your class. Also, provide ways for students to connect with each support unit or office without visiting campus—for example, by phone, email, text, chat service, and videoconference. Next, use content or activity instructions to remind students about specific support options that relate to that course content or activity. Here are some examples for you to modify:

- In your instructions for writing assignments, mention the writing center and how students might use it: "Contact the campus writing center to get help planning or proofreading your essay. The center in [**Campus Building A-235**] is open [**Monday to Thursday, 10:00 a.m. to 6:00 p.m. and Friday, 10:00 a.m. to 2:00 p.m.**]. If you cannot get to campus, submit a support request via their online form ([**yourcampus.edu/learning-resource-center**]) or email ([**writinghelp@yourcampus.edu**]) or call ([**555-765-4321**]) during the hours of operation."
- Similarly, tell students about online tutoring options for other types of assignments: "If you need help completing this assignment, our campus provides a free online tutoring option through [**name of tutoring service**]. Visit the campus web page at [**yourcampus.edu/online-tutoring**] to schedule an appointment."
- In your outline of a research project, direct students to contact librarians and to take advantage of library services. Libraries at some institutions aggregate and advertise services for online learners. If your institution does not have a page like this, you can use the examples in the following list (also included in Appendix C) to identify what you could put together for your students.
  o Broward College (Florida)—Online Library: libguides.broward .edu/bconlinelibrary
  o Coastline College (California)—Online Library: www .coastline.edu/student-life/online-library/index.php
  o Skyline College (California)—Library Online Services: skylinecollege.edu/library/libraryinfo/onlineservices.php
  o Tri-County Community College (North Carolina)—Library Resources for Online Students: tricountycc.libguides.com/ c.php?g=74586&p=1115199
  o Rasmussen College (multiple locations)—Online Library: guides.rasmussen.edu/library

SUPPORTING ONLINE LEARNERS BY PREPARING FOR THE FIRST DAY

One thing that is consistent about teaching any portion of the course online is that preparation typically takes place much earlier than for face-to-face courses. Hybrid and online instructors must be ready for the first day of class well before the first day, especially if it's your first time teaching in this format. Stakes are high for online classes, and although an increasing number of students register for online classes every year, studies show that they pass online courses 6% to 10% less often than in-person courses (Hart et al., 2015; Kaupp, 2012; Xu & Jaggars, 2011). You can prepare students for successful online learning by creating an orientation module, fostering a sense of belonging and community, and humanizing the course experience.

Technique: Create an Orientation Module

Many students enroll in online courses for flexibility and convenience (Allen & Seaman, 2011; Shay & Rees, 2004). Although some students recognize the time management and other learning challenges often associated with online courses (Bozarth et al., 2004), students taking online courses frequently underestimate the time and effort required to succeed in this format (Bawa, 2016). Factors such as reading rate and typing speed, important in classrooms, are critical in the online format due to the extensive amount of independent reading and posting required (Geiger et al., 2014). Therefore, when establishing learner expectations for your course, it's essential to include clear expectations regarding what it will take to be successful in the online format. It is also helpful to build in mechanisms that will help to alert you and your students within the first few weeks if they begin to fall behind.

Studies show increased success when institutions require students to review critical aspects of online learning through a course- or module-based introduction to online learning (Cintrón & Lang, 2012; Lorenzi et al., 2004; Lynch, 2001). If your institution does not offer a centralized course or module about online learning, create your own orientation module to convey your expectations and prepare online learners. At least 1 week before the first day of class, send a message that lists all expectations for the course and direct students to the orientation module for additional information on how to be successful in the online course. The following five steps describe how to create potential components of an orientation module:

1. *Overview video*: Use a free screencast tool like Screencast-o-Matic or Jing to create a 3-to-5 minute course overview video that outlines

(a) the work students need to complete to succeed and how you will grade that work; (b) how students should communicate with you and what your expected response time will be; (c) when key assignments are due, and how you will manage the class flow of information; (d) the importance of regular interaction with a community of learners, rather than completing the course alone; and (e) how to navigate the online environment and where students can go for technical help.

2. *Syllabus activity*: Create an activity that requires students to review and reflect on the course syllabus, such as a discussion forum for students to post questions or a "Learning Agreement" quiz for students to show they understand how to complete the course successfully and commit to doing so. Here are some example "Learning Agreement" quiz questions:

- Multiple-answer question: According to the syllabus, student responsibilities in the online environment include (mark all that are true):
   o Students are only responsible for making sure that their email is correct at the beginning of the semester, but not after that. (Incorrect)
   o The instructor will use the LMS as the primary method to communicate class-related messages. In addition to reading emails, students must read the messages posted each week in the Announcements forum. (Correct)
   o Students do not have to worry about their email. (Incorrect)
   o Students are responsible for making sure that their email is correct throughout the semester. (Correct)
   o Students who forward emails sent to campus accounts are responsible for maintaining their off-campus email boxes so that class-related messages do not bounce. (Correct)
   o Students in the class will follow the suggested netiquette guidelines. (Correct)
   o Students are responsible for completing the assignments on time. (Correct)
- Final, multiple-answer question: Carefully read each of the following statements. Checking each box means you understand and agree to that statement:
   o I agree to make time for this class—an average of 5 hours per week.
   o I understand that I must keep track of my own progress.

o I agree to keep track of important deadlines, including class deadlines (e.g., assignment due dates) and campus deadlines (e.g., switching to credit/no credit, withdrawal).

o I agree to ask questions as soon as I do not understand something. I will not wait.

o I agree to take responsibility for my own learning.

3. *Advice from former students*: Post student comments in the online course shell from previous semesters, such as anonymous feedback from student evaluations of teaching effectiveness or online student testimonial videos that you have solicited. Following are examples of written comments from former students:

- "At the beginning of this online class, my goal was to complete the course activities before they were due. Unfortunately, I did not fulfill those goals. Instead, I ended up cramming everything right before it was due. I regret putting off all of these assignments because I did not do a good job on them."

- "This online class challenged my accountability. There was no face-to-face instructor to whom I had to answer. Perhaps the most substantial outcome of this is that it forced me to take charge of my own learning, instead of depending on someone else to dispense it to me."

4. *Open forum*: Start an open forum for general questions about the class and require students to participate in this first forum over the first 2 to 3 days of the semester. For this forum, you may need to provide more prompting and participation than you will for later discussions. The goal here is to get students comfortable communicating with one another through the forum format and begin to build the online community of learning. Some instructors call this first forum the Student Lounge or Virtual Class Café. Topics may include (a) prior experience in online and hybrid courses and tips for success, (b) content areas students are particularly interested in learning about, or (c) concerns about taking this course online and suggestions for the instructor to consider to help everyone to be successful. Note that you don't have to act on every student's suggestion. Point out that each student's comment will be read and given consideration.

5. *Readiness survey*: Assign students to take an online learning readiness survey like the Online Learning Readiness Questionnaire from Penn State, accessible at http://tutorials.istudy.psu.edu/learningonline/learningonline2.html) or Wichita State University's (n.d.) Online Readiness Assessment (www.wichita.edu/services/mrc/elearning/online

_orientation/online_self_assessment.php). Create an activity that requires students to reflect and take action on their results from the online learning readiness survey. Link to resources to address common needs, such as the California Community College (n.d.; apps.3cmediasolutions.org/oei/modules/study-time/story/) system's tutorial about online study skills and managing time or Western Governors University's (2018; https://www.wgu.edu/blog/time-management-strategies-online-college-students1810.html) list of time management strategies.

6. *Time allocation activity*: Students put in-person class meetings in their calendars but often do not set aside time to work on online or hybrid courses. Require students to submit an image of a paper or digital calendar, highlighting that they have scheduled the required amount of time each week to work on your class.

7. *Synchronous chats or meetings*: Find a few times the first week of the semester for students to log in and chat in real time. This is an ideal time for students to get to know one another. A way to make this fun for many students is to suggest to students that they introduce a pet during these open discussion times. Students often enjoy seeing animals, and for some shy students, it is a way to talk to the group more comfortably. Use different titles to show the purpose of these synchronous events— "meetups" emphasize community and human connectedness, "study groups" focus on collaborative knowledge sharing toward academic goals, and "group question and answer (office hours) sessions" offer opportunities to ask questions in a group setting.

SUPPORTING ONLINE LEARNERS THROUGH UDL AND DESIGN FOR LEARNING EQUITY

If we are not careful, online and hybrid courses have the potential to exclude different types of learners from participating. Learners with disabilities are one of the most notable groups, but not the only one by any means! With careful planning, courses can be designed to be more inclusive and structured so that everyone is supported.

Creating a More Inclusive Online Learning Environment

There is a wide range of inclusion strategies, and although there is no "one size fits all" way to address inclusivity, there are commonalities from which everyone can draw ideas. Some tasks are the same regardless of the course format.

- *Create a diversity statement in your syllabus.* Set an inclusive tone for your class from the very start by adding a diversity statement to your syllabus. See Vanderbilt University's Center for Teaching guide "Developing and Writing a Diversity Statement" for ideas on creating a diversity statement (Beck, 2018; cft.vanderbilt.edu/guides-sub-pages/developing-and-writing-a-diversity-statement/). Also see Appendix 2.1 for a sample diversity statement.
- *Choose (or create) inclusive course content.* Saunders and Kardia (1997) provide guidelines for choosing course content that increases inclusion. Those guidelines are including multiple perspectives on course topics, including materials written by people of different backgrounds, including materials that address underrepresented groups' experiences, and being aware of how various groups are portrayed or represented. Use image galleries dedicated to accurate and equitable representation to ensure that the students in your class see themselves in the course content. Burst and Women of Color in Tech are free, while galleries like Lean In, Representation Matters, and Toni are fee-based. See "Image Galleries That Address Image and Representation Bias" by Kevin Kelly (n.d.; drive.google.com/open?id=123F5RnQ_vP_QDNzoJAV-EoBlwadTvhWK).

For online and hybrid teachers, creating inclusive course environments and activities takes on another dimension.

- *Make adjustments to your course and approach to students*: Jones and Sneed (2016) provided five strategies to foster inclusivity in your online course: (a) getting to know your students, (b) reviewing course activities for cultural awareness, (c) drawing from your students' backgrounds and experiences, (d) using technology to bridge cultural and socioeconomic gaps, and (e) working to create a safe and positive course environment. They also suggest a specific "Name Stories" activity—one of Paul Gorski's (n.d., www.edchange.org/multicultural/activityarch.html) Awareness Activities—that would work well as an online icebreaker discussion. In the Name Stories activity, students "write and share stories about their names and nicknames, what they mean, why they were given to them, and how they relate to them" (Gorski, n.d., para. 4).

Apply UDL and Universal Design for Instruction Principles to Increase Inclusion

Clemson University (2016) provided a rationale for applying UDL to distance education: "When designing your online courses consider UDL as a foundation for establishing a learning environment that not only supports your students with disabilities, but also fosters an environment where all students can thrive" (para. 3). K. Kelly (2014) suggested specific strategies to foster inclusion by applying UDL principles related to assessment, ranging from simple to complex. A simple strategy might entail allowing students to choose one of several questions you provide for each concept you assess through an essay test. A more complex strategy involves letting students submit their work in one of several formats, such as "an essay, an infographic, an audio presentation or podcast episode, a screencast or online presentation, a video, or a project of another media type that might be appropriate to the course" (K. Kelly, 2014, para. 8).

Brandon and Nemeroff (2016) provided a number of examples of how to meet universal design for instruction (UDI) principles. For example, to meet the principle related to "instructional climate," include a statement in your syllabus "affirming the need for class members to respect diversity" (Brandon & Nemeroff, 2016, para. 10). Their work is an adaptation of efforts by the UDI Online Project (2009), a project that has received grants totally over $3 million to develop UDI principles and applications throughout higher education.

Technique: Use Discussions to Foster Community and Belonging

Although technological factors, students' study habits, and personal behaviors all affect students' ability to complete an online course, social and psychological factors, such as community and belonging, also play an important role in online student persistence. This is just one reason of many that community and belonging are core elements of the design for learning equity framework.

Building a sense of community has been proven to counteract online learners' feelings of alienation and isolation (Croft et al., 2010; Rovai & Wighting, 2005). Sadera et al. (2009) found that "a positive relationship exists between students' sense of community and their learning success in online courses" (p. 282). Therefore, providing opportunities for student-to-student interaction early and often—starting the first day of class, if not before—is critical to student persistence and success.

Building on earlier research in the K–12 classroom (Dweck et al., 2014; Kizilcec et al., 2017) showed that social belonging and values affirmation activities closed achievement gaps for students facing stereotype threats in online courses. Thomas et al. (2014) found that nontraditional students in online courses highly valued a sense of belonging and persisted in those courses that fostered it.

To foster belonging, use one or more of the following discussion activities.

Facilitate a values affirmation discussion by asking students to take the following four steps:

1. List the three values that currently are most important to them.
2. Describe why those values are important to them at this point in their lives.
3. Describe how taking your course reflects or serves one or more of those values.
4. Validate the values described by two or more classmates.

Facilitate a social belonging discussion by asking students to take the following three steps:

1. Review quotes attributed to a diverse set of former students who successfully completed the class (e.g., first generation to attend college, nontraditional/returning students, different ethnicities and gender identities) that let the readers know they are not alone in any anxiety related to taking an online course for the first time and that they can complete the course successfully.
2. Reflect on their own experiences of learning in new environments and feelings about taking your online course based on reading the quotes.
3. Review and reply to other classmates' reflections with encouragement.

To foster community, use one or more of the following three discussion activities. Structure a discussion that encourages students to find commonalities with their peers.

1. In response to your prompt, ask students to share their academic goals and challenges, either in general or for your specific online or hybrid class, as well as personal facts such as their favorite food.
2. Ask students to find and reply to at least one student who has a common goal, another student who has a common perceived challenge, and a third student who has a common personal fact.

3. If the discussion tool in your LMS has social media functionality, allow students to "like" other students' posts or replies.

In a large class, use the group functionality in your LMS to keep discussions more approachable with 5 to 10 students per group. Be sure to participate in each discussion yourself to join the new community of learners.

NEXT STEPS

Now that you've reviewed a variety of methods to support online learners, reflect on how well you do the following:

- Incorporate appropriate policies in your online course syllabus
- Outline both academic and nonacademic support services available through your campus that are relevant to your class and your students
- Help learners assess their readiness for your online course and prepare to be an online learner
- Create a more inclusive online environment for your students
- Use discussions to foster community and social belonging

CHAPTER SUMMARY

Students come to our courses with individual life experiences that often create academic challenges, and many students struggle more in online environments than they do in face-to-face courses. There are many ways for online teachers to be proactive in meeting the needs of learners who may live far away or may be unable to get to campus for in-person support. This chapter includes many templates and suggestions for addressing the wide variety of ways an online instructor can help students to be successful: common policies for an online course syllabus that you may modify and use, examples of both academic and nonacademic student support services that are relevant to your class and your students, suggestions to help learners assess their readiness for an online course and prepare to be an online learner, descriptions of how to use discussions to foster community and social belonging, and ideas to help you to create a more inclusive online environment for your students.

Reflection and Discussion Questions

1. Describe how students may contact campus units or find campus resources designed to assist them if they need learning accommodations. To what extent do you know what services are offered through each office?

2. Are there differences in the level of support throughout your college or university with respect to on-site students and online students? Are the writing center, counseling center, disability services, and other resource centers used by online students? If so, how do they make this possible? If not, how might these resources be adapted to make it easier for online students to use them?

3. What would you see as the most critical component of an orientation module of a selected course you teach online? Describe a specific example that you feel would work well for students throughout your institution.

4. Describe how you build community in your online courses. What do you require of or offer students the opportunity to do that helps them feel like they are unique individuals within a caring course community?

APPENDIX 2.1

SAMPLE SYLLABUS POLICIES

Course Format

This [**three credit**] hour course will be entirely online, which means that all class meetings and activities are online, or virtual. By university policy, the amount of work you to do to complete this online class is equivalent to face-to-face [**three credit**] hour courses. For this course, please expect to work for [**up to 9**] hours per week. In the first week, you will be asked to share a picture of a paper calendar or screenshot of a digital calendar showing you have blocked off enough time each week to complete this class. The online learning environment we will be using is [**name of campus LMS**]. I am committed to this being a safe place for our course. Please do your part to maintain our class as a safe place to learn by respecting your fellow online learners and helping them whenever you can. There will be many online class discussions in this course. Online class discussions provide opportunities to try out ideas or to gain new knowledge or skills. You can ask any question at any time. Don't hold back, even if you think what you may say might be silly or trivial. Also, please provide thoughtful responses and new ideas. Everyone in the course is busy, so let's show respect to one another by posting conversations that are well worth the time it will take to read them.

Incomplete

The goal is that you will complete your work by the end of the semester and avoid an Incomplete in the course. Although you may be stressed or busy during the course, years of experience have taught us that schedules rarely get easier later in the semester. That said, one can never predict everything that may happen while you are in this course. If you cannot complete the course requirements by the end of the semester due to unforeseeable and justifiable reasons, you may receive an "I" grade (Incomplete). Although I am always disappointed when a student finds it necessary to take an incomplete, it will not change how I think of you. The grade of Incomplete is there to help you to be successful—if you must use it, then I will support your decision. You will have [**12 months**] from the last day of classes to complete the work. It is extremely important that we discuss and document in writing your plan for completing the course. If your completed work meets our agreed-upon requirements, I will work with you to file a grade change request. If you do qualify for and choose to take an Incomplete, you are responsible for getting your completed work (e.g., papers, exams, peer assessments) to me and for following up to make sure the appropriate grade change has been recorded.

Withdrawal From Course

If you are unable to complete a significant amount of work related to the course and are unable to finish, an Incomplete may not be the appropriate option. Incompletes are for situations in which there is a relatively small portion of the course remaining to complete. In cases in which a significant portion of the course work is not completed at the time you realize you cannot finish the course, the most appropriate option is to withdraw from the course. A "W" symbol will be recorded on your student transcript if you withdraw from the class. You can select this option after the last day to drop classes without a withdrawal through the end of the [**14th week**] of instruction. The "W" symbol is used to determine progress probation and is not used to determine academic probation.

Accommodation Statement for Students With Disabilities

Students with disabilities who need reasonable accommodations are encouraged to contact the [**name of Disability Resource Center unit**]. That office is available to facilitate the accommodations process and to determine which accommodations will be made available to you. [**The Disability Resource Center**] is located in room [**room number**] in the [**building name**] building. As this is an online course, you may not have to come to campus to identify appropriate accommodations! [**The Disability Resource Center**] can be reached by telephone (voice/TTY [**555-123-4567**]) or by email ([**email@yourcampus.edu**]). I will work with you to provide whatever accommodations are afforded to you through [**The Disability Resource Center**]. Please be aware that I want to help you to the greatest extent I am able. If you request and are granted an accommodation, then I will certainly provide that accommodation. Please note that by law, as much as I would like to, I am not allowed to provide any accommodation for you that is not granted by [**The Disability Resource Center**].

Academic Integrity and Plagiarism

Academic integrity refers to the "integral" quality of the search for knowledge that a student undertakes. This means that all work you produce and claim to be your original work must be entirely yours; it should result entirely from your own efforts. A student will be guilty of violating academic integrity if he/she: (a) knowingly represents work of others as her/his own, (b) uses or obtains unauthorized assistance in the execution of any academic work, (c) gives fraudulent assistance to another student, or (d) engages in any behaviors that increase the grade in the course through dishonest statements or actions.

Plagiarism is cheating that occurs when a person misrepresents or claims the work of another as his or her own. Plagiarism may consist of using any amount of text written by another without appropriate acknowledgment. In some cases, the content may be as few as three words in a row. Plagiarism also includes paying or allowing another person to write work that a student then submits as his or her own. In some cases, having another person alter work without acknowledging that work can be considered plagiarism. If you are uncertain as to whether to cite something, please see the course plagiarism guide or contact the online support for the writing center. In all cases, when in doubt, check it out.

It is also essential to give credit for any images you use for this class. Many of the images found on Google and other online search engines are copyright protected. If you do use them, be sure to cite them appropriately. University of Virginia's Health Science Library has an excellent page on how to give proper credit for images, aptly titled "How Do I Properly Cite Images in a Presentation or Publication?" (https://www.hsl.virginia .edu/services/howdoi/how-do-i-properly-cite-images-presentation-or-publication). There are many images with a "Creative Commons" (CC) license (e.g., you can filter for CC images on Flickr, Google, and other websites), which means you can use the image for free as long as you follow the artist's requests. Here's a link to a helpful infographic that describes CC licenses and how to give credit for CC images: "Foter—How to Attribute Creative Commons Photos" (2015; http://foter.com/blog/how-to-attribute-creative-commons-photos/).

Some sites have images that are free to use and do not require that you provide a citation. That said, if you use images from those sources and image credit is available, it is always nice to give credit to the person who created the image for the work done. Three popular image sources are Unsplash (https://unsplash.com), Pixabay (https://pixabay.com), and Canva (https://canva.com).

Last, some image galleries do a poor job of representing our diverse population accurately and equitably. There are a few free image galleries designed to address this shortcoming, such as Burst (https://burst.shopify .com), Nappy (https://www.nappy.co), and Women of Color in Tech (https://www.flickr.com/photos/wocintechchat/). Regardless of the gallery used, be aware of how people are or are not represented, and cite your sources.

As per university policy, any plagiarized assignment will receive a grade of zero points. Instances of plagiarism in this class may be reported to the dean of the college or the university judicial affairs officer for further action. Not knowing the rules regarding plagiarism is not a defense for plagiarizing.

Late or Missed Assignments

All work must be submitted on time to give me time to grade the assignment or exam. All assignments will have a deadline for submission, and all assignments will have stated penalties for work that is submitted late. Points will be deducted from any assignment submitted late. Please note that computers freeze at times, the internet goes down, and files can be difficult to locate. It is best to plan to submit work well before the minute it is due. Under extreme circumstances only, you may contact me by email to request an exception: [**youremail@yourcampus.edu**].

Resources for Citing Sources

All sources for your written work, both paper and online, must be cited using the American Psychological Association (APA) guidelines. The following links are helpful resources for APA protocols:

- Purdue Online Writing Lab (OWL)—APA Style and Formatting Guide (https://owl.english.purdue.edu/owl/resource/560/10/)
- Rochester Institute of Technology—Wallace Library—APA Citation Format (http://lgdata.s3-website-us-east-1.amazonaws .com/docs/1366/837696/apa6.pdf)

Student Responsibilities in the Online Environment

I will use [**name of campus LMS**] as the primary method to communicate class-related messages (e.g., Announcements). You are responsible for reading all messages and making sure that the correct email address is attached to your [**name of campus LMS**] account throughout the semester. If you forward your campus emails to another service (e.g., Gmail, Yahoo Mail), then you are responsible for maintaining your email boxes so that class-related messages do not bounce. See the Campus Student email service website—[**link to correct webpage**]—to review how to forward your address, and so on. I also use a free, opt-in service called Remind .com to send text message versions of important announcements. You will find the link to sign up to get text message announcements in the "Getting Ready" module in our course.

Please support your fellow learners by respecting them (even if they have different opinions), providing constructive feedback and giving encouragement. We will follow the Lake Superior College Netiquette Guidelines (http://blogs.lsc.edu/expectations/netiquette-guidelines/) as we interact online.

Basic Needs Security

Any student who has difficulty affording groceries or accessing sufficient food to eat every day or who lacks a safe and stable place to live and believes this may affect their performance in the course is urged to visit the campus Basic Needs website—[**link to campus basic needs webpage**]—for information about food security resources, or contact Health Promotion and Wellness at [**email link for campus health and wellness**] for support. If the campus is closed and you cannot access the food pantry, you can find other food pantries close to you with tools like FoodFinder (2020; foodfinder.us). Furthermore, please notify your instructors, if you are comfortable in doing so. This will enable us to connect you with any resources that we may possess.

Respect for Diversity

It is my intent that students from diverse backgrounds and perspectives be well served by this course, that your learning needs be addressed both in and out of class, and that the diversity that students bring to this class be viewed as a resource, strength, and benefit. I strive to present materials and activities that are respectful of diversity: gender, sexuality, disability, age, socioeconomic status, ethnicity, race, and culture. Your suggestions to increase diversity—for example, materials that present course topics from other perspectives or more inclusive activities—are encouraged and appreciated. Please let me know ways to improve the effectiveness of the course for you personally, or for other students or student groups. Last, I ask that everyone respect the diverse identities, backgrounds, and cultures of their fellow classmates and encourage others to share their perspectives.

2.2

CREATING AND MAINTAINING YOUR "INSTRUCTOR PRESENCE"

FACULTY–LEARNER INTERACTION IS A foundation of quality instruction in any setting. Studies consistently show that online learners highly value interaction with, and availability of, their instructor, and educational developers encourage online teachers to be visible and accessible to students in a variety of ways. These strategies stave off feelings of isolation that learners typically feel in online environments and increase their motivation. During the COVID-19 pandemic, faculty soon found that connecting with students became a central focus. Multiple resources emerged that encouraged faculty members to not forget about the instructor-learning connection. For example, in the opening sentence of her blog, *The Scholarly Teacher*, Harriet Schwartz (2020) stated: "How we are with our students throughout this pandemic will teach them at least as much as the content of our courses" (para. 1). Campuses that close, whether due to pandemics, hurricanes, or other natural disasters, come with many stressors for students. In such cases it is particularly important to connect with students. That said, under the best of circumstances, online students run the risk of feeling isolated from the campus and having an instructor who demonstrates concern is greatly appreciated by those students.

This chapter will support you in (a) letting students know who you are, (b) making connections with students, (c) building learning communities, and (d) guiding students through the learning process in a way that feels personal to them.

UDL, DESIGN FOR LEARNING EQUITY, HUMAN CONNECTIONS, AND INSTRUCTOR PRESENCE

The design for learning equity framework pulls together a variety of research-based concepts that help instructors address equity issues in any type of course. There are several frameworks within higher education that suggest addressing the human aspect of learning, particularly in the online environment. Dee Fink's taxonomy of significant learning (2003) includes the "human dimension" (learning about oneself and others) and "caring" (developing new feelings, values) as higher levels of student learning. Michelle Pacansky-Brock has been writing and speaking for several years about both why and how we should design human-centered learning experiences, or humanize our online courses (see brocansky.com/humanizing for excellent resources on humanizing). Human-level concepts are even gaining traction within the educational technology space. For example, a startup company named Pronto (pronto.io/education) makes student engagement software (e.g., chat and video tools) for teaching and learning and gives out T-shirts at educational conferences and conventions that say "Be Human." (Please go to Appendix C for links to the online resources mentioned in this chapter.)

Humanizing various aspects of your course follows UDL principles. By recording video messages for students, you both allow students to see you as a person and provide an alternative to text-only messages. By allowing students to participate in online class discussions using either text or Flipgrid videos (which are automatically captioned), you allow students to connect with each other more deeply and offer multiple media for communication.

Human connection has an impact on teachers and learners alike. Instructor–student interaction and faculty engagement are critical factors in online student retention and success (Crews et al., 2015). Notably, an online instructor's "presence"—the degree to which students feel the instructor is visible and actively participating—affects students' persistence, motivation to participate, and even final grades in online courses (Garrison et al., 2000; Liu et al., 2009; Savery, 2005). Further, as with face-to-face courses, your presence online has multiple dimensions—your persona, your role in the course learning community, and your actions to guide learners (R. Kelly, 2014). The following are practical examples of how to increase your instructor presence throughout the course experience.

Letting Students Know Who You Are

Creating several brief videos (shorter than 5 minutes in length) establishes an online presence on, or even before, the first day of the course. There are several ways to create videos with very little work. Videos can be created easily by using your smartphone or free, online screencast tools. If your campus offers software to online faculty, ask if they provide tools like Camtasia or Relay by TechSmith. Each of the following examples is provided as a guide. Adapt them as appropriate and establish your own presence in the course.

- *Personal introduction*: Students want to know more about you as a person, so share personal information to the extent you are comfortable related to (a) the course (e.g., what excites you about the course topics and how your real-world experiences relate to the course), (b) your academic role and experiences (e.g., what inspired you to become an instructor in the area in which you are teaching and how you overcame academic hurdles as a student in this area), and (c) personal hobbies and interests you have to the extent you are comfortable sharing with your students, particularly if you intend to ask students about their hobbies and interests. This recording can be made informally by using a smartphone or laptop to record yourself in an informal setting that represents you in some way, such as a home office, your backyard, or your favorite local coffee shop.
- *Course overview*: In their study of online students' perceptions about instructor presence, Sheridan and M. Kelly (2010) found making course requirements clear is one of the most important things you can do. A course overview message is an excellent place to begin that process. Review the learning objectives and connect them to students' lives—how they'll use knowledge, skills, and attitudes from your course in subsequent courses, in the workforce, or both. Go over important aspects of the syllabus, such as important due dates, your grading policies, and how often you will communicate and participate in online activities. Although you will be covering administrative topics, you can still share your personality and energy. If you make a mistake that you find funny, consider leaving it in the video or using it as an outtake.
- *Course welcome message*: In addition to a more traditional overview of the course syllabus and student expectations, create a "trailer" welcome video designed to pique students' interest in the course and its learning objectives. Let the students know that you care about their success, how you intend to support them in this particular course, and how you plan to make the class engaging. One option to create this video is to intersperse video footage of yourself with images related to the course topics. Pacansky-Brock (2013a) suggests creating a "welcome mat"—a video preview of your course using images and voiceover narration—with a tool called Animoto.

- *Course environment navigation tutorial:* Students in your hybrid or online class will have varying degrees of experience with the LMS or online course environments. Use a tool like Jing (www.techsmith .com/jing-tool.html) or Screencast-o-Matic (screencast-o-matic .com/) to record a brief introductory screencast video, narrating as you navigate through the important elements of your course to help them to get started in the course. Identify any weekly patterns students should follow, such as "Review the recorded mini-lecture each Monday and take the quiz. Each Wednesday, participate in the online discussion. Every other Friday, submit your reflection paper." Also, tell students where they can get technical help (e.g., campus help desk or LMS help guides) and academic help (e.g., librarians, online writing support, or online tutors).

- *Introduce the first lesson or module:* This video should achieve the goals of (a) outlining the objectives and instructions to complete the first week's activities successfully and (b) establishing student motivation and interest in the topic(s). After you have established an online presence in the first week, have videos prepared in advance to introduce each new module, lesson, or topic for each week of the course. Tell students how each module aligns with the course objectives and if the lesson relies on prior learning. To avoid remaking videos, avoid references to specific dates or holidays in videos that have consistent messages from one academic term to the next. For example, if you teach the same online course in the spring that you taught in the fall, a reference to Thanksgiving break will quickly date your work when you make it available to students in January!

Guiding Students in a Way That Feels Personal

Building your presence online can be done at multiple levels. For example, announcements reach every student, but students will need individual attention that increases your overall presence, too. Timing and tone are two aspects of this individualized presence. The first day sets the tone for any course, so it is important to establish an online presence no later than the first day of the course. Sheridan and M. Kelly (2010) found that being responsive to students' needs was another important aspect of instructor presence. The online students in their study did not expect an immediate response but did want an answer within a day.

As we mentioned in chapter 1.1, online students bring a diverse set of personal goals and needs to our classes. Although you aren't trying to be every student's BFF (best friend forever), it doesn't take much to show empathy, to be positive and friendly, or to add a personal touch. In an ice-breaker activity, ask students by what name they prefer to be called, then keep a list of their preferred names handy and use those names when you reply to their forum posts and email messages. If you are comfortable, also ask students their preferred pronoun. Be aware that as difficult as it might be based on your personal background and learning, there is an increasing trend to use "they" as a gender-neutral pronoun for an individual (as is done in the following sentence). If a student starts to fall behind, provide a concrete plan showing how they can catch up, if that's possible, and end your email with a supportive "You can do this!" For some of us, using they as a singular pronoun may be challenging, but making adjustments to our past practices is at times necessary to create a more inclusive community now and in the future.

Use Smartphone, Tablet, or Webcam Videos to Humanize Announcements
Many instructors send announcements in a text format—usually through the LMS announcements feature or email. An easy way to humanize those announcements is to pull out your smartphone or tablet, or turn on your webcam, and record the same message. Then upload the video and add a link to it from the announcement or email. Kevin, the lead author of this book, likes to record those videos from different locations, such as a running trail or an airport terminal. For example, "Hi everyone! Before I start my morning jog here on the San Francisco Bay Trail, I wanted to remind you to get started on this week's reflection essay . . ." or "Hey, everybody. Just letting you know that I've been reading and scoring your discussion posts on a long Uber ride to LAX airport. I really like how so many of you are providing strong suggestions for classmates to take their ideas further . . ." You do not have to involve exercise or air travel, of course, but letting students see you away from a desk allows them to connect with you as a person and models that, with online education, one can be working and learning in any environment.

Use Screencast Videos to Provide Feedback on Activities and Assignments
In addition to timing and tone, you can adopt practices that humanize the online environment. Although course welcome videos and video announcements allow students to see who you are collectively, assignment feedback videos perform the same function individually. Henderson and Phillips (2015) found that undergraduate and graduate students preferred 5-minute video feedback to text-based feedback. LMS solutions like Canvas (native) and Moodle (through plugins) allow video feedback for

assignments. If your LMS doesn't have this capability, you can use screencast tools and link to your videos.

If you're wondering how video feedback works, here is an example. Pull up a student's assignment, such as a problem set for a STEM field; an essay for English, humanities, or social sciences; an image of creative work for the arts; or a video of a physical skill like welding. Review the student's work with your rubric or guidelines. When you have scored the work, create a screencast video in which you make comments on what the student did well and how they can improve. Use a highlighter or pen tool to identify a specific math problem, idea from an essay, or aspect of a creative work that you describe. Use a tool like Coach's Eye (coachseye.com by TechSmith) to give feedback on something that involves movement, such as dance or sewing sutures with a practice kit and a silicone suture pad. Focus on criteria from your rubric or guidelines. Let them know what needs to be improved, but also how they can improve.

It is also possible to give video feedback about a presentation. Use VoiceThread (voicethread.com) or Edpuzzle (edpuzzle.com) to embed comments in a video created by your students. This allows you to provide feedback or even augment their materials in a way that is both interesting and informative for your students.

General Tips for Using Video

Making effective educational videos for your online course is not as challenging as most believe. Here we offer a few concepts to get you started. For additional tips and ideas, a quick web search will give you guidance in any area you desire. There are also several excellent books on this specific topic, such as *99 Tips for Creating Simple and Sustainable Educational Videos* by Karen Costa (2020).

- *Preparation*: Write out a complete script for each video. You do not have to read every word of the script when you record the video, but writing it out will help you to think through what you wish to say and determine the video's approximate length using the total word count and video tools like Edge Studio's (n.d.) time calculator (www.edgestudio.com/production/words-to-time-calculator). If the script requires scrolling, try using a teleprompter app to keep your hands free. Once you record the video, revise the script for any changes you made and use it as a transcript or text for video captions.
- *Tone and animation*: Maintain an upbeat tone of voice throughout the video and be at least somewhat animated. Even if you are describing something technical like how to navigate your online

course, avoid sounding like you are tired, reading from a script, or bored with the topic. Remember, you are projecting your persona along with conveying important information. As you prepare, think of how you might sound if describing the same process to a class in person.

- *Length*: It is generally best to make feedback videos as short as possible. Even though they are videos, as opposed to written comments, students will want to get through them as quickly as possible. Do not be cryptic, but do be concise.
- *Placement*: If possible, embed the videos in high-traffic areas. For example, students should see your personal introduction and welcome messages when they first enter your course. If you cannot embed the videos directly on your course pages, then place a screenshot or still frame taken from the video next to each link to an actual video. Also, link to personal introduction and welcome message videos from the announcement you send before the class starts. Link to the course navigation tutorial and the first module introduction from the announcement you post on the first day of class.

MAKING CONNECTIONS WITH STUDENTS AND BUILDING A LEARNING COMMUNITY

Along with a variety of videos, you can use other small touches to set the stage with your presence. Edit your profile in the LMS to include a photo and brief bio. If you don't like using pictures of yourself, choose an image or icon that represents you in some way and explain that connection to your class. Create an icebreaker forum (e.g., "Introduce yourself" or "Share a memorable learning story") and write the first post, following the same prompt you give to your students. At this point, you've completed activities to establish your presence before the students enter the online course environment. Now it's time to turn your attention to maintaining that presence, making connections, and building community.

Use Announcements to Maintain a Regular Presence

Announcements allow you to maintain your presence at regular intervals, so set a schedule that makes sense for your class. For example, kick off each week with a note about the new course topic(s). Tell students how they'll use or build on what they've learned earlier and what they'll be expected to complete. In the middle of the week, try occasional "midweek motivation" messages to encourage students to space out their study or to share an interesting article or video related to current course topics. Toward the end of each week, send a reminder announcement with due dates and tips for how students can succeed or meet expectations. Some LMS solutions like Canvas allow you to schedule your announcements in advance. In addition to "taking care of business," include interesting facts or an image that relates to the announcement information. Call out an interesting quote from one of the students' discussion posts that week. As we noted previously, mix things up by creating a video version of an announcement.

Consider selecting students or asking for volunteers to make contributions to your regular announcements. Do not have the students post these announcements directly to the class, but have them send the announcements to you for review. As you comment on student contributions, you are making an additional connection with the student and also modeling good behavior for the student that they may use later in a job. Many managers motivate work teams with regular announcements on Twitter and Facebook pages created specifically for a workgroup. These same processes can be used in the classroom setting, with students taking the lead on announcements and motivating posts.

Use Videoconference Meetings to Foster Connections in Asynchronous Classes

If your online class is asynchronous with no class meetings, create opportunities for students to connect with you and other students. Use informal videoconference meetings, or "meetups," to give students chances to interact with you and other students. Even if you have a completely asynchronous class, consider having a mandatory meeting at the beginning of the semester—before the add/drop deadline—to allow students to see your face and ask questions and to get a verbal commitment from students that they intend to complete the course. If you have a large class and you do not have a set day and time for your class, provide multiple time slots over a few days to give options to students who work or have other obligations. Follow that with voluntary meetings, such as virtual office hours, optional test prep sessions, or video discussions about real-world events related to your course.

Building a Learning Community

Your presence plays a significant role in whether or not students feel they are part of a learning community. If you're not sure why you'd bother trying to create a community with and among your students, consider how that community can affect your students' learning. Without a sense of community, online students are mainly together in learning alone. Zhao and Kuh (2004) found that fostering a community enhances students' academic performance, increases interaction with the teacher, and encourages cooperation on learning tasks. Gabelnick et al. (1990) found that learning communities "provide opportunities for deeper understanding and integration" (p. 19). Vincent Tinto (2003) stated that learning communities support shared knowledge, shared knowing, and shared responsibility. McGee and Reis (2012) added psychological and social benefits for students participating in communities, such as giving them a sense of belonging and providing a support or collaboration network.

Your first responsibilities in that community include setting up environments and setting expectations. Environments might be a discussion forum, a wiki, a group activity that persists throughout the academic term, or a complete course section or module with community resources and activities. Kunal Chawla (2015) recommends sharing information that will "reveal the diverse nature of your class to your students and work towards making the learners identify with their peers" (para. 7). Instructors like Michael Wesch, a cultural anthropologist from Kansas State University, engage online and offline learning communities through projects that involve the whole class. In one project that Wesch (2007; www.youtube.com/watch?v=dGCJ46vyR90) put together, 200 students made 367 edits to a Google Doc in the process of making a 4-minute and 44-second video that has now been viewed over 5 million times.

Expectations define what students will do together, such as sharing how they plan to apply class concepts in the workforce or their personal lives. Students should know how to join the community, connect with their classmates, participate and contribute, and support and encourage each other. Set small and large community goals that address needs that arise; achieve a curricular or cocurricular task; provide students with chances to connect with you, their classmates, experts and practitioners in the field, or the community beyond campus; or align class activities with civic engagement or service-learning work. See Figure 2.2.1 for a detailed example of community expectations and goals that you may adopt or adapt for use in your syllabus or as part of a message to students explaining how your class will create and sustain a learning community.

Participate in Community Settings, but Don't Dominate Them
After creating a space for the community to interact, establish a presence there. To make a successful learning community, participate on a regular and active basis (Vesely et al., 2007). Your value here is as a "guide on the side," so strike a balance between answering questions yourself

Figure 2.2.1. Example community expectations and goals.

About our learning community: In this online class, we'll get the best results when we work together. You will complete most of this class on your own time, but you will not complete it on your own. It's easy to feel isolated or alone when you don't meet in a classroom, but online environments can be just as social.

Goals
- Grow your network: Use the Student Lounge forum to connect with as many classmates as possible. When you reply to other students in class discussions, choose different students each time. Trade contact information with two or three students who are willing to answer questions privately or to be virtual study buddies.
- Solve problems together: Peer instruction is one of the most effective ways to learn. What's more, research shows that diverse groups are the most successful. I'll create specific collaboration opportunities throughout the course.

Expectations
- Participation: You'll get more out of this course when you put more into it. Contribute original ideas and helpful feedback in discussions. Be sure to visit discussions more than one time, so you can respond to people who reply to you.
- Challenge: Challenge yourself to do more than the bare minimum, and challenge your classmates by asking them to contribute or to expand on their contributions.

---

and encouraging students to solve problems together. Point students to comments by classmates who had the same question and received an answer, or directly ask more experienced online students to support those who are new to online classes.

In the Course Information or Instructor Participation section of your syllabus, let students know how often and to what extent you will be participating in online discussions and activities. To model good online communication, strive to do what you ask the students to do—for example, create an original post answering the prompt and reply to two students' posts. If you cannot answer every student, make sure to reply to students who have no replies yet. We'll cover online teacher participation strategies in more detail in chapter 2.3, Facilitating Engaging and Meaningful Online Course Activities. For now, remember that students will know when you are present or absent from online activities. Avoid being a "lurker," or someone who reads everything without participating. Also, model the types and depth of replies and feedback you want students to provide for each other.

Let Students Know That "We're in This Together"

When your expectations are high, set a collaborative and supportive tone by reminding students that you will be reaching them together. Create community goals that encourage students to help each other, such as "help" participation points. Urge everyone to complete an activity by offering bonus points for everyone if the whole class submits an assignment. Also, let them know that this course, as with almost any class in higher education, will be challenging at times and certainly more challenging to some than for others. Challenges are not an indication of general intelligence, but rather prior learning in the area taught. The message "we're in this together" becomes even more important if your campus is forced to close for an emergency situation that lasts for more than a couple of days.

Keep Equity in Mind

The students will represent and showcase a variety of cultures and communication preferences in the learning community. When you watch carefully, you will see vast differences in comfort levels of students who were raised in collectivistic versus individualistic cultures in terms of their sharing of personal information. Never assume that students will want to talk about themselves and their families. They may desire to do this, but they also may feel very vulnerable doing so. Todd Zakrajsek, an author of this book, recalls speaking with a student who stated he would be going home to another country for a few weeks as his parents had passed away in a train accident. He had never discussed his parents previously, so this sharing of information was a surprise. He also explained that he was not sure he would be returning to the United States, as he had spoken out publicly about safety issues with the train, and he was not sure whether he would be arrested upon going home to attend his parents' funeral.

Differences will also emerge in terms of access to equipment, prior experience with digital technologies, and general trust concerning the internet. Allow students to contribute their ideas with the community in different formats—such as text, audio, video, or annotated images. Be responsive to the tone of students' comments and replies to one another. Give feedback about any negative comments that detract from the sense of community you want to build or replies that are critical without offering suggestions for improvement. Building on Figure 2.2.1, see Figure 2.2.2 for additional introductory language, goals, and expectations that can be adopted or adapted to create and sustain an inclusive and equity-minded learning community.

Figure 2.2.2. Example community instructions that showcase an equity-minded approach.

About our learning community: In this online class, we'll get the best results when we work together. You will complete most of this class on your own time, but you will not complete it on your own. It's easy to feel isolated or alone when you don't meet in a classroom, but online environments can be just as social. Every one of you has valuable contributions to make, and we want you to make them.

Goals
- Foster awareness and sensitivity: We all belong to more than one group or community. Whenever it's appropriate and relevant to our discussion topics, we invite you to share viewpoints from another community. We all benefit by seeing the world from different perspectives and by practicing how to interact respectfully with those perspectives.

Expectations
- Respect: It's okay and even expected to disagree, but we can disagree and still show respect. Support your ideas with references and ask questions that encourage others to share different points of view.

NEXT STEPS

Now that you've reviewed strategies for establishing your presence in the online course environment, it is time to begin to do it yourself or to add to what you currently do:

- Develop a video or some other way to introduce yourself to your students that is different from what you have done previously. What information to which they can relate are you willing to share, such as your own history as a learner or your passion for the discipline?
- Draft out how you will introduce the course to your students. How will you create a friendly and engaging approach to sharing the course topics? How will you make sure the course requirements are clear?
- Plan one project that will build and maintain a community of learners in your online class.
- Identify ways to add personal touches to your approach to guiding individual students and small groups.

CHAPTER SUMMARY

Teaching is more than conveying content to students and then assessing the extent to which they have learned what was taught. Teaching is supporting, encouraging, and motivating students to achieve as much as possible in the course, perhaps even more than they themselves realized they could accomplish. In this chapter, we consider ways to help students, know who you are as an instructor as well as methods for you to connect with them in a professional yet meaningful way. Impactful teaching is not about covering content; it is about uncovering possibilities.

Reflection and Discussion Questions

1. If you have taught face-to-face courses, how have you introduced yourself to your students? In what ways do you feel personal introductions might differ in a face-to-face versus an online course?
2. Think about routine behaviors in your life that suggest good places from which to make videos to connect with your students. Describe three videos you could create, where you would create them, and how that might help form connections with your online students.
3. Explain a project that could be done by the entire class that would meet the goals of the course and also be a benefit to society in some way. How might this project be laid out to instill a solid learning community among the students?
4. Interview five individuals you know and ask them how comfortable they would feel sharing personal information pertaining to travel, family, and food preferences with their students if they were teaching a college or university course. Explain the differences you noted and why those differences may exist. You may well see differences based on ethnicity, gender, age, amount of teaching experience, and perhaps even academic discipline.

2.3

FACILITATING ENGAGING AND MEANINGFUL ONLINE COURSE ACTIVITIES

*T*HERE IS A PLETHORA of research showing that using active and engaged learning strategies brings about much better learning outcomes than long lectures or other presentations of course material (e.g., Freeman et al., 2014; Major et al., 2016). Engagement in online course activities is one of the most critical elements both to effective course design and to effective course facilitation in the digital environment. Based on a review of the research and interviews with online education specialists, Johnson et al. (2015) found that "regular and effective interaction is essential to establish a successful online learning environment" (p. 11). At the same time, engaging online students is very challenging, and it is one area in which online and hybrid teachers frequently struggle. This chapter provides strategies and tools for engaging learners in a variety of ways, both as individuals and also through online group activities.

MAKING STUDENT ENGAGEMENT REGULAR, EFFECTIVE, AND SUBSTANTIVE

Teaching strategies that bring about student engagement are not just good evidence-based practice to enhance student learning; at times engagement is also required. The U.S. Department of Education, various states' codes of regulations, and regional accreditation bodies all require regular and substantive interaction and/or regular and effective contact. For example, as a regulatory requirement for federal student aid (Title IV) eligibility, "All Title

IV eligible programs, except correspondence programs, must be designed to ensure that there is regular and substantive interaction between students and instructors" (U.S. Department of Education, 2014, para. 32 [A9]). Similarly, Section 55204 in the California Code of Regulations states that distance education courses must include "regular effective contact between instructor and students, and among students, either synchronously or asynchronously" (Westlaw, 2017, para. 2). In general, these regulations provide little guidance as to what regular, effective, or substantive look like in an online course, so we have included the following examples.

- *Regular and effective teacher–student contact via announcements*: One way to achieve this is to create a consistent announcement schedule (regular) that supports effective online learning practices (effective). On Mondays, send students a "What's Due & What's New" message to provide one last reminder about a Monday deadline and to outline the expectations for the upcoming week. On Wednesdays, send students a "Midweek Motivation" note to share ideas from early student posts, to remind students to spread out online coursework, to provide encouragement, and to share real-world examples. On Fridays, send a "Weekend Update" announcement to remind students what will be due the following Monday. At least once per week create a video version of your announcement. Use free, opt-in text message services (e.g., remind.com) to send announcements to students who might not check email regularly.

- *Regular and effective student–teacher contact through "meetups" and "work sprints"*: Meetups are informal gatherings for people with similar professions or interests. Hold videoconference meetups regularly throughout the academic term—for example, once every 2 or 3 weeks—to provide opportunities to review course concepts. Unlike some virtual office hours, you can encourage students to support each other. *Work sprints* are group study sessions or work sessions. Invite students to join a videoconference session to work on class activities together. Students first state their goals for what they want to accomplish, then work for 25 minutes, stopping only when necessary to ask questions. Everyone then takes 5 minutes to share what they achieved and to take a short break. Repeat this 30-minute cycle as often as you like. The accountability and community setting make these productive work time for students.

- *Regular and substantive student–student interaction*: There are numerous ways to establish and maintain regular and substantive student–student interaction. One way is to conduct a small group discussion in each module. Keep students in the same groups throughout the term. Start with a low-stakes activity, where students identify their role(s), share their personal goals and barriers to participation, and create group norms. Follow with a meaningful activity, like a values affirmation exercise. Use prompts to keep discussions tied to course topics and to guide substantive student replies to one another. Help students use the LMS and other tools to contact each other if some students are missing from the conversation for too long.

UDL, HUMAN CONNECTEDNESS, AND DESIGN FOR LEARNING EQUITY STRATEGIES TO ENGAGE ONLINE STUDENTS

Have you wondered how you can genuinely engage online students? Do you struggle when trying to determine how best to increase student activity in the online course? Motivating online students is surprisingly similar to motivating students in any learning environment. Students are more engaged when faculty ensure there is a diversity of activities in both how information is learned and how students produce work based on what they have learned. Motivation improves when faculty set clear expectations as to what the student is to do. Explaining to the students why the activity helps them to learn the course content material increases student motivation.

Additionally, use specific LMS settings designed to help present content in ways that motivate students. Key to engaging your online students is going beyond the content ("what") and the teaching methods ("how") to also consider the students, or "whom" we are teaching (Tanner, 2013). Tanner's (2013) set of five categories of "equitable teaching strategies" (p. 322) designed for classroom biology is also helpful in thinking about engaged learning strategies for online courses. In this chapter we briefly describe approaches that support equitable online teaching, some of which are based on ideas from Tanner's categories.

Give Students Opportunities to Consider and Discuss the Content

In face-to-face teaching, one important strategy to encourage students to participate is "wait time," or the amount of time you wait for students to think about your questions and respond before telling students the correct response to that question. In an asynchronous, online environment, "wait time" will simply not work. However, it is still essential to give students time to think about material before formulating a response or joining a discussion forum. For example, for a one-page reflective essay, provide an organized set of questions that students should answer to meet rubric criteria. These prompts will encourage students to think about the content and assignment before starting. Asking students to reframe the most important element of a post and then use that reframed sentence as the foundation for a contribution also helps students to think a bit before writing.

UDL Guidelines encourage faculty members to "provide scaffolds that can be gradually released with increasing independence and skills" (CAST, 2018b, para. 2). One way to scaffold in the online environment is to have students learn about how to learn with mobile devices. To scaffold this, students might write a plan that describes how they will explore using mobile technology to complete learning tasks for school, for work, or at home. For the first plan, you might provide a set of questions, a rubric, and a template that students can use to structure their writing. For subsequent plans, give a set of questions and the rubric without the template.

Another example might include helping students to formulate good responses on an essay exam. For the first exam, give students a framework for answering responses. For the second exam, provide a few bullet points but much less of a framework. For the third exam, students respond with no guidance. As long as students know the exams will change in terms of support (i.e., scaffolding), this system will help students to become better essay response writers by encouraging them to think about how to formulate responses.

Encourage, Expect, and Actively Manage the Participation of All Students

Students often do not know what participation expectations are in an online or remote course. There is a wide range of diversity among the faculty at any institution, such as gender, age, ethnicity, culture, and life experiences. These differences result in different expectations of student participation in each course. Even faculty members in the same department who seem very similar may have vastly different expectations. Given this, students will respond differently based on their interpretations of faculty expectations in a course. If you expect students to participate in a meaningful way, prompt them to do so, and be sure to provide meaningful responses. When this happens, more students will respond. Expecting meaningful responses from everyone in the online course is an excellent example of the influence of a positive expectation.

There are many strategies to getting all students to participate in an online course. Assign small group discussion summaries to different students each week. Across the semester or academic term, most courses have multiple online discussions. Break your class into small groups of five to 10 students for these discussions, and assign a different student to summarize the discussion each week. Give the summarizers clear goals, such as the following example:

> (a) Identify the three to five ideas that generated the most discussion and summarize each idea in one or two sentences. (b) Identify at least one idea that had no or very few replies to date, and explain in one or two sentences why the group may not have discussed that topic. (c) List the questions that the group generated but could not or did not have time to answer.

As UDL principles suggest, this strategy fosters collaboration and provides a structure for the summarizers to manage the information from their group discussion.

Explore Your Own Role in Engaging Students

Sometimes what you convey—your expectations and even your belief that all students can meet them—may not be enough. *How* you express those ideas can have an impact too. Being a "warm demander" (Kleinfeld, 1975, p. 335) is an equity-based approach that aligns with both learning equity and human connectedness. The process begins with relationship building through personal warmth, moves to active demanding that includes challenging negative stereotypes, and requires affirming effort and ability (Pacansky-Brock et al., 2020). During a virtual Online Teaching Conference in June 2020, Michelle Pacansky-Brock, Aloha Sargent, and Fabiola Torres applied the warm demander concept to supporting minoritized college students in online courses (Online Teacher's Conference, n.d.; http://tinyurl.com/warm-demander for presentation recording and other helpful resources). To be a warm demander, they advocated being present, knowing your students, and viewing your class through your students' eyes (Pacansky-Brock et al., 2020).

Different thought leaders have informed aspects of being a warm demander for specific student groups. In a 2019 interview with the Office of Community College Research and Leadership (OCCRL), J. Luke Wood encouraged higher education teachers to engage men of color by building "relationships that are typified by trust, mutual respect, [and] authentic care" (Keist & Wood, 2019, p. 3). He challenged teachers to ask themselves, "So, am I someone who knows how to validate students? Can I create relationships with students, learn about them, and use that information to better support them, engage them, and teach them?" (Keist & Wood, 2019, p. 3). Getting to know your students will take effort, but it will create an environment that fosters both academic rigor and real engagement. The warm demander approach provides a way to engage your students and to reengage students who may have stopped participating for a while.

Build an Inclusive and Fair Online Class Environment for All Students

Ladson-Billings (1995) outlined three elements of culturally relevant pedagogy: (a) students achieving academic success while (b) developing cultural competence and (c) developing critical consciousness. Earlier in this book, we looked at academic success through an administrative lens by addressing students passing a class or completing a certificate or degree goal, and through a student lens with a discussion of meeting a personal goal regardless of course-related outcomes. The APA defines *cultural competence* as "the ability to understand, appreciate, and interact with people from cultures or belief systems different from one's own" (DeAngelis, 2015, para. 1). Ladson-Billings (1995) described critical consciousness as developing "a broader sociopolitical consciousness that allows them to critique the cultural norms, values, mores, and institutions that produce and maintain social inequities" (p. 162). Culturally relevant pedagogy provides strategies to help faculty members to make classes more inclusive and fairer for all involved.

Design for learning equity encourages connecting—and asking students to connect—course activities and content to their personal goals and sociocultural backgrounds, or to people who have different goals or experiences. Such connections also go a long way in humanizing an online course. As an online instructor, your role in helping students reach these goals includes providing a more diverse set of examples of your course topics than might be found through one source, such as a textbook. As you cannot always see your online students, it will be challenging to know which examples are most meaningful to which students. Strive for as much diversity as you can, making sure to include perspectives that may resonate with students who typically have larger online success gaps (e.g., first-generation, Hispanic/Latinx, and African American/Black students). One of the best strategies is to let students know you would like to have an environment in the course that is as inclusive as possible and in order to accomplish that, you will need their assistance. Ask students to add examples of a course topic that are culturally relevant to them and to politely note whenever any aspect of the course feels like it is not as inclusive as it could be. Don't be surprised if students define *culture* differently than you do. You may see examples that represent communities that are not always included, such as LGBTQ or Deaf and Hard of Hearing.

Do not be overly concerned or overly apologetic if you make a mistake concerning inclusiveness. It is extremely important that students know you are attempting to create an inclusive learning environment. Let students know inclusivity is vital to you and that you have a growth mindset with respect to inclusion. This means that you anticipate that you will make unintentional mistakes, and when you do, it is imperative that individuals politely point out these errors to allow for corrections. If you ask students to help you with inclusiveness feedback, they will tend to be very forgiving. If you are concerned about how to approach a specific situation, the Office of Diversity and Inclusion is an excellent resource on your campus.

Monitor Behavior (Your Own and Students') to Cultivate Divergent, Inclusive Thinking

It is easy to fall into a pattern of thinking and acting in a similar way over and over. Part of this is simply a lack of realization that there are multiple ways to think about anything. Also, the more one does something, the easier it becomes, which is also why trying something new always takes more energy. That said, an important aspect of being educated is that one thinks of things in new and innovative ways. In teaching, we must be careful not to always teach in the same way. It is vital to think continually of new and innovative ways to teach, and at times that is to teach about thinking that embraces new and innovative approaches.

Keep an eye on how you and your students respond to each other. Design for learning equity suggests showing students that both diversity of and participation by every student are of value in your course. If students answer a prompt incompletely or share a value that is not common, think about how to reply in a way that will not discourage those students from participating in future online activities. In addition to avoiding a judgmental tone, you can structure activities so that all ideas are welcome at the beginning, after which the discussion will turn to clarifying misconceptions and identifying what students should retain. For example, your instructions might say, "Let's get as many different ideas as possible on the table first, then discuss which ones are best supported by course materials or other trusted sources."

Teach All of the Students in Your Online Class

You can adapt valuable classroom assessment techniques to your online class as another way to increase equity for all students. In the next part, we'll talk about assessing teaching and learning in more depth, including instructions for how you can turn the One-Minute Paper activity—where students share what was clear and unclear from a classroom session—into a One-Minute Thread discussion. In the context of equitable teaching, take a few minutes to determine what individual students did not understand and what the entire class struggled with collectively. For individuals, you can provide additional resources or check-in via email. For concepts that many students did not fully grasp, you can create a mini-lecture or follow-up activity.

Pay Equal Attention to All Students

Design for learning equity asks us to manage potential biases in how we interact with our students. A recent Stanford study found that online teachers show bias in discussions by replying more often to students who are likely to be White men than to other students based on student names (Baker et al., 2018). These results mirror those from a study of instructor response rates to graduate student requests for mentoring, again based on student names (Milkman et al., 2015). To be more inclusive and check your potential for this type of bias, try one of these techniques:

- If your class is large enough that you cannot reply to every student in each discussion, then respond to a certain percentage each time (e.g., 10%–20%). For example, in a class of 50 students, reply to at least five to 10 different students in each discussion, starting with students who have not yet received replies from any other students. Create a list or spreadsheet to track how many times you reply to each student over the entire length of your class. Make sure that students have a similar number of replies by the end of the semester or term. This technique will also help you identify and reach out to students who are not engaging in discussions. In your syllabus, tell your students how you intend to be more equitable when participating in discussions and how often they can expect a direct reply from you.
- If you teach a hybrid or face-to-face class, use a similarly equitable, classroom-based strategy in which you keep an index card for each student in a pile. For each class discussion, select the top name from the stack to answer your question. If that student gives an incomplete or incorrect response, ask them if they want help from the next person in the stack. After class, note the date and discussion on those cards, and put them on the bottom of the pile. Once you get to the bottom of the stack, shuffle them and start again. This classroom strategy also encourages students to come to class prepared, knowing the probability their name will be selected.

Engage Students in Activities Beyond the Computer Monitor

Faculty members who teach in digital environments often fail to realize students do not always need to be interacting through their computers or handheld devices. Later in this chapter, we outline in detail three techniques that showcase different ways to increase online student motivation. Before we get to those, we wanted to share another possibility for engaging online students. Not all distance learning activities require being at a device. Today's untethered learners can engage anytime and anywhere in authentic, meaningful work related to your course. Ask students to get up from the computer, perform a course-related task in the real world, and then report back and/or reflect on that work. Claiborne et al. (n.d.) described several activities that online, hybrid, and even face-to-face students could complete. These activities are not space- or technology-dependent and can be implemented "outside the classroom," including field trips, community engagement activities, place-based learning, assessing field experiences, and other experiential learning exercises. Here are a few ideas to implement this strategy in different disciplines:

- English and English-as-a-second-language teachers can ask students to take pictures of grammar errors on billboards and share those pictures in a photo gallery or discussion forum. They can require students to suggest the correction(s) for the images they submit, or they can ask all students to correct the mistakes on every submission and identify the underlying grammatical rule.
- For her online art appreciation course, Michelle Pacansky-Brock asked her students to complete an Art Visit activity. Students were "required to view art in person" at a museum or gallery opening. They needed to include a selfie photo or other photo of themselves as evidence that they attended. They were also expected to write about viewing art in person compared to on a computer screen and reflect on their favorite artwork and the overall experience (Pacansky-Brock, n.d.a, pp. 8–9).
- Science instructors can ask students to contribute to data collection for citizen science projects or science projects that invite the general public to participate in some aspect of the work. After they collect data, students can work in groups to analyze those projects' data sets and submit reports with their conclusions or recommendations. These can be especially effective for engaging nonmajor students (Kridelbaugh, 2016) and increasing retention of underrepresented minority students (Cardamone & Lobel, 2016).

- Students can create a "commercial" that features a specific component of the course. The project might include writing a script, finding friends to participate, directing the "actors" during the shoot, and editing the material to create the final product.
- During the COVID-19 pandemic, individuals were encouraged to stay in their homes for many weeks and, in some cases, months. Many course-related activities may be done remotely from home and away from the computer. For example, assign students to find one item at the back of a kitchen cupboard that has been there longer than it should and then develop an advertisement designed to get individuals to consume that product. Various communities came together to share resources related to converting difficult topics, such as arts (music, dance, studio art), STEM labs, career and technical education, service-learning, and physical education. We have pulled together links to many of those resources in Appendix A.

In addition to rethinking where students engage, also reconsider how you ask students to engage, how well you outline your expectations for student engagement, and how you set up the online environment to encourage engagement. To help you reimagine what student engagement looks like, we next describe an online teaching technique for each of these in detail.

Technique: Assign Roles in Online Discussions

As you plan online discussions for your class, it is important to create activities that motivate students to participate and engage them in higher-level thinking. Studies have shown online role-play discussions to be an effective way to do both (Bender, 2005; Darabi et al., 2010; Lombard & Biglan, 2011; Waesche, 2017). Further, online role-play provides opportunities for students to practice solving complex, unstructured problems and group decision-making (Hou, 2012; McLaughlan, 2007). Students themselves have reported the benefits of online role-play discussions, including meeting learning objectives through both exploring multiple perspectives and using critical thinking (McLaughlan, 2007), as well as appreciating real-world relevance (Lombard & Biglan, 2011).

Online role-play discussions work best when you break students into groups of four to six students and assign a specific role to each student. For students to represent their assigned perspective effectively, first assign preparation work to study their roles (e.g., see the Instructions and Guidelines sections in Figure 2.3.1). In using online role-plays, students may be assessed or graded on components of participation: assessment of student preparation, participation (e.g., number of posts and replies, ability to "stay in character," and representing the appropriate perspective when discussing the issue), group work (e.g., ability to create a mutually agreeable solution), and individual reflection.

Figure 2.3.1. Online role-play discussion example.

INTRODUCTION TO POLITICAL SCIENCE OVERVIEW

Political conversations in the United States frequently and quickly become shouting matches. Such escalations happen all too often in town hall meetings, on televised news shows, at political events, and on social media. CivilPolitics .org notes that it is possible to disagree productively, represent different viewpoints, and even compete to recruit voters—all while respecting each other throughout the process. In this course, we will create guidelines that allow for civil disagreement during political discussions on social media.

Scenario. It is 4 weeks before the next presidential election in the United States. Among the items on your ballot is a statewide measure to ban the sale of all soda drinks in K–12 schools. The initiative has become a hot topic, and people on social media have become very disrespectful of one another. You serve as a member of a small focus group to create guidelines for using social media for political purposes that allow for individuals to disagree productively and to represent different viewpoints respectfully.

Each group member will be assigned one of the following six (6) roles:

- A voter with strong feelings in favor of the ballot measure to ban the sale of soft drinks at schools
- A voter with strong feelings against the ballot measure who wants the sale of soft drinks at schools to remain
- An independent voter with no strong feelings yet on the ballot measure regarding soft drink sales in schools
- A journalist from the mainstream media (newspapers, cable TV news)
- A staff member for a well-funded political action committee supporting the ballot measure to ban soft drink sales in schools
- A staff member for a nonprofit organization working against the ballot measure who wants the sale of soft drinks to continue

Instructions. In this online role-play discussion, you will complete the following activities:

(Continues)

Figure 2.3.1. (*Continued*)

WEEK 1: You will study the role you are assigned in your small group and create a one-page profile (50 points maximum value). The profile should include:

- General (up to 10 points): An overview of your role. Provide details about the person you are playing.
- General (up to 10 points): An interview of one person who shares the same beliefs as the role you were assigned. The interviewee can be someone in your family or community or someone you choose from the teacher's list. Document their answers to the following questions: (a) How do you, or could you, use social media to inform others of your political position? (b) How do you, or could you, use social media to recruit others to vote for or against a particular ballot measure or political position? (c) When you use social media for political purposes, how do you balance being effective in reaching your goals and being civil and respectful?
- General (up to 10 points): A review of social media posts by people in the role you were assigned. Outline the underlying motives behind why people in your role adopt specific approaches to using social media.
- Specific (up to 10 points): A brief statement on how someone in your role might feel about the ballot measure on banning soda from schools.
- Specific (up to 10 points): A brief statement on how someone in your role might use social media concerning the ballot measure on banning soda from schools.

WEEK 2: In your small group, you will analyze and debate the use (and misuse) of social media for political purposes. This discussion is worth up to 50 points total.

- First, answer the following questions as a person in your assigned role might answer them (up to 5 points per question for a possible total of 25 points):

  o Why would someone in your role turn to social media after hearing about the ballot measure?
  o What aspects of social media would someone in your role find helpful when considering the ballot measure?
  o What aspects of social media would someone in your role find unhelpful, harmful, or offensive when considering the ballot measure?
  o How could others use social media to engage someone in your role in a civil discussion (or disagreement) about the ballot measure?
  o How could someone in your role use social media to engage others in a civil discussion about the ballot measure?

Figure 2.3.1. (*Continued*)

Then reply to every other person in your group, outlining how someone in your role might respond to what they each presented (up to 5 points per reply for each question for a total possible of 25 points).

WEEK 3: Each group will create a set of guidelines applicable to anyone using social media to share political views, ranging from active politicians (from any party) and people who work for political organizations (political action committees, nonprofits) to concerned voters and citizens. As there are so many different perspectives, you will need to compromise!

- Based on your Week 1 research and Week 2 discussion, work with your small group to create a set of 5 to 10 guidelines that anyone could use to engage others in civil dialogue or civil disagreement (up to 50 points per team, everyone gets the same score).

Guidelines. (Following in part adapted from Waesche, 2017).

- *Get to know yourself*: Go beyond the class materials to research more about the role you are portraying.
- *Keep it in perspective*: Answer the prompts and your group members based on the assigned role. Remember to keep your personal opinions in check while you play your character.
- Start each post and reply by restating your role—for example, "[ROLE NAME]: From my perspective, I think..." or "Based on my experience as a ___, I think..."

Technique: Outline Expectations for Online Discussions

Students frequently dislike discussions and small group activities in both online and face-to-face courses. One reason many students loathe group work is because they lack instruction about how to engage in productive group work or discussions. If we are going to tell students that discussions and group work are essential, we should teach them how to do these activities well. Like good classroom discussions, online discussions are not merely informal chats. Good course discussions have a well-developed structure, and to help students reach learning objectives, students must know how that structure facilitates learning. Defining expectations is known to improve student performance in online discussion activities (Dennen, 2005; Jung et al., 2002; Rovai, 2007). Clear instructions and activity rubrics are two excellent ways to outline those expectations (Rovai, 2007).

Expectations provide information regarding both how to accomplish learning tasks and how to interact with classmates (Benfield, 2002). Discussion expectations can be quantitative (e.g., number of times participating in a discussion, word or paragraph count, and number of citations). Discussion expectations may also be qualitative (e.g., the content included, the justification of a position, or the expressed support for opposing viewpoints). Behavioral expectations define how to best interact with peers. They include what you as the faculty member of the course consider appropriate. Rules and expectations for interacting with classmates may refer students to internet etiquette resources like the Lake Superior College (n.d.) Netiquette Guidelines (http://blogs.lsc.edu/expectations/netiquette-guidelines/). If you use your syllabus to provide expectations about student behavior for the entire course, it is helpful to provide a link to remind students where to find those expectations.

Potential Expectations for the Overall Discussion
- Create specific deadlines for each part of the online discussion (e.g., students must submit original posts by Tuesday and reply to each other by Friday of the same week). Multiple checkpoints foster better student dialogue than one single deadline.
- Give students an idea of the amount of time they should invest in the activity.
- Describe the overarching goals or specific objectives for each discussion. The instruction can range from a formal, graded discussion with a concrete learning objective to an informal, ungraded discussion to allow students to work on team projects.
- Include the activity's grade value and specific measures of participation.
- Provide context (e.g., how does the activity tie to course materials, activities, or assessments?).

Potential Expectations for Original Posts or Contributions
- Outline the elements of a complete post (e.g., what constitutes a "good" answer).
- Ask students to create a new subject line in the discussion forum, rather than use the default provided by the LMS.
- Refer to multiple sources to support an argument. There are a wide number of checklists and tutorials about evaluating websites. The example assignment in Figure 2.3.2 asks students to evaluate the credibility of web-based information.

Potential Expectations for Replies to Other Students
- Tell students how many replies are required (state the minimum), as well as how many responses will earn points (state the maximum).
- Give students specific tasks that foster peer interaction, such as building on or suggesting adjustments to their classmates' posts.
- Guide students about how to respect diverse opinions, even if they do not agree with them.

Figure 2.3.2. Example online discussion instructions outlining expectations.

FIX FAKE NEWS OR REPORT ON ALTERNATIVE FACTS: OVERVIEW

As an increasing number of individuals get their news primarily from the web, it is critical to confirm that the articles you read, the videos you see, or the podcasts you hear contain facts that have been supported by trustworthy sources. This entire course takes place online. Although I have provided research and evidence to support everything you learn in this class, I will ask you to explore a variety of topics in more detail. To start this process, we will evaluate websites with the authority, bias, content, date, and evaluation, or ABCDE, method (hilo.hawaii.edu/library/evaluating-sources/abcde).

I encourage you to use skills from this class in your other courses, for training at work, or to teach yourself new skills. For example, before you start a do-it-yourself (DIY) construction project at home, how do you make sure you have found the best information, not just the information that is easiest to find?

Objectives. This activity aligns with the following objectives:

- *Course objective*: Evaluate web-based information (e.g., for validity, reliability, bias)
- *Activity objective*: Support your work with citations that are appropriate and credible

Time Commitment. You should spend roughly 25 to 70 minutes on this activity.

- 15 to 20 minutes to write an original post responding to the following prompt—this includes research time
- Five to 10 minutes to write each reply to another student—this includes searching for sources to support each reply

(Continues)

Figure 2.3.2. (*Continued*)

Value. You may earn up to 50 points for this activity.

- Earn up to 25 points for your original post.
- Earn up to 25 points for replying to posts by classmates. You may earn up to 5 points for each reply and must complete a minimum of two replies and a maximum of five replies.

Instructions. By Tuesday: Submit an original post that does the following:

Step 1: Provide a link to a fake news article, OR a video, website, speech, science report, or whatever containing "alternative facts" (up to 5 points).

- If you do not know where to look for fake news, you can use this list of fake news sites: en.wikipedia.org/wiki/List_of_fake_news_websites

Step 2: Rewrite the fake news article so it is correct, or report on how the alternative facts are inconclusive by the evidence you find (up to 15 points).

- NOTE: Stick to the facts! Avoid sharing your opinions or commentary. You may feel very strongly about the topic you find, but your argument will be more compelling if you present your case professionally. We will deduct points if you submit your opinion as part of the paper.

Step 3: Cite at least two credible sources that refute the fake news story and support your rewritten news story—in other words, show how or why the news is false or the alternative facts are made up (up to 5 points).

- Cite the sources using the APA format outlined in the syllabus.

Step 4: Write a new headline showing what you revised or corrected.

- In 10 words or fewer, summarize your rewritten article and use it as your headline in the title (subject) of your discussion post.

By Friday: Reply to at least two other threads that do not have two replies yet (up to 5 points per reply).

- Provide feedback about how well the rewritten article debunks the fake news. For example, does the rewritten article leave any misconceptions unaddressed? Is there a connection between the article that they rewrote and your own?

Figure 2.3.2. (*Continued*)

- Provide at least one unique additional source to support the rewritten article.
- It's okay to encourage each other, but you will not earn any points for replies that are too simple, such as "Good job! :-)."
- Remember that we all follow the Lake Superior College Netiquette Guidelines to inform online conduct in our discussions (see http://blogs.lsc.edu/expectations/netiquette-guidelines/)

See the following rubrics on how original posts and replies will be scored. I look forward to seeing your entries!

Rubric for Original Posts

Criteria	Complete 5 points	Developing 3 points	Not Yet 0 points
Identify a fake news story	Your post identifies a fake news story and shows how it was determined to be fake.	Your post identifies a story but does not show how it was determined to be fake.	Your post does not identify any fake news or alternative facts.
Provides a new article or report	Your post provides a new article or report to correct the misconceptions from the fake news story.	Your post provides a new article or report, but it does not correct all misconceptions from the fake news story.	Your post does not provide a new article.
Cite credible sources that refute the fake news story	Your post cites two or more credible sources to refute the fake news story.	Your post cites one credible source to refute the fake news story.	Your post does not cite any credible sources to refute the fake news story.
Avoid sharing opinions	Your post avoids sharing opinions altogether.	Your post shares opinions that are supported by facts.	Your post shares opinions.
Provide a new headline as the discussion post subject	Your post provides a new headline as the discussion post subject.	Your post provides a new headline, but not as the discussion post subject.	Your post does not provide a new headline.

(*Continues*)

Figure 2.3.2. *(Continued)*

Rubric for Replies to Other Students			
Criteria	**Complete** **5 points**	**Developing** **3 points**	**Not Yet** **0 points**
Provide a complete response to a classmate	Your reply provides appropriate feedback **and** at least one unique additional source to support your classmate's article	Your reply provides appropriate feedback **or** at least one unique additional source to support your classmate's article, but not both	Your reply provides neither appropriate feedback nor at least one unique additional source to support your classmate's article

Note. Minimum two replies required, maximum five replies to earn points.

Technique: Change Forum Settings to Promote Interaction in Online Discussions

When planning classroom discussions, teachers regularly consider physical aspects of the classroom environment that impact the quality of student-to-student interactions: seating arrangements, proximity of students to one another, size of the class, and their own physical placement with respect to the students. Although the specific considerations are different for online courses, there are ways to change the "layout" of the course. The best place to start is forum settings in the online environment designed to promote increased interaction among students. There are many considerations, such as establishing the size of discussion subgroups, making group work visible to other groups, assigning students to take leadership roles, fostering student-led appreciation, and providing extrinsic incentives (e.g., points) for participation quality.

Group Size
Studies collectively suggest no ideal group size, but these studies have also shown that group size affects the quantity and/or quality of students' contributions to online discussions (Kim, 2013; Qiu & McDougall, 2015). Online discussions require a critical mass (minimum number for students to engage with one another), but when the number of students grows too large, students face information overload. This overload can lead to lower student participation frequency and quality (Jones et al., 2004) or students skipping future class discussions altogether (Kim, 2013). AbuSeileek (2012)

found the best results with five students per group, and other studies saw negative issues arise in groups larger than eight to 10 (Qiu & McDougall, 2015). That said, in very large classes over 100 students, Kim (2013) found that groups of 25 to 30 students could be productive and engaged.

All major LMS solutions—for example, Canvas, Moodle, Blackboard, D2L—and stand-alone forum tools like Piazza and Zoom allow you to break a class into smaller groups. In most cases, creating groups themselves—and their size—is a separate process from choosing between whole class and small group discussions. For example, in Moodle select the Groups link in the Administration block, then click the Create Group button or Auto-Create Groups button. In Canvas, go to the People tab and click the Add (+) Group Set button. In both cases, you can create a specific number of groups or assign a specific number of students per group. You may reuse the groups throughout the academic term to increase the sense of community or create new groups for different discussions to diversify students' connections among their classmates.

Group Visibility

Qiu and McDougall (2015) learned from student interviews that students appreciated being able to "overhear" other group discussions to find perspectives beyond those presented in their own group or to augment their group's ideas. Instructors can increase this strategy's effectiveness by encouraging the whole class or specific groups to review individual comments or entire group discussions.

LMS solutions handle group visibility differently. For example, in Moodle you can set the group visibility for each activity—the "visible groups" setting allows students to see other groups' work, while the "separate groups" setting does not. In Canvas, groups are not visible to each other. To allow students to see other groups' ideas, create a different whole class discussion forum for each group that is clearly labeled (e.g., Red Group, Blue Group, One Group, Two Group). Be sure to list the members of each group in the instructions or attach a spreadsheet with group assignments.

Group Roles

Hew and Cheung (2008) learned that peer facilitation increased overall student participation in online discussions. Build facilitation techniques by assigning your students to take leadership roles. Encourage student leadership that models and fosters student-led interactions. Students take turns summarizing their group's discussion each week, personally inviting nonparticipants to contribute, asking classmates to clarify or elaborate on another group member's idea, or sharing their personal experiences to add meaning to a discussion topic (Hew & Cheung, 2008).

Some LMS platforms allow you to assign group leaders. For example, when you create or edit a Group Set in Canvas, you may automatically assign a student group leader—either the first student to join the group or a random student. All students in a group can use Canvas group page features to post announcements, send files, and more. There is no group leader functionality in Blackboard or Moodle, so name the group leaders in the discussion instructions, along with a list of tasks the leaders must perform to keep the discussion moving. In Moodle go to the gradebook's Setup tab and add a new Grade Item in the gradebook to assign points for being a discussion leader.

Students Showing Appreciation
As part of their study, Hew and Cheung (2008) found that "showing appreciation increased student participation in a discussion because it made students feel that they were worthy contributors" (p. 1119). Although this study described students expressing appreciation through their comments, social media functionality (e.g., "likes") provides another way for students to show encouragement or recognition for their classmates' posts and replies.

You may add social media functionality to discussions in multiple LMS discussion forums. For example, in Canvas, select the Edit button for a specific discussion, then select the Allow Liking option. Canvas also allows you to sort the discussion by the number of likes earned by each post. In Moodle, first create a new rating scale (Administration block > Grades > Scales) with one rating item ("like"). Then go to the appropriate forum and select Edit settings. On the settings page, expand the Ratings category, select Scale as the rating Type, select your new scale with one rating item, and choose "Everyone can rate posts."

Extrinsic Incentives
Some research indicates that instructors giving points to students as an incentive increases the quantity of student participation (number of postings) in online discussions (Dennen, 2005; Hew & Cheung, 2008). You can reward students quantitatively in different ways, such as counting the number of posts, providing more points for original posts and fewer for replies, and giving points for posting on multiple days throughout the discussion period. Instructors also give points to improve the quality of student participation, often through rubrics. Rubric criteria might include how well their posts address the discussion prompt, connect peers' comments to course material, refer to course readings or lectures, or cite external references to support their ideas.

Points are the easiest way to apply the concept of incentives to online discussions, and all LMS environments make it possible to assign points to student participation. When you edit a discussion in Canvas, check the Graded option, assign the number of points possible, and choose how to display each student's grade (e.g., show points, complete/incomplete). If you want to use a participation rubric, go to the discussion page and select Add Rubric from the settings menu. In the window that appears, you may select an existing rubric or create a new one. In Moodle, find the appropriate forum and select Edit Settings from the settings menu. Scroll to the Ratings category and choose how you will score the forum posts and how many points the forum is worth. If you want to use a rubric in Moodle, create an Assignment activity in addition to your Forum activity. In the Assignment settings, name it "XYZ Forum Feedback and Scoring," uncheck all of the submission types so students cannot submit anything, and select rubric as the grading method. Prompts will guide you to find or create a rubric to score the discussion via the assignment.

NEXT STEPS

Now that you have explored a wide variety of strategies for engaging online learners, consider the following as you prepare to try some of them yourself:

- Review the UDL and design for learning equity strategies. Do you scaffold the process for students to complete core assignments successfully? Are you managing potential biases in how (and how often) you interact with each learner?
- Review your descriptions of expectations for online activities. Clarify and expand as needed.
- Identify at least one way to engage students "beyond the computer monitor" by asking them to interact with the world, reflect, and report back in your online class.
- Do a web search for LMS discussion forum settings and look for ways to optimize participation.

CHAPTER SUMMARY

As with all learning, the more students engage in the process, the more they will experience deep learning. Engagement in the online environment is challenging, and finding ways to create active online classes is a frequent request of faculty members in higher education. Maintaining a goal of creating an inclusive online learning environment is important in teaching all of the students enrolled in the course. The more we teach with inclusivity in mind, the easier it is to create inclusive classrooms. Students often express a dislike in regard to working in groups and do not inherently understand the value of group work. Set clear expectations and give multiple examples to help students to understand the value of engaged learning and working in groups and to provide a better opportunity to be successful.

Reflection and Discussion Questions

1. If you email a colleague requesting a review of a short paragraph regarding the tone of something you intend to send out to a large group of faculty members, what would seem to you to be a reasonable length of time for that colleague to respond? If an undergraduate student sends the same request to you, what do you think their response expectation would be? Discuss the similarities and differences of these expectations. How are expectations such as these set, and how might they be adjusted, if needed?

2. It is often easier to connect with students who we perceive to be similar to ourselves. What are strategies to connect more meaningfully with students who are very different from ourselves?

3. Create one new assignment that might be given to students to engage them in an activity that is "beyond the computer monitor" and directly related to an anticipated educational outcome for the course. Consider how students might be involved in creating this assignment.

4. Think back across the group projects in which you have been a group member. Did you tend to have a consistent role in these projects? If so, do you feel you ended up in that role because of your skill set or because of work that needed to be accomplished? If you did not have a consistent role, why did your role change based on the group project?

2.4

MANAGING YOUR WORKLOAD WHEN TEACHING ONLINE

*F*ACULTY MEMBERS ARE REGULARLY overworked individuals who always seem to be scrambling to get a stack of papers graded, running to get to a committee meeting, finding new information for an upcoming class module, or doing one of the millions of various things we are all asked to do. For contingent faculty members, there is often the extra work of another job or two. These are just a few of the many items that demand time, and this discussion does not even touch on family responsibilities and finding just a bit of space to take care of oneself. Overall, being a faculty member is particularly challenging because of three essential elements of the position: (a) faculty members are very bright individuals, (b) faculty members are committed to helping others, and (c) the role of being a higher education educator is ill-defined. When you put bright and committed individuals into an ill-defined job, it is no wonder the result is a habitually overworked group of people. The same holds for faculty members who work entirely on campus and teach face-to-face courses as it does for faculty members who teach only online courses for multiple institutions and, of course, every configuration in between.

Teaching itself is a demanding profession. Teaching a course for the first time is additionally challenging. Teaching a course in a new format is also very arduous. Experienced face-to-face faculty teaching an online course for the first time will find the online format requires a very different approach to teaching. In this circumstance, it is best to think of teaching such a course the same as a "new prep," even if you have taught that same content for many years. Overall, teaching is a difficult and challenging process. As a faculty member, in order to be successful it is imperative

159

that you find a way to manage your workload in a systematic way. This chapter outlines how to manage (a) "start-up" factors that affect workload for anyone teaching online for the first time, (b) student expectations (and your own), and (c) your workload through implementation strategies.

MANAGING THE START-UP AND ONGOING COSTS OF TEACHING ONLINE

Are you new or relatively new to teaching online? Have you been asked to convert some or all of an in-person course to a remote format in an emergency response or campus closure situation, such as a hurricane, wildfire, polar vortex, or pandemic? Have you taught online before, but still feel it takes more time than your face-to-face classes? If so, then you may be facing the start-up costs associated with moving your class(es) online. If you're not familiar with the term, *start-up costs* are expenses one must pay *before* a new business is up and running. For example, before you can open a café, you will need start-up funds to pay initial costs. Consider the financial liability of a physical space, payment for any renovations necessary to turn it into a café, purchasing equipment for making coffee and other drinks, and buying furniture for customers to sit and relax. Second, consider costs for inventory, including your first round of supplies such as tea, coffee beans, syrups, cups, and napkins. Third, prepare a budget for operational costs to train your first employees, and so on. A reliable market analysis and business plan increase the chances the business will generate revenue that sustains the enterprise. When not planned appropriately, such costs appear as surprises, with more expenses to follow. Without adequate planning and prep work, start-up costs accelerate quickly, often resulting in insufficient funding that threatens the viability of the entire project.

Once the business gets rolling, *ongoing costs* must be accounted for. The better you are at identifying recurring expenses and budgeting for them, the better you will be at managing your time.

Before you teach online the first time, it is valuable first to carefully consider the start-up costs related to teaching that specific course. In this context, the start-up costs are factors that affect your workload. Those factors include, but are not limited to, gaining skill and experience with technologies that are new to you, modifying your current teaching and learning activities for online use, or adopting teaching techniques that are new to you. Many individuals fail to consider that costs vary by course, by the institution, by students, and by format. An introductory, online, two credit hour language course taught to 10 students who struggle online is very different from a senior level capstone course taught to 20 or more experienced online learners. The start-up costs and ongoing costs are essential considerations in teaching well in a face-to-face, hybrid, or wholly online environment.

Becoming Adept in Using the Appropriate Technologies

There are many technologies, both current and emerging, that can reduce ongoing costs of time but vary significantly by the amount of start-up time costs. Some instructors who start teaching online already have used online tools to supplement their face-to-face classes and/or have taught hybrid courses that use those tools to replace face-to-face activities. We introduced some of those tools in earlier chapters of this book, such as tools to create and share course content in chapter 1.4 and tools to facilitate engaging activities for online students in chapter 2.3. These tools may be part of an LMS for quizzes, discussion forums, and assignment tools in Canvas, Moodle, (D2L) Brightspace, or Blackboard. Some online tools are integrated into an LMS, such as plagiarism detection tools. Stand-alone tools may be used separately to record lectures as screencasts, like Screencast-o-matic, or to facilitate course projects, such as Wikipedia.

If you have not used these tools for technology-enhanced, traditional, or hybrid classes, then the knowledge and skill needed to begin teaching online may seem daunting. In that case, treat this book like a buffet, but don't overfill your plate. There will be plenty of options, but start with a small number of tools at first to find those that work for you, your students, and your course topics. Keep in mind a general rule when it comes to implementing new technology: It will take more time than you think. You can always go back to the buffet for more at a later time!

Translating Teaching and Learning to the Online Environment
Have you ever learned a new language or studied in another country? Until you become fluent in that new language, it seems like every conversation takes a lot of energy and requires extensive mental effort. Sometimes you come across a word, phrase, or idea that doesn't translate properly. Even worse, you may encounter what the French call a *faux ami* ("false friend")—a word in your native language that seems like it should be the same but has an entirely different meaning in the new language.

Trust us; we know firsthand about false friends. When Kevin studied abroad in college, he told his entire French host family how processed snack cakes have long shelf lives thanks to all of the sugar and preservatives. In that moment, he guessed that the word *préservatifs* was the French word for "preservatives," inspiring much laughter. It turns out *préservatifs* means "condoms" in French. Kevin should have said *conservateurs*. Kevin had found a false friend, which resulted in his new friends laughing at his choice of words.

The same false friend concept holds when translating face-to-face class activities to the online environment. For example, it can seem natural to post a 45-minute lecture video you recorded the previous semester during an in-class session. Although that lecture recording would support face-to-face students who want to revisit what they experienced in person, it would not work as well for an online student. Instead, rerecord the lecture in 10- to 15-minute chunks that include a summary statement of major concepts for each chunk. As you record, prompt the students to pause the video to complete specific learning tasks, such as writing down what they already know about a new topic, completing a worksheet, or applying what they have just learned. The general rule for posting digital recordings is to keep in mind what is lost when students are not sitting in a classroom and able to interact with you directly, particularly to ask questions. Typically, recorded material must be more descriptive and more transparent regarding the learning process than must be done for live presentations.

Trying Entirely New Teaching Techniques
Gaining familiarity with and confidence in using new teaching techniques are additional start-up costs you may face as a new or relatively new online teacher. For example, you may have extensive experience giving lectures each week in your classroom, but you may not typically include facilitated discussions as part of your teaching strategies. In that case, you will need to learn not only how to use the technology to set up a discussion but also facilitation strategies to engage online students. Once you consider start-up costs regarding your time, it makes even more sense to start small and build over time, which might mean conducting discussions once every 2 or 3 weeks at first, rather than once every week.

Managing Student Expectations (and Your Own)

Thanks to sophisticated online and phone-based support for businesses, like Zappos, Southwest Airlines, and Amazon, students today are accustomed to robust support centers that answer any question at any time of day. Along the same lines, thanks to learning platforms like Udemy and Coursera, students are used to seeing sophisticated online courses produced by well-equipped teams designed to maintain high production values. Following are strategies to help you manage everyone's expectations about your online course.

Make Yourself Available, but Not Always Available
Whether it's the only time they can get to it or it's the time of day when they think of it, online student activity increases dramatically from the late afternoon until after midnight. In an era of services that operate 24 hours a day, 7 days a week, everyone seems to expect to receive assistance as soon as it is requested. If you are looking over credit card statements late at night and find a discrepancy, you likely expect to be able to call the card company and get someone who can assist you, even at 2:00 a.m. If you decide to take a vacation and want to buy an airplane ticket at midnight, you would expect to be able to call the airline and get help at that time. The same is true for students in our online courses. Students often expect immediate replies to their discussion forum and email questions. It is not that students feel entitled or impatient, but instead, it is often simply that the world they live in provides airplane tickets and customer service desks on-demand and 24 hours per day. Unfortunately, answering student email messages as soon as they arrive at all hours of the day is neither reasonable nor efficient. Unlike airlines and credit card companies, we do not have phone banks of individuals to respond to queries. Best practice in online teaching is to pick specific blocks of time when you are going to answer students' questions (Bregman, 2012) and let students know when that will be.

Kevin teaches his online courses as an adjunct, which is his second job. To manage expectations, he puts the following information in the Communication section of his syllabus:

- Regular communication: Use the ITEC 299 Community Café—an open forum in iLearn (Moodle)—for general questions. *[text links to a discussion forum for general questions]*
- Emergency or private communication: Use the previous email link to send me a private message (please include "ITEC 299" in the subject, or I may not see it).
- NOTE: I will reply to all questions via the discussion forum and email within one business day: usually between 6:00 p.m. and 10:00 p.m., Monday through Friday.

Although responses to messages may occur early in the morning (before work) or at lunch, he is committing to responding within one business day. You may decide to answer questions during your office hours, before your day begins, or at the end of the day, like Kevin. Whatever days and times you pick, choose specific blocks of time that you have available regularly. Most online instructors do get back to students within one business day.

If you are new to online teaching, please be aware that students are not on campus and cannot drop by to see you during office hours. Similarly, if you are only teaching online, you may not have an office to visit! As a result, responding to requests promptly through email is essential to your students' success.

Start Small and Build Over Time

It can take hundreds of hours to build a quality online course. In an ideal world, you would add online activities to your fully face-to-face course, then convert it to a hybrid course, and finally turn it into a fully online course. That would allow you to build over time, but often that time is not available. If you are a new online teacher and do not have the luxury of a large block of time to build your course, pick a small number of strategies for assessment, engagement, and content sharing that you can repeat each week. Do be careful of both the start-up time cost and the ongoing cost. Carefully supplement your core set of learning strategies with more robust activities that might take more time to implement. For example, you might have weekly quizzes but ask students to write essays only once a month. Each time you teach the course, you can continue to refine it and add new activities to enrich the student experience.

Implementation Strategies for Managing Your Workload

As you begin developing your online course and determining how you will facilitate discussions, pay particular attention to your workload. You do not want to start teaching online, only to realize there are not enough hours in the day to do what you have planned and promised! The workload management strategies that follow will help you to be successful by considering carefully how to spread out the load, share the load, and create resources and activities that can survive the test of time.

Spread Out the Load

Kevin's wife works as a horticulturist, installing and maintaining gardens at people's houses and a few commercial buildings. From time to time, she and her business partner order a load of mulch—small bits of organic material like wood chips or tree bark that you put around the base of plants. The mulch keeps moisture from evaporating, adds nutrients to the soil, slows down erosion, and so on. You can buy it in bags at a nursery, or you can order a delivery that comes in units of cubic yards. If you haven't seen a cubic yard of mulch before, it's enough to cover the entire floor of a 10-by-10-foot room, 3 inches deep. When a dump truck deposits 5 cubic yards of mulch in a pile at the end of a driveway, it is impressive

. . . and intimidating. Kevin's wife and her business partner have a phrase they use to keep moving and to avoid feeling overwhelmed: "Don't stare at the load." They grab shovels and start moving the mulch, one bucket or wheelbarrow at a time.

The same concept works for online teachers. After you filled out Table 1.5.5 to map your assessment strategies, activities, and course materials to your learning outcomes, you ended up with a rough checklist of everything you would need to teach a hybrid or online course. For a 16- or 17-week semester, that checklist typically contains a lot of items! Your load of mulch may take a while to distribute, so consider creating a first version of your course that is both functional and minimal. You can revise and augment it each semester afterward.

Share the Load

If you are teaching a course that has multiple sections, talk to the other instructor(s) at your institution and offer to collaborate on developing course materials and/or online activities. If there are not multiple sections, seek out individuals who teach the same or a similar course and ask about a collaborative approach whereby you share resources and ideas. Keep in mind that we live in a globally connected world, so these other instructors may be at a campus where you also work full time to teach face-to-face courses. Still, they might also be colleagues you meet at a teaching conference who teach a course similar to your course in another country. Networking is more important than ever, so use conferences as opportunities to grow your online teaching support system. When you meet others who teach online courses similar to yours, suggest a collaboration that will allow each of you to save time as well as to get feedback on your work.

Reduce, Reuse, Recycle

A famous phrase in environmental protection and conservation is "reduce, reuse, recycle." However, it also works as a workload management mantra for online teachers. For example, you can apply one or more of these strategies when grading:

- *Reduce*: Identify ways to do the same amount of work in less time or energy. Use rubrics to reduce grading time by focusing your grading on specific criteria (Stevens & Levi, 2012). Anglin et al. (2008) found that computer-assisted grading rubrics increase efficiency even further. To that end, LMS solutions like Canvas include streamlined rubric tools that allow you simply to click the level of achievement for each criterion and save the final score directly to the grade book.

You may also reduce time by providing video feedback. Simply record short screencast videos in which you highlight student work on an essay or project as you narrate your feedback. Finally, you may reduce the amount of time grading by requiring less material to be turned in to you for grading or having students do a round of peer editing.

- *Reuse*: Look for ways to use the same material elsewhere in a course or the next time you teach the course. Create a library of written comments that you can reuse when another student achieves a common goal or makes a common mistake. After you type a new comment for the first time, copy it to a "library" document where you can find it again. Have that document open on your desktop while grading each paper so that you can easily copy and paste any number of comments. Not having to retype basic comments will save you time. Watch specifically for statements you type over and over, such as "Please provide additional sources to support this statement." You can still customize them, of course!

- *Recycle*: Identify ways to adapt resources to make them better or different the next time they are needed. Take a message that you used to address common mistakes after they happened, and turn it into a section of instructions for future activities to prevent those mistakes from happening again. You can do this later in the same semester or in future iterations of your class. For example, if students shrink margins and expand spacing to meet page requirements, put in the instructions that the paper must be 12-point font and standard margins. If students frequently include references that are not in APA format (or whatever format you use), then include that in the instructions. Do not spend energy ruminating over what the students should know with respect to your course. If the error is common, add it as an instruction. Getting students to read the instructions can also be a challenge. One strategy is to have a grading rubric that includes these elements and have students grade their paper with the rubric and then include that self-graded rubric with the writing they are submitting. Recycle rubrics as needed for future courses.

Another way to recycle is to find what has worked for others. Much is online now, including grading rubrics, syllabi, and assignments. Do a quick web search for just about anything you require of your students to see what might be available for adaptation. The best practice is to contact the instructor who posted the information to ask permission to use and perhaps adapt. It is becoming common practice to use things from the web in other courses. Most instructors are pleased to be contacted about the use of their materials elsewhere, and you can volunteer to share your information, thereby creating another online teaching colleague.

UDL, DESIGN FOR LEARNING EQUITY, HUMAN CONNECTIONS, AND MANAGING YOUR WORKLOAD

The workload management strategies presented in this chapter can help you as you start applying UDL and design for learning equity techniques to your course. You can spread out the universal design load by splitting up the work required to offer alternatives for audio or visual content or to give students multiple pathways to show what they know. As you prepare a class before each semester, you can create one new instructional material—or a new type of material—to support student learning. In their book about UDL, Tom Tobin and Kirsten Behling (2018) call this "plus-one thinking" (p. 11). For example, the first time you teach a class, you might provide presentation slides with the previous semester's lecture recordings from the classroom. Over the winter or summer break, you can record a few new lectures—enough that you can stay a few weeks ahead of when students will watch them. If you prepare lecture notes or even scripts for the recordings, you can upload those too. The third time you teach a class, you might make a few concept maps as advance organizers to help students see connections among course topics. And so on.

Sometimes this will happen organically. Throughout this book, we have made references to Mary-Ann Winkelmes and her Transparent Assignment Template. Kevin learned about the template at the end of one spring semester he was teaching. Like the UDL framework, it provided a "what, why, and how" explanation for each activity and learning material. Winkelmes and her colleagues found the template had increased success for first-generation students, and more of those students were (and still are) coming to Kevin's campus each year. He decided to convert the instructions for every activity to the transparent assignment format over the summer. Like you, Kevin wondered if the extra work would be worth the effort. Amazingly, he did not have to wait long to find out. A student who had failed the previous semester's class retook it after Kevin made his assignments transparent. That student not only passed but earned an A in the course. The student wrote an end-of-semester email telling Kevin that he thought the assignment instructions had helped him the second time around—"I knew what to do." Spreading out the load had an unexpected consequence—it provided a window to see what works for students.

When it comes time to incorporate learning equity techniques, you can share some of the load with your students. If it's your first time teaching a course online, you will be working hard to get that course ready and may not have time to research connections between course topics and different sociocultural backgrounds. So, make it part of the assignment that students explore, share, and discuss the connections between each topic and their backgrounds. If your campus does not have the resources to caption your mini-lecture videos, offer bonus points for students to type up a transcript as they review 5-minute segments. Once they have typed it up, have them use bold and highlight to mark the ideas that they think are most important. They are getting to know the content more thoroughly while you are getting a rough transcript and a sense of what students take away from the materials. This sharing of the load of creating content for the course will also significantly impact the human connection aspect of the online course. The more students participate, the more they will recognize that you see them as a valuable member of the course and not simply a name on a course roster.

NEXT STEPS

Now that you have read about some factors that affect your workload and strategies to help reduce it, perform a self-check:

- Ask experienced faculty members what they consider to have been their primary "start-up and ongoing costs."
- Identify a workload management strategy that we shared that will help you the most as you design, develop, and deliver your hybrid or online course.
- Identify a workload management strategy that will help you apply UDL, design for learning equity, or human connection.

CHAPTER SUMMARY

Managing your time may well be the most important determinant as to whether you will be a successful online instructor. Students face more independence when taking online courses, and you will face more independence in teaching these courses. If you are a part-time faculty member, you may never have the opportunity to interact with your campus colleagues. As a result, you will need to find ways to build collaborative networks and identify ways to manage your time well. The good news is that there are a plethora of resources to help you to manage your time. Find which have reasonable start-up costs in terms of time and which will demonstrate the best return on investment in terms of saving ongoing time costs.

Reflection and Discussion Questions

1. List the start-up costs that come to mind for teaching a course online that you have taught previously multiple times in a face-to-face format. Which of these start-up costs concern you the most? Explain why and what first steps you would take to address those costs.

2. Describe one challenge you have had in a previous course (face-to-face or online) or one you can identify from your time as a student in a given course. Identify one learning technology that may well address that challenge. Explain the intended outcome if the learning technology works as you think it might.

3. Describe your planned strategy for being available to your students, but not becoming overwhelmed by the responsibility of being available all the time for everyone. From where did you identify this strategy? Was this something you developed on your own or one that is adapted from a strategy you have seen another faculty member use previously?

4. Describe three things from a previous course you have taught: one that you can reduce next time, one that can be reused, and one that can be recycled. If you have not taught before, identify things you have experienced as a student that you might be able to reduce (not do something another faculty member unnecessarily allotted time to), reuse (with attribution), or recycle (with attribution).

PART THREE

MAKING ADJUSTMENTS TO YOUR ONLINE COURSE

3.1

ASSESSING TEACHING ONLINE

*A*SSESSMENT IS CRITICAL IN higher education, as it shows what students are learning and, in so doing, helps to demonstrate which instructional strategies are effective and which are not. There is no difference between online and face-to-face courses concerning collecting data to help make decisions based on the extent to which intended course outcomes have been realized. In chapter 3.2, we will look closely at assessing student learning. In this chapter, we highlight different ways to evaluate teaching effectiveness in virtual environments. We start by turning our attention to gathering information and advice before the term begins and finalizing course preparations. We then look at collecting formative feedback during the course to suggest where instructional adjustments might be needed and finally turn our attention to identifying ways to collect summative feedback after a course ends to make adjustments for the next term.

ADOPTING A GROWTH-MINDED APPROACH TO TEACHING ONLINE

Throughout education much has been written about the importance for learners to have a growth mindset (Dweck, 2017) and for instructors to encourage all students to see they have the ability to succeed—especially students of color (Wood, 2015). Further, Kundu (2020) promotes increasing learning agency for all students, especially those who come from disadvantaged backgrounds. One way to help students realize their ability to succeed and for them to have increased agency is to ensure students understand the importance of having a growth mindset. Growth-minded individuals believe that success comes from effort. Fixed-minded individuals, however, believe that success comes from innate talents. One of the most important aspects of growth-mindedness is the belief that feedback is informative and that feedback helps a person to grow and to improve. If a person takes a math test and does not do well, a fixed-minded person might blame the test, the teacher, or believe that they are simply "bad at math." A growth-minded person, in contrast, would see poor performance on a math test as evidence that they need to work harder on learning math. Growth versus fixed mindedness is not an all-or-none proposition in every aspect of a person's life. A person can be growth minded toward math (e.g., I need to study and work hard to better understand the concepts) and, at the same time, be fixed minded with respect to public speaking (e.g., I am bad at giving speeches).

Although it would be ideal if all faculty members were growth-minded, some certainly have a fixed mindset. It may be relatively easy to think of a teacher you recall as a "naturally born good teacher." That is fixed-minded thinking, believing that someone is just naturally good or bad at something. In actuality, there is no such thing as a teacher who is naturally good at teaching. Some teachers learned early in life to be socially adaptive and very caring toward others, both important characteristics for good teachers to have. That said, there are many dimensions to being a good teacher, and good teachers work hard at learning a variety of things that result in them being good teachers. Growth-minded teachers see the world differently than do fixed-minded teachers. For example, when it comes to end-of-the-course student evaluations that are critical (informative and critical, not the mean ones), growth-minded teachers see areas for improvement. In contrast, fixed-minded teachers see a flawed system of gathering evaluations. Although most faculty agree that student evaluation systems need improvement, there is a good deal of information in the assessment of our teaching provided by students through those forms. That is, if they are viewed with growth in mind.

Similarly, assessment and evaluation data about a course can be beneficial to a growth-minded faculty member. Online teachers benefit from soliciting feedback and conducting self-assessments early and often. Instructional design models usually include evaluation as one stage of a long process. One popular model, although there is a question as to its origin, is the ADDIE model (Molenda, 2003). If you follow the ADDIE model, you *assess* the learners' needs, *design* and *develop* your instruction or course, *implement* with your students what you have built, and then *evaluate* how well it worked. However, we challenge you to evaluate what you are doing at every stage, not just at the end. Borrowing from an old orange juice commercial, one might say assessment "is not just for breakfast anymore!" In this chapter, we'll look at ways to conduct assessments before, during, and after each online course.

In addition to expanding the "when" of assessment, we'll also expand what to assess. Traditionally, we understand teaching effectiveness according to the course's quality and the teacher's practices. We will define teaching effectiveness more broadly by looking at several factors that affect student success—quality, accessibility, inclusion, and equity.

Last, as we've increased the scope of work, it would only be fair to increase the size of the team. Rather than tackling this task on your own, bring others into the review process. We will share strategies to ask your students what works and what you might change, as well as ways to ask peers at and beyond your institution for feedback.

Strategies for Assessing Your Online Course (and Your Online Teaching)

Assessing your own course design and facilitation is a cyclical process. Before your course begins, you can review it yourself in different ways and ask colleagues and former students for feedback on course updates. If you do this over the summer, take a break for at least a couple of weeks after the spring term so you look at course materials with fresh, or at least somewhat rested, eyes. As you teach your class, you can collect feedback from students and keep notes on changes you want to make before you teach it again. You can make small tweaks as you teach, but making some changes during the class would be too disruptive for learners. After the class ends, combine the feedback you collected with information from the student evaluations and other sources. Now let's look at that timeline for online teaching assessment in more depth.

Before Your Course

If your campus does not require some sort of review process before you begin teaching an online course, take the time to conduct a self-assessment or to ask a colleague to give you feedback. Even if you are an experienced online teacher, it's useful to review your course against a checklist or rubric related to course design or course quality. Another option is to have someone else review your course environment. Find a trusted colleague who is not familiar with the course topic you are teaching and ask for feedback regarding your learning outcomes, activities, assessments, and other course elements. In particular, ask them to determine if what you are attempting to achieve in the course is clear.

To support self-assessment, informal peer review, and more formal review processes, several statewide or nationwide initiatives have created online course review rubrics. Most of these rubrics include criteria or entire sections that echo common quality indicators of online courses identified in related literature (K. Kelly, 2019b; Shelton, 2011).

The most common criteria addressed in online course review rubrics include the following:

- *learning objectives or learning outcomes*
- *course design*
- *content presentation* and *instructional materials*
- faculty–student and student–student *interaction*, including fostering a *learning community*
- *assessment*
- *course technology*
- *learner support*, specifically helping students learning at a distance
- *accessibility*, including both the course environment and everything that goes in it
- *course evaluation*, such as through anonymous student feedback

Some of the most widely known rubrics are listed here by organization, in alphabetical order (see Table 1.1.3 for list with full details and links).

- California Community Colleges (CCC)—OEI Course Design Rubric
- California State University (CSU) system—Quality Learning and Teaching (QLT) Rubric
- Illinois Online Network (ION)—Quality Online Course Initiative (QOCI) Rubric
- QM—Rubrics and Standards
- State University of New York (SUNY) and the Online Learning Consortium (OLC)—Open SUNY Course Quality Review (OSCQR) Rubric

There are also a few noteworthy rubrics and guidelines created by individual institutions, such as University of Wisconsin-La Crosse's—Online Course Evaluation Guidelines.

Once you have a good sense of what appears to be designed well and what areas need attention, you can lay out a solid foundation for your online course.

During the Course

At the beginning of your course, an icebreaker activity may include asking students to share their expectations—that is, what they want to get out of the course—as part of an "Introduce Yourself" discussion. In a summary post, identify common goals and note some interesting, unique goals as well. In a moment, we'll describe how to circle back to these goals and expectations as part of a midsemester feedback survey. It's important to note that students who have jobs, who have children, or who act as caregivers for elderly relatives may question the value of icebreaker discussions, as they have limited time and do not want to participate in what they perceive to be "fluff" or meaningless activities. This feeling of time pressure makes it even more important to convey how creating a learning community supports their learning. For example, identifying students who face similar circumstances, they can create a support group that will answer questions about the class.

Throughout the course, try collecting feedback from students in microbursts. For example, use One-Minute Threads (discussion forum) as a virtual alternative to the traditional classroom assessment technique called the One-Minute Paper (K. Kelly, 2008a). One-Minute Threads provide an asynchronous venue for students to share what was clear, what was unclear, and what questions they have about each online module or the work they complete each week. It also offers opportunities for students to help each other by answering classmates' questions before you, the teacher, get to the discussion forum. We will outline the steps involved in conducting a One-Minute Thread activity in more detail in the next chapter.

If you decide you want fewer feedback loops, conduct a midsemester evaluation survey. Some LMS platforms offer anonymous, ungraded survey tools through their Quiz functionality (e.g., Canvas) or a separate Survey functionality (e.g., Moodle, D2L, Blackboard). If you would prefer to use a third-party tool, both SurveyMonkey (surveymonkey.com) and the Free Assessment Summary Tool (toofast.ca) allow anonymous responses. They can make sure students only take the survey once. Some campuses provide access to survey tools like Qualtrics (www.qualtrics .com/), which have the same capabilities. Be sure to dedicate a few questions on your assessment form to address students' expressed needs. Ask students at the beginning of the class to share their expectations (e.g., "What do you want to get out of this class?"), and then ask them to rate their progress in meeting those expectations or provide a text area for them to state what would help them reach their personal goals. Midsemester feedback is also valuable. Four questions you may want to ask at the midpoint of the semester or a few times during the semester are: (a) What am I doing that is helping you to be successful in this course? (b) What could I do to help you to be even more successful? (c) What are you doing to help yourself to be successful? and (d) What could you do to help yourself to be even more successful? A midsemester feedback form could be given for any component of the course. For example, after an exam, you could make slight adjustments to these same four questions and gain feedback about the exam.

Once you have collected the feedback, do something with the information you have collected. Students will get frustrated if they take the time to provide feedback and feel that it went into a black hole. Start with a brief summary of the suggestions and an honest appraisal of what is feasible for you to address. For example, if students noted on the feedback forms that they would like additional virtual office hours, let them know that you will hold virtual office hours more often during each week before a major assignment is due. If students complained about the course organization, you could tell them that you will not be able to change the course organization at this point in the semester, but you can create aids like brief videos or downloadable handouts that explain each module more clearly and share that you will look at organization carefully for the next course. If students ask for more opportunities to interact with each other, let them know you are responding directly to this request with weekly discussion forums or chats. The key is to take action quickly and inform the students of the changes you made based on their feedback and explain why some requested changes cannot be made at this time.

At the end of the academic term, most institutions require a student evaluation of teaching effectiveness. Even if your campus doesn't require a student evaluation, be sure to conduct one, as the information obtained can be extremely helpful in making changes in future courses. Some campuses provide an online course evaluation system, but if your campus still uses a paper instrument, then create your own, analogous survey using a tool that provides true anonymity (see the previous tool recommendations for midsemester evaluation surveys). A plus/delta activity is a less formal method for collecting student feedback at the end of the term (K. Kelly, 2008a). In this exercise, students share what they liked (plus) and what they would like to change (delta). For fully online classes, this activity could be done asynchronously using a discussion, Google Doc, or survey. It could also be done synchronously using a videoconference or Twitter chat.

After the Course
With the feedback that you've gathered over the academic term, it's a good idea to make one last pass through the course with an online course review rubric. You are bound to be ready for a break, so it does not have to be extensive. However, it will be easier to recall issues that arose throughout the course while the experience is still fresh in your mind. At the very least, make a list of items that you want to change or fix before the next time you teach the same course online.

Figure 3.1.1. Online course assessment timeline.

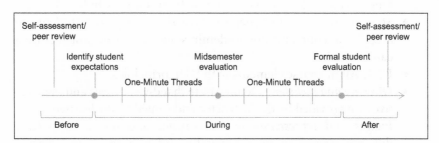

Now you have closed the assessment loop, having conducted assessments before, during, and after teaching your course online. Figure 3.1.1 shows an online course assessment timeline that includes each strategy we described, but there is always room for more. Check with your colleagues or any instructional designers at your campus to determine if there are any other simple ways to assess your course.

Assessing Accessibility, Inclusion, Universal Design, and Learning Equity

Usually, online teachers check their courses for quality, but as we mentioned previously, many of the course review rubrics also include criteria related to accessibility for students with disabilities. In chapter 1.6, Making Your Course Accessible, we covered a variety of ways to accommodate students with different needs related to vision, hearing, cognitive processing, attention, and more. Those strategies addressed making content pages and downloadable files accessible, primarily through *text formatting*, *descriptive text*, *table formatting*, and the *use of color*. The online course environment itself and everything you add to it—from what students will download to what students will review online—should be checked for accessibility. The OEI Course Design Rubric listed previously has more than 20 criteria related to content accessibility. Go beyond the content and check your activities and assessments as well. To get an outside perspective, visit your campus unit that supports students with disabilities to see if they have any staff or know any students who might review your course for accessibility.

As we've done throughout this book, we recommend assessing your course for inclusion and equity as well. Peralta Community College District (2019) in Oakland, California, has created a comprehensive rubric to review online courses for learning equity issues (web.peralta.edu/de/equity-initiative/equity/), using the following criteria:

- *Technology:* Provide technology pathways, alternatives, and assistance so all students can complete activities successfully.
- *Student resources and support:* Provide avenues for students to access academic and nonacademic support that do not require a campus visit.
- *UDL:* Align course elements with UDL principles.
- *Diversity and inclusion:* Demonstrate that diverse ideas and perspectives are provided by the instructor and valued by the learners.
- *Images and representation:* Use images and media to portray different groups of people equally and accurately, and discuss potential stereotypes or inaccuracies of specific media.
- *Human bias:* Identify and manage different types of bias (e.g., implicit bias, cultural bias, interaction bias) in course materials, activities, or assessments.
- *Content meaning:* Use course materials that have meaning for students from multiple backgrounds, and create activities that require students to connect course topics to their backgrounds or the backgrounds of others.
- *Connection and belonging:* Facilitate connections with and among learners, and demonstrate a genuine interest in learners' success and participation at different levels.

The equity rubric development team suggested a way to conceptualize the changes from the most recent update—namely, having rubric ratings align with specific levels of student engagement. Meeting the criteria could mean you are generating awareness among students about learning equity. Exceeding the criteria could mean you are driving students to take action related to learning equity. The Peralta team also launched an Online Equity Training course that they shared freely and openly in the Canvas Commons (Stark, 2019; lor.instructure.com/resources/f35cd7a09da64112 aff13a98b7ddf0cd). Individuals can go through the course on their own, or campuses can use it to support cohorts of faculty. It scaffolds the process for online teachers—(a) participants learn about each equity criterion, (b) they analyze a sample course with the rubric, and (c) they build learning equity into their own online course(s).

NEXT STEPS

Keep in mind that you do not have to assess your online course by yourself. Campus staff, your colleagues, and even your students can support your efforts. Using Table 3.1.1 as a guide, identify people you might approach

TABLE 3.1.1
Potential Sources of Online Course Feedback

	Quality	Accessibility	Inclusion and Equity
Before	Self, peers, instructional design staff	Self, accessibility staff	Self, previous students
During	Students, self, peers	Students, self	Students, self
After	Self, peers	Self	Self, peers, equity staff

to get feedback (a) about different aspects of your online course—that is, quality, accessibility, inclusion, and equity, and (b) at different times during your course cycle—before, during, and after you teach the course.

CHAPTER SUMMARY

The only way to improve is to know how things are going. Maintaining a growth-minded perspective toward teaching will necessitate feedback as the information to allow the course to be improved. Collecting assessment data before the course starts will allow for building a solid foundation and launching the course well. Collecting assessment data during the course will allow for corrections as the course progresses and will show students that we can all benefit from shared information on how to make the course a positive learning experience to the greatest extent possible. Collecting assessment data after the course will allow you to make adjustments to the overall course to help create the best learning environment possible for your students.

Reflection and Discussion Questions

1. Why do you think most individuals find it difficult or anxiety provoking to assess the performance of students and colleagues? If you were going to help a colleague who noted that it was extremely difficult to give students feedback about their performance when they do poorly, what would you say to help the faculty member reframe the feedback?
2. Locate one of the course design rubrics listed in this chapter and complete it for a course you will be teaching. Explain what you found and specifically note anything that surprised you regarding your course design readiness.

3. Design a midsemester feedback form. Explain what you included in the form and why it is included.
4. Explain one nontraditional method you might use to collect end-of-the-course assessment data to be more inclusive in terms of student responses. That is, decide how you might get assessment data from students who may otherwise not participate in assessing the course or your instruction.

3.2

ASSESSING LEARNING ONLINE

*A*SSESSING STUDENT LEARNING IS a fundamental responsibility for all faculty members. Assessment results provide students with necessary feedback on their performance for several reasons. Feedback lets students know how best to gauge their effort in learning course material. Feedback is important to reinforce that students are on the correct path to learning. Constructive feedback indicates how students need to make adjustments to receive the appropriate level of recognition for work completed. And feedback conveys that students have received academic credit for their work. These are just a few reasons feedback is important to students and to the learning process. Because of the many values of feedback, assessment is critical as it provides the information used for feedback. Assessing student learning and providing feedback are among the most critical aspects of being a faculty member.

Assessment in online courses needs to be even more clearly executed than in face-to-face courses, as students in online courses tend to work in more independent circumstances. Similarly, instructors must convey assessment expectations just as clearly in advance. In this chapter we discuss (a) how to apply UDL and design for learning equity principles to give students multiple pedagogical and technological pathways to show what they know; (b) what tools and strategies work best for authentic and/or higher-level thinking activities—for example, assessment of writing, presentations, projects, and teamwork; and (c) how and when we can make our assessment feedback more personal while saving time.

WHAT TO CONSIDER WHEN CHOOSING YOUR ASSESSMENT STRATEGIES

When choosing an assessment strategy for your course, the following fundamental questions transcend all course types and delivery formats:

- To what extent is it possible to create a robust and authentic assessment plan (e.g., assessment plans should include data from multiple sources)?
- From whom can we collect assessment data (e.g., self-assessment, peer review, instructor feedback, and even review by other stakeholders)?
- Are individuals completing the assessment able to provide complete and accurate assessment data regarding their own learning (e.g., those providing assessment data should have experience and knowledge in the assessment methods used)? Although this may seem like an automatic "yes," there is a plethora of research in psychology that suggests otherwise. People certainly are capable of reporting on their perception of their own learning, but there are conditions in which they are distinctly poor at self-assessment of resulting behavior (e.g., Kruger & Dunning, 1999; Marsh & Butler, 2014).

As you develop ways to assess student learning in your online or hybrid course, four factors to keep in mind are authenticity, validity, variety, and frequency. The previous chapter introduced these factors within some of the course design rubrics listed. We'll describe each factor briefly, then give you more detailed assessment ideas and provide examples of using specific techniques.

Authenticity

As per the backward design model we discussed previously in this book, all assessments should connect directly to module-level outcomes, course-level outcomes, or student learning outcomes. Recall that in backward design, the first step is to determine an anticipated outcome and then an assessment strategy that will allow you to determine the extent to which a student has reached the desired outcome. These outcomes may address any level of achievement, according to the taxonomies we shared earlier related to knowledge, skills, and attitudes. In addition, it is advantageous to make the outcomes as authentic as possible. Jon Mueller (2016) defined *authentic assessment* as "a form of assessment in which students are asked to perform real-world tasks that demonstrate meaningful application of essential knowledge and skills" (para. 1). Frequently, online career and technical education courses use authentic assessment strategies as preparation for real-world work performance expectations learners will experience once they enter the workforce. For example, a business or entrepreneurship instructor may ask students to create an invoice rather than provide a quiz about the parts of an invoice. Of course, not every assessment can be a sample of potential work duties assigned on the job. If you're using a traditional educational assessment, such as a test or term paper, ask yourself questions such as the following:

- Is there a way to incorporate questions that relate to a real-world context?
- Is there a way to use that test or written assignment to prepare students to perform an authentic, real-world task?

Validity

Validity is used to describe how well an instrument/tool measures what it is intended to measure. At a basic level, your assessments are valid if they align with your learning outcomes. If you use test pools provided by a publisher, check each question that you plan to include on the test to ensure it measures the outcome you intend for it to measure. In many cases, the textbook publishers' questions cover every possible topic in the book. Make sure the questions you use relate to something you've asked students to learn. As a quick tip, if you select 10 questions at random from a pool of questions, always make sure that the pool contains questions that are unique and relevant. As test banks may have hundreds of questions, a random selection of 10 items could result in many of the items measuring the exact same concept or concepts not covered in your class.

Exemplary teaching practice includes telling students which learning outcomes are going to be measured. You may remember the Transparent Assignment Template from Mary-Ann Winkelmes that we described in chapter 1.2, (Re)Writing Learning Outcomes for Your Online Course. That template asks you to restate the outcomes as they apply to each assignment or assessment. Just as easily, you can add the outcomes being assessed to a brief purpose statement in the instructions for a quiz, an assignment, or a graded discussion.

Variety

Incorporating a variety of assessment strategies can be as simple as implementing two types of assessment throughout the semester. First, consider using formative assessment, such as lower-stakes quizzes or discussions to help students judge their progress and gaps in their knowledge. Second, use summative assessment, such as a high-stakes midterm, final exams, or papers designed to determine the level of student performance. Ideally, each course will contain different types of formative and summative assessments that may serve both functions. For example, use both quizzes and graded discussions to help students identify if they are ready for a final project. A wide variety of options are available online through an internet search of "classroom assessment techniques." UDL suggests giving students multiple opportunities to show what they know. Not all students are great test-takers, so they are supported by having other ways to demonstrate they understand and can apply course concepts.

Frequency

Assessment frequency refers to conducting multiple assessments throughout the course. Establish frequency through a combination of (a) spacing assessments at regular, consistent intervals throughout the course and (b) providing timely feedback to students.

- *Clearly note in your syllabus if there will be a regular pattern for assessments*: For example, "Each module will last 3 weeks. In the first week of each module, you will review the mini-lecture videos and take a quiz. In the second week, you will participate in a graded discussion about the module topic(s). In the third week of each module, you will write a reflection essay about how you applied a concept from the module to your life."
- *Indicate in the syllabus how quickly you'll return student work with feedback*: For example, "I will review essays with a rubric—a scoring guide that you will have in advance—and provide personalized feedback (written or video) about how you can improve on the next essay you submit. I will strive to return essays within 7 days after the due date so you can apply the feedback to the next assignment."
- *Use the LMS calendar to note assessment dates, as well as assessment preparation dates*: When you set due dates in the LMS settings for quizzes, discussions, and assignments, they automatically appear in most LMS calendars. Take it one step further and add calendar events for the start of a discussion, as a reminder to study for a quiz more than 1 day before the quiz is due, or when they should think about starting the essay they'll turn in as an assignment. Given most faculty members teach multiple courses, it is good practice when selecting assessment dates to lay out on a calendar all assessment

obligations across all courses. It is easy to accidentally have a due date for term papers in one class that is within a few days of an essay exam in another course and feedback on a role-play activity in a third class. Space out assessments to give yourself as much grading time as possible.

APPLYING UDL AND DESIGN FOR LEARNING EQUITY STRATEGIES TO ASSESSMENT

Throughout this chapter (and this book), we have been promoting the concept of giving students multiple ways to demonstrate they have reached your course outcomes. Now let's look at specific methods to apply UDL principles to assessment—offering students a choice regarding the assessment task, the submission format, the difficulty level, or some combination of these three choices (K. Kelly, 2014).

- *Offer a choice of assessment task*: Although you need to have control over how students show their knowledge or skills, it is possible to provide students with a small degree of choice. For example, give students more than one essay prompt or essay test question that will show they understand a course concept and let them pick one that they want to answer or that is most relevant to them (K. Kelly, 2014, para. 7). Use the same rubric or grading criteria, regardless of which question they choose.
- *Offer a choice of submission format*: In chapter 1.4, Finding, Creating, and Sharing Course Content, we promote following UDL principles by sharing course content in multiple formats (e.g., PowerPoint, PDF, and screencast versions of a mini-lecture). Similarly, you can give students a choice of submission format for some assessments in your class. Rather than give them a completely open-ended choice, provide them with a list of acceptable formats. For example, for a lab report, allow them to submit a written report, presentation slides with audio narration in VoiceThread, or a video made in the lab to describe the setup, process, results, analysis, and other required information about the experiment.
- *Offer a choice of difficulty level*: In almost any LMS there are three common tools available to provide progressive levels of difficulty (K. Kelly, 2014)—you can assess information recall and concept comprehension via quizzes, assess concept application and analysis via discussions, and assess students' ability to evaluate and create

via assignments. You can spread these out over time to scaffold the learning process or give students a choice of one strategy to show they have reached specific outcomes.

The design for learning equity framework offers several strategies related to creating equitable achievement pathways, using equitable feedback methods, and fostering persistence in and beyond the course. You may have noticed in the previous list that we referenced providing feedback using text or video. Doing so is a learning equity practice because it serves first-generation, nontraditional, and other students who face additional barriers to success. Here are samples of assessment and feedback practices that increase learning equity:

- *Provide just-in-time, in-line links to appropriate support*: Most instructors use the syllabus to alert students to support services like library faculty, online tutors, and writing support. That's helpful information, but it's also information that falls to the wayside after the first weeks of the semester. Take it one step further by linking to the appropriate support services in the instructions for an assignment—for example, "If you have questions about how to research your essay topic, contact a librarian using the library chat tool. When you are ready to write your essay, you can schedule a video session with the writing center team." Use the phrases "contact a librarian using the library chat tool" and "schedule a video session with the writing center team" as your descriptive link text. (Remember to use the accessibility techniques from chapter 1.6!)
- *Manage cultural bias within assessments or activities*: Just as the world around us, our class rosters keep getting more diverse. In some cases, and with care, we can make assumptions about the learners in our online classes—for example, they all use the same language (usually English) equally well, eat the same foods, are familiar with the same historical figures or older pop culture references, have the same level of previous experience leading up to the course material, and so on. Although there are similarities, there will also be many differences, some of which are not obvious. Some students will be affluent, yet wear clothing that does not indicate their affluence. Some of your students likely have food or housing insecurities, but you may never know how hungry they really are or that they have no secure place to sleep (Barnes & LeDuc, 2018). Conversely, there may not be any difference, but as faculty, we may inadvertently assume

there are differences. Brown University's Education Alliance (2020; www.brown.edu/academics/education-alliance/teaching-diverse-learners/question-iv-0) provides a helpful resource to manage cultural bias in assessments. Please go to Appendix C for links to the online resources mentioned in this chapter. The team at Brown lists practical ways to manage potential bias without having to remove cultural references altogether. For example, ask yourself, "Are there enough supporting details so that students can comprehend the cultural content?" When considering an example, ask, "Are members of different cultural groups positively portrayed?"

- *Provide alternative pathways for students to create and submit their work*: Although faculty hold a common assumption that all students have access to a computer, adequate internet, and all required software, that is not true for every student. As we noted in the previous bullet, significant numbers of students face housing insecurity and homelessness—up to 16% of students at 2-year institutions and 11% of students at 4-year institutions (Goldrick-Rab et al., 2019). These students will likely be completing courses from a smartphone, so offering alternative pathways to create and submit work is critical. For example, allow students to send a clear phone picture of their handwritten math or science problems. Allow students to share a link to a Google Doc instead of a Word document. For students with no devices, create a free Google Voice phone number and allow them to read their handwritten essays as a voicemail message. These strategies also support students who share a limited number of devices with others in emergency, shelter-in-place situations.
- *Provide meaningful prompts for students to give each other feedback that respects diversity*: Have you noticed how easy it is to write several paragraphs for a discussion forum prompt, and how easy it is to write very little as an instruction for discussion replies? For some teachers, "Give feedback to two other students" is as sophisticated as it gets. It's time to start creating more meaningful prompts for how students should give each other feedback. As we do this, we can also encourage students to seek out and respect diversity. Here's an example:

Your replies will compare and contrast your viewpoint about the discussion topic with other students' viewpoints. Reply to at least one student whose viewpoint is similar to yours and at least one student who has a viewpoint that is different from yours. For the students with a similar viewpoint, share a new resource that will expand their thinking about the topic. For the students with a different viewpoint, ask them two or three questions that will help you better understand their point of view.

- *Increase students' sense of belonging and connectedness*: A fair number of students may not feel they belong in your class, in your field, or at your institution. Nontraditional students who take courses while working and/or caring for family may see classes as a requirement to complete. First-generation students taking online courses may get lost when they have to manage time and take responsibility for completing assignments regularly. Select demographics of students—for example, women, LGBTQ, or minoritized students—may not envision themselves ascending to important positions in disciplines such as STEM fields when they do not see themselves represented in those roles in mainstream media. With all this in mind, provide assessment feedback throughout the course to foster a greater sense of belonging and connectedness at those different levels. To promote institutional belonging, suggest in a class announcement that students participate in a campus event (live or streamed via video) as a reward for a high class average on a test. To foster belonging in your course, email students who have not participated in every discussion, telling them that you are interested in hearing their thoughts. To foster belonging in your discipline, construct prompts that allow students to make connections to their personal experiences and cultural perspectives. In your feedback for each assignment, copy and paste a different, relevant quote from a notable woman, a person of color, or a person who identifies as trans from your field.

- *Make assessment feedback more personal*: A number of studies (e.g., Lumadue & Fish, 2010; Mathisen, 2012; Stannard, 2007, 2008) have stated that multimodal feedback—for example, instructor screencasts narrating as they review each students' work—can be both more impactful for and more personal to students. This type of feedback gets its power in part because it follows our now common UDL theme of providing information—even feedback for students—in multiple formats. Along the lines of learning equity, it also humanizes another part of the learning experience. In online courses where students do not get to meet with the teacher or other students very much or at all, screencast videos in which the teacher gives feedback about students' coursework create a more profound sense of connection. If possible, add an on-camera greeting before switching to screencast mode.

ASSESSING HIGHER-ORDER THINKING AND AUTHENTIC ACTIVITIES

Online faculty members sometimes find it difficult to facilitate two types of assessment: higher-order thinking and student performance of authentic activities. If you use these strategies in your in-person classes, then you should try to use them in the online environment as well. If you normally do not use these strategies, then you may want to consider them as a way to increase the variety of assessment for your students. Following are some ideas to help you address the challenges these types of assessment bring with them.

Higher-Order Thinking

Online learners can demonstrate any and all levels of thinking, doing, and feeling as well as classroom-based learners, as we described in our chapter on rewriting learning outcomes (see chapter 1.2). It's up to you to determine the level of achievement you want your students to reach. Paul (1993) outlined a strong rationale and provided recommendations for assessing higher-order thinking, paying extra attention to critical thinking in multiple areas—elements of thought, abilities, affective dimensions, and intellectual standards. He offers a rich set of assessment examples in each area. He addresses what to ask students to do and even writes example multiple-choice questions that require higher-order thinking. Although some argue it is not possible to assess higher-order thinking by way of multiple choice questions, this is simply not true.

Higher-order thinking activities can be as simple as asking students to describe why they did something, such as explaining their thinking when solving a physics problem. In this case, the students are analyzing their own actions. These activities also may be designed to show achievement of campus-wide student learning outcomes in areas such as critical thinking, civic engagement, or global learning. The exercises themselves might involve problem-solving, writing, presentations, projects, and/or teamwork.

- *Inform students of the higher-order thinking skills that you will be assessing*: Mansbach (2015) shared five types of online activities for teaching and assessing critical thinking—reflection, peer review, discussion, small group, and digital storytelling activities. For each type, she described an example of an online exercise and a digital tool to help facilitate the process. Although Mansbach identified some stand-alone tools to support these activities, most

LMS solutions offer the same capabilities. For example, assess peer review activities through a discussion forum or assignment tools in your LMS or an integrated, third-party tool with peer review features, like Turnitin.com.

- *Use or create rubrics or rubric criteria that assess higher-order thinking*: The Association of American Colleges & Universities (AAC&U, n.d.; www.aacu.org/value-rubrics) developed "meta-rubrics" for a variety of assessment activities. Among the 16 instruments, they included rubrics to assess critical thinking, creative thinking, teamwork, problem-solving, civic engagement, intercultural competence, ethical reasoning, global learning, and integrative learning. Review these AAC&U rubrics in applicable areas to see if you can use or modify them, or even just a few criteria, for your assessments.

Authentic Assessment

Remember our earlier assertion that learning in online courses can take place anywhere? That students do not have to sit behind a monitor 100% of the time? Some forms of authentic assessment are perfect examples of what we mean. Observation logs and ePortfolios are possible strategies for this type of evaluation:

- *Observation logs*: For physical workforce skills courses (e.g., welding, aviation maintenance, fire technology), clinical practice courses (e.g., nursing, kinesiology), internships, or cocurricular work, even online students must perform specific tasks or work on-site with experienced professionals. As some online students live far away from their home campus, consider how to partner with professionals or higher education campuses in different locations so students do not have to travel far to demonstrate skills. In those cases, after the students have gained enough proficiency to be tested, provide any on-site professionals with an observation log template to complete and sign. The student can then submit the observation log as evidence that they have achieved specific outcomes for a course and/or program. In some cases, the students may be able to produce smartphone videos that you could review yourself to see if they performed a kinesthetic task correctly and generated the desired results.
- *ePortfolios*: Have students assemble examples of work they have done to demonstrate achieving outcomes. This collection of work is called an electronic portfolio, or ePortfolio, and taken as a whole can be very powerful. It doesn't get much more authentic than

asking students to produce or do something in anticipation of real-world work expectations. ePortfolio tools like Pathbrite (pathbrite .com) and Digication (www.digication.com/) allow students to share their work with you and their classmates for academic purposes, and again with career center advisers and prospective employers for career bridging purposes. First, students upload digital work products (e.g., an accounting ledger for a business-related internship), images of physical work products (e.g., a spliced cable for aviation electronics), videos of themselves performing specific skills (e.g., evaluating shoulder range of motion for physical therapy), or other types of evidence. Then, they write reflection statements to describe their experience, explain how they arrived at certain conclusions, discuss how each artifact ties to the course or program outcomes, or answer other prompts. Note that guiding students through the process of *collecting* their work, *selecting* artifacts to serve different purposes, *reflecting* on what each artifact means in a specific context, and *building* an ePortfolio requires planning and effort. We recommend checking to see if your campus has an ePortfolio initiative or program that can support you as you get started and reading books like *High-Impact ePortfolio Practice: A Catalyst for Student, Faculty, and Institutional Learning* by Bret Eynon and Laura Gambino (2017).

In addition to our observation log and ePortfolio ideas, look at Appendix A: Resources for Putting Difficult Topics Online to see if there are resources for your discipline. Some of those resources include ideas for assessing authentic activities.

TECHNIQUE: ASSESSING STUDENT LEARNING WITH ONE-MINUTE THREADS

The One-Minute Paper, a commonly used classroom assessment technique in face-to-face courses, is designed to prompt students to think about and answer a few questions about the class session in one minute (Major et al., 2016). Questions should help gauge students' learning or reactions. For example, after a classroom meeting, you might ask the following three questions:

1. Which concept from today's class is most clear, helpful, or meaningful?
2. What concept from today's class is still "muddy" or unclear?
3. Do you have any additional comments to share about today's class?

Student responses may be anonymous, or you may ask students to include their names on their answers and assign points for completing the activity. When you collect the One-Minute Papers, look for patterns or areas that are generally clear or unclear to students. You can address problem areas at the beginning of the next class meeting before introducing new material. Less common comments can be reviewed by posting additional resources, such as journal articles or links to websites that cover a problem area in more depth.

One-Minute Thread

Kevin Kelly developed the One-Minute Thread as an online version of the One-Minute Paper (K. Kelly, 2008a). Questions are similar to the face-to-face One-Minute Paper (e.g., "What concept from this module was most clear?" or "What concept from this mini-lecture is still unclear?"). In hybrid and traditional courses, One-Minute Threads support students who need a bit more time to formulate a response, including international students or students who need more processing time. For particularly challenging classes, all students may need time to review their notes from the face-to-face class, to translate any unfamiliar terms and ideas, and sometimes to discuss the concepts in small groups. The One-Minute Thread activity allows for this additional time. In online courses, One-Minute Threads help students feel supported and will enable you to respond to students' questions quickly and efficiently.

To use a One-Minute Thread in your course,

1. Determine two or three questions you want to pose to the class to assess students' learning or get their reactions to course content.
2. In your discussion forum, create a single thread or discussion topic for each of your questions. For example, if you were using the three questions outlined in the One-Minute Paper section, you would create three threads: one for the clearest point, one for the muddiest point, and one for an additional comment.
3. Adjust the forum settings to require students to reply to your prompts. For example, in Moodle, choose "Standard forum for general use" and "No discussions, but replies are allowed" as the forum settings. If your LMS or other discussion forum tool does not have this setting, write clear instructions for students to answer each of the three prompts rather than starting a new discussion thread as a means to ensure that the forum remains organized.
4. As the discussion will likely be asynchronous, set a deadline (e.g., 24 hours) for students to answer the questions. Select a deadline

that gives you enough time to respond to students before the next online class meeting or module deadline.

5. When assigning the One-Minute Thread, encourage students to provide short, concentrated answers rather than lengthy passages. If students are completing this activity for the first time, it is helpful to share examples. The following is an example from a biology student: "clear—understanding the basic structure of the cell and what keeps the cell alive," "unclear—I don't get the four phases of mitosis/cell division and if the phases are different for different kinds of cells," and "comment—please show more animations and pictures . . . they help a lot."

6. Once students have submitted their responses, reply to individual students' posts that are of particular importance, and encourage students to respond to one another.

7. Identify patterns regarding what is clear and unclear to students. Share a summative post that addresses problem areas by providing necessary clarifications and useful resources and describes any modifications you will make to course materials based on recommendations students offer.

TECHNIQUE: ASSESSING STUDENT LEARNING WITH EACH ONE TEACH ONE

Each One Teach One is an activity in which students teach a course concept to a classmate or back to the instructor. The strategy helps deepen their learning and understanding of the topic (Karpicke, 2016) and allows instructors to check for student understanding (Major et al., 2016). To use the Each One Teach One technique to check for student understanding, start by teaching a topic, then have students prepare to teach that concept back to you, and use the results to inform future instruction.

Before the Activity

1. Select a course topic that former students may have found difficult or that you think is particularly challenging.

2. Write a prompt that includes specific criteria or steps for what you would like students to teach.

3. Select, adapt, or create course materials, such as short videos, PowerPoint presentations, or articles that clearly present the topic. Identify short content segments—for example, a 5-minute segment of

a recorded lecture or screencast video or specific pages from a reading assignment—that students can easily review multiple times.

4. Develop a rubric with two to five criteria that allow you to check for student understanding. Criteria might include completeness ("explains each step in the process"), application ("demonstrates how to solve the provided practice problem"), or real-world application ("shares at least one example of how to apply the mini-lesson concept to a real-world scenario").

5. Develop written assignment guidelines, use a video-capture program, or plan for a live videoconference to establish clear directions for students. Be specific about what students should produce, in what format they should provide it (e.g., written, infographic, video, screencast), and where they should post or submit it. Figure 3.2.1. gives an example of Each One Teach One activity instructions.

During the Activity

1. Teach the topic, synchronously or asynchronously, with your selected course materials.

2. Provide students with the assignment guidelines, including the prompt, helpful resources, and the assessment rubric, along with a deadline for completion.

3. Encourage students to submit any questions they have in a question-and-answer forum accessible to the full class and promptly respond to their questions.

4. Once students have submitted their lessons, use the rubric to provide specific feedback, and recommend any adjustments.

After the Activity

1. Review the collective results from your students' submissions. Make a note of common misconceptions, errors, and knowledge gaps.

2. Compile a list of additional resources you will share with students to help them fill the knowledge gaps you identified.

3. Prepare a summary of your findings as a screencast or written description and share it in a course announcement. Your summary should address the following: How did the class perform as a whole? What did students teach well in their lessons? What gave students difficulty? What will you do to help students fill knowledge gaps or correct errors? Share the additional resources as part of this announcement.

Figure 3.2.1. Example of Each One Teach One activity instructions.

During our class meeting today, we discussed how to write slope-intercept equations. Now it's your turn to be the teacher! In this Each One Teach One activity, you will do the following:

1. Design a mini-lesson to teach me how to write a slope-intercept equation using the sample problem in the following prompt. Be sure to

   a. use your own words;
   b. provide a brief but complete overview of writing slope-intercept equations, covering the points listed in the previous prompt; and
   c. explain how to answer the example problem provided.

2. Use VoiceThread.com to create the presentation (must be less than 5 minutes).
3. Share a post in the discussion forum that uses your topic as the title and links to your VoiceThread presentation.
4. Submit your post by Wednesday at 11:55 p.m.
5. On Friday, review my feedback via the rubric (see as follows) and written comments. I will also share a course announcement with additional feedback and resources.

In general, the slope-intercept equation is written as $y = mx + b$. Using the following sample slope-intercept equation, you will teach me how to write a slope-intercept equation:

Sample slope-intercept equation

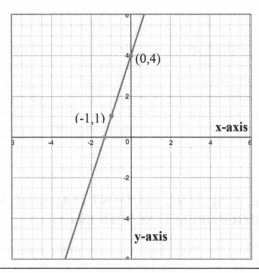

(Continues)

Figure 3.2.1. (*Continued*)

- First, teach me how to solve for b by finding the y-intercept of the line. Explain b as the point where the line crosses the y-axis.
- Next, using the two given points, teach me how to solve for m by calculating the change in y divided by the change in x. Explain the difference between positive and negative slope.
- Last, teach me how to write the new equation by substituting values for m and b.

Course materials for reference are short recorded mini-lesson from my presentation slides and the Khan Academy lesson on this topic (located at https://www.khanacademy.org/math/algebra/two-var-linear-equations).

Criteria for Success

The following rubric provides a range for students to gauge their level of achievement.

Slope-Intercept Rubric

	Exemplary	Proficient	Not Yet
Prepare viewer to complete a practice problem.	Student teaches the viewer how to complete the practice problem and explains each concept clearly.	Student teaches the viewer how to complete the practice problem but does not explain all of the concepts clearly.	Student does not explain any concepts clearly and does not teach the viewer how to complete the practice problem.
Use your own words to teach.	Student explains everything without copying language from the resources provided.	Student explains most concepts using original language but copies some of the resources provided.	Language from the resources provided outweighs any original student explanations.

TECHNIQUE: ASSESSING STUDENT LEARNING WITH A MISCONCEPTION/PRECONCEPTION CHECK

Misconception/Preconception Check is a classroom assessment technique designed to identify inaccurate knowledge or erroneous beliefs that act as obstacles to student learning (Angelo & Cross, 1993). In classroom settings, teachers can review misconceptions and preconceptions as they go through results from quizzes or clicker activities. For hybrid and online classes, there is an inherent challenge with the immediacy of addressing incorrect or incomplete understandings, which are diminished by the asynchronous flow of learning activities. To overcome this challenge, use any of the following techniques:

Identify potential misconceptions in advance by (a) looking through historical data, such as quiz results from previous semesters, and (b) conducting an internet search for common misconceptions related to a course topic. You may also talk to colleagues who have taught the same course.

As an example of reviewing historical data, use LMS tools to conduct an item analysis for each quiz question, or download quiz and survey results as a spreadsheet. Tables 3.2.1 and 3.2.2 show Moodle's Item Analysis (Quiz > Results > Statistics) results for multiple-choice quiz questions. Table 3.2.1 shows a multiple-choice (single answer) question about effective search strategies. More than one third of the students selected the same incorrect answer, confirming a known misconception. Table 3.2.2 shows a multiple-answer question about verifying a web page author's qualifications. Half of the students selected the same incorrect answer option, signifying a potential misconception.

TABLE 3.2.1

Analysis of Responses for a Multiple-Choice (Single Answer)
Quiz Question

Question: Which of the following describes an effective search strategy on its own?

Attempts: 44

Response	Partial Credit	Count	Frequency
Ask someone who already completed the research assignment for the resources they used (Incorrect)	0.00%	0	0.00%
Evaluate search results from any tool against a checklist of criteria for website evaluation (Correct)	100.00%	27	61.36%
Perform a normal Google search and use the results ranked as most relevant (Incorrect)	0.00%	16	36.36%
Search relevant hashtags on Twitter to find information about a topic (Incorrect)	0.00%	1	2.27%

TABLE 3.2.2

Analysis of Responses for a Multiple-Answer Quiz Question

Question: When evaluating websites for accuracy, how do you determine if a web page author is qualified to publish information about a topic?

Attempts: 44

Part of Question	Response	Partial Credit	Count	Frequency
359153	Check the "about us" or "philosophy" links (Correct)	33.33%	37	84.09%
359154	Find and research the publisher if there is no individual author (Correct)	33.33%	36	81.82%
359155	Check the author's credentials (Correct)	33.33%	43	97.73%
359156	See if you recognize the author's name (Incorrect)	–33.33%	4	9.09%
359157	If there is no author listed, then move on (Incorrect)	–33.33%	5	11.36%
359158	If the site looks like a professional web designer built it, then the information is probably reliable (Incorrect)	–33.33%	22	50.00%

Prepare students to think critically about what they know by (a) modeling how to debunk common misconceptions, or (b) highlighting common misconceptions and providing additional information to guide students as they review their work. As an example of modeling how to debunk a common misconception, create a "think aloud" screencast recording in which you verbalize your thought process as you review possible answers to a quiz question. Identify common misperceptions and other erroneous thinking that might lead a person astray to show students it is important to consider different perspectives. Figure 3.2.2 is an example of how you might question why answers on a particular quiz or survey are correct or incorrect.

As an example of guiding students as they review their work, use the LMS quiz tool settings to allow students to see their answers and your feedback but not the correct answers when you create a quiz. For questions that test for preconceptions or misconceptions, enter automated feedback for each possible response—both correct and incorrect. Provide some

Figure 3.2.2. Example script for a "think aloud" screencast for a class on human biology.

Hi, everyone! Let's take a look at the following question about foods that affect human growth:

Question: Coffee stunts human growth. True or false?

To begin, I ask myself, "Does this answer represent a fact or an opinion? How can I tell?" While this is something that many of us have heard, for it to be a fact, we have to be able to prove it. Mark Pendergast (2010) found that "no one has ever turned up evidence that drinking coffee has any effect on how much children grow" (as cited in Stromberg, 2013, para. 4).

Next, I ask myself, "What is an alternative way to think about this question, and why might an alternative view be incorrect?" Even though no one has turned up any evidence, that doesn't mean we can assume coffee does not affect growth. There is little research that examines the issue.

Last, I ask myself, "What evidence, if any, supports this answer?" Only one study looked at the impact of caffeine intake in adolescents over 6 years. That study found that caffeine had no impact on bone density or bone gain so, for now, we have to say this statement is false due to a lack of contrary evidence.

rhetorical thought prompts to support reflection. At a minimum, direct students to specific pages or resources to review the material. Figure 3.2.3 gives an example of potential feedback for responses to a question about beginning sentences with different parts of speech.

Figure 3.2.3. Example feedback for correct and incorrect question responses.

Question type: Multiple choice
Question text: Which of the following parts of speech are not acceptable to begin a sentence?

Choice 1: You must never begin a sentence with a gerund, such as "complaining" or "lying." (Incorrect)
Feedback: It is acceptable to start a sentence with a gerund, such as when used as a subject of a verb ("Complaining about the heat won't make it cooler."). Before you move on, take a moment to reflect: Why did you choose this answer? What led you to adopt this belief? Once you have reflected on your response, check *The Chicago Manual of Style* to learn more about acceptable ways to begin a sentence with a gerund.

(*Continues*)

Figure 3.2.3. (*Continued*)

Choice 2: You must never begin a sentence with a verb, such as "ask" or "give." (Incorrect)

Feedback: It is acceptable to start a sentence with a verb, such as when used as to express commands ("Give me a break."). Before you move on, take a moment to reflect: Why did you choose this answer? What led you to adopt this belief? Once you have reflected on your response, check *The Chicago Manual of Style* to learn more about acceptable ways to begin a sentence with a verb, such as to express commands (imperative mood).

Choice 3: You must never begin a sentence with a conjunction, such as "but" or "and." (Incorrect)

Feedback: This is a common misconception about grammar. It is acceptable to begin a sentence with a conjunction ("And God said, Let there be light."). Before you move on, take a moment to reflect: Why did you choose this answer? What led you to adopt this belief? Once you have reflected on your response, check *The Chicago Manual of Style* to learn more about acceptable ways to begin a sentence with a conjunction.

Choice 4: All of the previously listed parts of speech are acceptable to begin a sentence. (Correct)

Feedback: Well done! You avoided a common misconception about grammar. If you did not guess, what led you to this conclusion? Check *The Chicago Manual of Style* to learn more about acceptable ways to begin a sentence with a gerund, a verb, or a conjunction.

Include students directly in the analytical process by (a) asking students to rate their confidence in their quiz answers or (b) engaging students in an analytical review. As an example of asking students to rate their confidence in their quiz answers, devote specific questions to conduct a misconception check with your students. Figure 3.2.4 offers an example question to assess a common misconception about what causes the Earth's seasons.

Figure 3.2.4. Example question for a Misconception/Preconception check.

Question text: The location of the Earth in its orbit around the sun determines the season—spring, summer, fall, or winter.

    a) I'm certain this is true.
    b) I'm pretty sure this is true.
    c) I have no idea if this is true or false.
    d) I'm pretty sure this is false.
    e) I'm certain this is false.

Figure 3.2.5. Example discussion prompt for a Misconception/ Preconception Check.

On our quiz this week, one question stated: "The location of the Earth in its orbit around the sun determines the season—spring, summer, fall, or winter."

- Roughly half of the class answered that they were certain or pretty sure this is true.
- Roughly one quarter of the class had no idea if it is true or false.
- Roughly one quarter of the class answered that they were certain or pretty sure this is false.

Before we look at the correct answer, let's discuss how you arrived at your conclusions. How did you arrive at your answer? What evidence do you have to support it?

As an example of engaging students in analysis, use online tools— an asynchronous forum or synchronous videoconference—to conduct a virtual quiz review. Before providing the correct or incorrect answers, ask students to question or support their responses. Figure 3.2.5 provides an example discussion prompt.

NEXT STEPS

In this chapter, you reviewed a range of strategies and tools that give students multiple opportunities to show what they know, that support authentic and/or higher-level thinking activities, and that make our assessment feedback more personal while saving time. We also provided specific examples of some online assessment techniques. As you apply information learned in this chapter, ask yourself the following questions:

- Have you checked the overall assessment approach in your course for authenticity, validity, variety, and frequency?
- How can you apply UDL and design for learning equity strategies to how you assess online learners?
- Are you asking students to demonstrate higher-order thinking?
- How are you supporting students who do not live near your campus, but who need to demonstrate proficiency performing certain skills or tasks?

CHAPTER SUMMARY

Assessing student learning is a critical task for all teachers, regardless of the course delivery method. Assessment can be either formative or summative, depending on the purpose of the assessment. Assessments, particularly summative assessments, should be authentic, valid, varied, and frequent. This is also an important area to consider UDL, learning equity, and human connectedness, as assessment is such an essential aspect of the educational experience. It is often said that we measure what we feel is important, and if equity, inclusion, and connectedness are important, these components need to be part of any assessment plan. Included in this chapter are just a few of the dozens and dozens of online teaching techniques designed to assess student learning. Internet searches of "classroom assessment techniques" will reveal many strategies that may be adapted relatively easily to the online environment.

Reflection and Discussion Questions

1. Identify at least one assignment in your course that allows for authentic assessment. Explain the learning outcome and the assessment measures and why both this assessment and the outcome are important aspects of your course.

2. Describe some of the variety among students you have seen in your courses in the past. Identifying and discussing a variety of students' circumstances and backgrounds is not designed to pity any student or group of students or to identify who is better than whom. This exercise is to help us recognize that students have different preparations and experiences, and for all students to be successful, we must recognize these differences.

3. What types of feedback do you typically give on examinations, papers, and assignments? Describe ways you have developed to allow for personalized feedback without having the process take an excessive amount of time to complete.

4. Select one of the online teaching techniques described in this chapter that you have not used previously. Adapt the technique to your course. Describe how the technique was adapted and why. Explain how it may be modified even further in a future course.

APPENDIX A

RESOURCES FOR PUTTING DIFFICULT TOPICS ONLINE

Arts

Music

- Christopher Bill's (n.d.) Guide to Remote Music Education—list of software, apps, and resources for music educators: https://docs .google.com/document/d/1SoERjaLMA1Tro1FTf5i8iLckaLo3bL8X uugr7el77Iw/
- Colloquium Listings (n.d.)—Music Scholarship at a Distance—virtual colloquium for music scholars: https://musicscholarshipatadistance .com/?fbclid=IwAR0KUz7mDFy6q63Ge_y2w_RLz-OGv4x2bTbcN 7x1M3on0YLvyDT5wOsCL2s
- Royal Academy of Music, Denmark (2020)—Zoom in Music Mode—how to adapt Zoom settings for music rehearsals and instruction: https://www.youtube.com/watch?v=50NoWIiYECA&feature
- Texas Tech University (2020) School of Music—Teaching Music Courses & Lessons (Online)—strategies and technologies to support disrupted music teaching: https://www.depts.ttu.edu/ tlpdc/Teaching_Music_Courses_Lessons.php
- Trinity University (n.d.)—Collaborative for Learning and Teaching—online teaching resources for specific approaches/disciplines (includes music): https://sites.google.com/trinity.edu/keepteaching/ teaching-guide/specific-approachesdisciplines

Dance
- Dance Studies Association (2020)—Resources for Moving Dance-Based Pedagogy Online: https://dancestudiesassociation.org/news/2020/resources-for-moving-dance-based-pedagogy-online

Art (Painting, Sculpture)
- Crowdsourced document—Teaching Ceramics Online—Ideas for Teaching Clay Online (n.d.): https://docs.google.com/document/d/1oL9zp1UlMItlUgWq5earU_UAML9-sYhMQwyobxfMCUI/
- Facebook group—Online Art & Design Studio Instruction in the Age of "Social Distancing" (2020)—online resource/discussion page for faculty of studio based art and design instruction to share strategies, pedagogy, and support for instruction in the age of "Social Distancing": https://www.facebook.com/groups/2872732516116624
- The Museum Computer Network—The Ultimate Guide to Virtual Museum Resources, E-Learning, and Online Collections (Byrd-McDevitt, 2020)—list of museum and museum-adjacent online resources and collections: https://mcn.edu/a-guide-to-virtual-museum-resources/
- University of North Carolina—Art & Art History (n.d.)—Remote Teaching Resources for Studio Art and Art History—remote teaching tips and online resources: https://art.unc.edu/home/remote-teaching-resources-for-studio-art-and-art-history/

Media Production
- University Film and Video Association—crowdsourced list of resources for remote teaching of practical media production courses (Proctor, n.d.): https://docs.google.com/document/d/115zQ_t-mS-iuhJj6GKiK9vHkteIwWo6yAw2Rh8SJm1c/

Physical Education

Free physical education lessons (many of these resources released new lessons for free due to the COVID-19 pandemic)

- OPEN: Online Physical Education Network (n.d.)—website with curriculum resources, professional development and media for teaching physical education: https://openphysed.org/
- PE Central (n.d.)—website with lessons, assessments, best practices, professional development, discussion boards, classroom management strategies and media for teaching physical education: https://www.pecentral.org/

- The PE Geek (n.d.)—website with a blog, podcast, and community space for teaching physical education: https://thepegeek.com/
- SHAPE America: Society of Health and Physical Educators. (n.d.)— website with professional development, standards and guidelines, events and conferences, and resources and publications for teaching physical education (e.g., Shape America guidance for K–12 Online Physical Education): www.shapeamerica.org

Science, Technology, Engineering, Mathematics

- Professional and Organizational Development (POD) Network (crowdsourced list)—Online Resources for Science Labs (n.d.)— Remote Teaching: https://docs.google.com/spreadsheets/d/18iVSIe OqKjj58xcR8dYJS5rYvzZ4X1UGLWhl3brRzCM/

Career and Technical Education

- California Virtual Campus—Online Education Initiative (2019)— Improving Online CTE Pathways Grant Program—70 different grant career and technical education (CTE) project summaries describing how and why are putting the collective schools courses online: https:// cvc.edu/pathwaysgrant/grant-summaries/

Clinical Practice

- C. Bavitz (2020) (Harvard University)—Clinical Teaching and Practice—Working From Home—presentation slides describing remote teaching practices for clinical disciplines: https://hls .harvard.edu/content/uploads/2020/03/Work-from-Home-Clinics-03-27-2020-Bavitz.pdf

Nursing

- Clinical Simulation in Nursing (INACSL Standards Committee, 2016): INACSL Standards of Best Practice—Simulation Debriefing: https://www.nursingsimulation.org/article/S1876-1399%2816% 2930129-3/fulltext
- Montgomery College (2020)—Nursing Simulation Scenario Library—resource for nursing educators in all settings and made possible by the generosity of the Healthcare Initiative Foundation: https://www.montgomerycollege.edu/academics/departments/ nursing-tpss/nursing-simulation-scenario-library.html

- National Council on State Boards of Nursing (2015)—Nursing Regulation Recommendations for Distance Education in Prelicensure Nursing Programs: https://www.ncsbn.org/15_DLC_White_Paper.pdf

Community Service-Learning

- Minnesota Campus Compact—Center for Digital Civic Engagement Service-Learning in Online Courses (n.d.)—articles and other resources related to service-learning in online environments: https://cdce.wordpress.com/service-learning-in-online-courses/

Journal Articles Regarding Service-Learning Online

- anak, M. et al. (2018). Improving students' learning outcomes through e-service learning based on authentic learning strategy. *Innovative Teaching and Learning Journal, 2*(1), 8–16. http://161.139.21.34/itlj/index.php/itlj/article/view/13
- Bharath, D. (2020). Using eservice-learning to practice technical writing skills for emerging nonprofit professionals. *Journal of Nonprofit Education and Leadership, 10*(1), 62–81. https://js.sagamorepub.com/jnel/article/view/9420
- Hervani, A. A. et al. (2015). Service learning projects in online courses: Delivery strategies. *Journal of Learning in Higher Education, 11*(1), 35–41. https://files.eric.ed.gov/fulltext/EJ1141925.pdf
- Waldner L. S. et al. (2012). E-service-learning: The evolution of service-learning to engage a growing online population. *Journal of Higher Education Outreach and Engagement, 16*(2), 123–150. https://d3tb2mkdocc4em.cloudfront.net/oce/wp-content/uploads/sites/134/2014/08/E-Service-Learning-The-Evolution-of-Service-Learning-to-Engage-a-Growing-Online-Student-Population.pdf
- Waldner, L. et al. (2010). Extreme e-service learning (XE-SL): E-service learning in the 100% online course. *MERLOT Journal of Online Learning and Teaching, 6*(4), 839–851. https://jolt.merlot.org/vol6no4/waldner_1210.pdf

APPENDIX B

TECHNOLOGIES FOR ONLINE TEACHING AND LEARNING

Technology (in alphabetical order)	Technology Category	Technology Link	Technology Found in Chapters
Acrobat Pro	Document editing tool	https://acrobat.adobe.com/	1.6
Acrobat Reader	Document review tool	https://get.adobe.com/reader	1.4
Ally	Accessibility tool to check files shared in a learning management system	https://ally.ac	1.6
Animoto	Video creation tool	https://animoto.com	2.2
Big Blue Button	Video conferencing	https://bigbluebutton.org	1.4
Blackboard	Learning management system	https://blackboard.com	1.4, 1.6, 2.3, 2.4
Blend Images	Image gallery	https://blendimages.com	1.4
Brightspace (D2L)	Learning management system	https://d2l.com	1.6, 2.3, 2.4
Bubbl.us	Concept mapping tool	https://bubbl.us	1.4
Burst	Image gallery	https://burst.shopify.com	2.1
Camtasia	Video editing tool	https://www.techsmith.com/video-editor.html	1.4, 2.2

209

Canva	Infographic design and creation tool	https://www.canva.com/create/infographics/	2.1
Canvas	Learning management system	https://instructure.com	1.4, 1.6, 2.3, 2.4
Captivate	eLearning authoring tool	https://www.adobe.com/products/captivate.html	1.4
Coach's Eye	Video feedback tool	https://coachseye.com	2.2
Collaborate	Video conferencing	https://www.blackboard.com/teaching-learning/collaboration-web-conferencing/blackboard-collaborate	1.4
Contrast Checker	Accessibility tool to check webpage contrast	https://webaim.org/resources/contrastchecker/	1.6
Coursera	Online course provider	https://coursera.org	1.4, 2.4
Creative Commons Search	Image gallery search tool	https://search.creativecommons.org	1.4
Digication	ePortfolio tool	https://digication.com	3.2
Echo360	Screencast recording / lecture capture tool	https://echo360.com/	1.4
EdPuzzle	Video augmentation tool	https://edpuzzle.com	1.4, 2.2
EdX	Online course provider	https://edx.org	1.4
Facebook	Social networking site	https://facebook.com	2.2
FlipGrid	Video communication tool	https://flipgrid.com	1.6, 2.2
Google Docs	Desktop productivity tool	https://docs.google.com	3.1
Grackle	Accessibility tool for Google suite	https://www.grackledocs.com/	1.6
Ilos	Video communication tool	https://www.ilosvideos.com/	1.4
Infogram	Infographic design and creation tool	http://infogr.am	1.4
Jing	Screencast recording tool	https://www.techsmith.com/jing-tool.html	2.2

Khan Academy	Online course provider	https://khanacademy.org	1.4, 3.2
Lean In	Images gallery	http://leanin.org/getty	1.4
LinkedIn Learning	Online course provider	https://www.linkedin.com/learning	1.4
Loom	Video communication tool	https://www.useloom.com/	1.4
Microsoft Office	Desktop production tools	https://office.com	1.6
MindMeister	Concept mapping tool	https://www.mindmeister.com	1.4
Mindmup	Concept mapping tool	https://www.mindmup.com	1.4
Moodle	Learning management system	https://moodle.org	1.4, 1.6, 2.2, 2.3, 2.4, 3.2
Nappy	Image gallery	https://www.nappy.co	1.4
OER Commons	Open educational resources platform	https://oercommons.org	1.4
Panopto	Screencast recording / lecture capture tool	https://www.panopto.com	1.4
Pathbrite	ePortfolio tool	https://pathbrite.com	3.2
PDF Accessibility Checker (PAC 3)	Accessibility tool for PDF files	http://www.access-for-all.ch/en/pdf-lab/pdf-accessibility-checker-pac.html	1.6
Piktochart	Infographic design and creation tool	http://piktochart.com/	1.4
Pixabay	Image gallery	https://pixabay.com	1.4
Prezi	Interactive presentation tool	https://prezi.com	1.4
Pronto	Student engagement tools (video, chat)	https://pronto.io	2.2
Qualtrics	Online survey tool	https://www.qualtrics.com	3.1
Relay	Screencast recording / lecture capture tool	https://www.techsmith.com/lecture-capture.html	1.4, 2.2
Representation Matters	Images gallery	http://representationmatters.me	1.4
Screencast-o-matic	Screencast recording tool	https://screencast-o-matic.com/	1.4, 2.2, 2.4

Skills Commons	Open educational resources platform	https://skillscommons.org	1.4
Skype	Video conferencing	https://www.skype.com/en	1.6
SoftChalk	eLearning authoring tool	https://softchalk.com	1.4
SurveyMonkey	Online survey tool	http://surveymonkey.com	3.1
TooFast	Online survey tool	http://toofast.ca	3.1
Turnitin	Plagiarism detection tool	https://turnitin.com	3.2
Twitter	Microblogging platform	https://twitter.com	2.2, 3.1
Udemy	Online course provider	https://www.udemy.com	2.4
Unsplash	Image gallery	https://unsplash.com	1.4
Venngage	Infographic design and creation tool	http://venngage.com/	1.4
Vimeo	Video hosting platform	https://vimeo.com	1.4
VoiceThread	Interactive presentation tool	https://voicethread.com	1.4, 1.6, 2.2, 3.2
Women of Color in Tech	Image gallery	https://www.flickr.com/photos/wocintechchat/	2.1
Words to Time Calculator	Conversion tool	http://www.edgestudio.com/production/words-to-time-calculator	2.2
YouTube	Video hosting platform	https://youtube.com	1.4, 1.6
Zoom	Video conferencing	https://zoom.us	1.4, 1.6

APPENDIX C

URL LIST

The following alphabetical URL list (by chapter) contains links to helpful online resources noted throughout the book. An up-to-date list of clickable links can be found at the book's companion site (www.ExcellentTeacher Series.com/AdvancingOnlineTeaching).

Links From Chapter 1.1

Link	Link Source	Link URL
About UDL	Center for Applied Special Technology (CAST)	http://cast.org/our-work/about-udl.html
Blackboard Exemplary Course Program Rubric	Blackboard	https://www.blackboard.com/sites/default/files/2020-02/2020_Blackboard ExemplaryRubric_Vert5.pdf
California State University— Quality Learning and Teaching (QLT) Rubric	California State University system	http://courseredesign.csuprojects.org/wp/quality assurance/qlt-informal-review/
Design for Learning Equity Framework	Design for Learning Equity	http://learningequity.org
Illinois Online Network— Quality Online Course Initiative Rubric	Illinois Online Network	https://www.uis.edu/ion/resources/qoci/
Online Education Initiative— Course Design Rubric	California Virtual Campus— Online Education Initiative	https://onlinenetworkof educators.org/wp-content/uploads/2020/06/CVC_OEI_Course_Design_Rubric_rev_April_2020.pdf
Open SUNY Course Quality Review (OSCQR) Rubric	State University of New York	https://oscqr.suny.edu/get-oscqr/

Quality Matters (QM) Higher Ed Course Design Rubric	Quality Matters	https://www.qualitymatters.org/qa-resources/rubric-standards/higher-ed-rubric
UDL Universe	UDL Universe	http://www.udluniverse.com
UW–La Crosse Online Course Evaluation Guidelines	University of Wisconsin–La Crosse	https://www.uwlax.edu/globalassets/offices-services/catl/guidelines.pdf

Link From Chapter 1.2

Link	Link Source	Link URL
Transparent Assignment Template (PDF)	Transparency in Learning and Teaching (TILT) Higher Ed	https://tilthighered.com/assets/pdffiles/Transparent%20Assignment%20Template.pdf

Links From Chapter 1.3

Link	Link Source	Link URL
Humanizing Online Learning	Michelle Pacansky-Brock	https://brocansky.com/humanizing
Transparency in Learning and Teaching (TILT) Project	Transparency in Learning and Teaching (TILT) Higher Ed	https://tilthighered.com

Links From Chapter 1.4

Link	Link Source	Link URL
Blackboard Collaborate	Blackboard	https://www.blackboard.com/online-collaborative-learning/blackboard-collaborate.html
Blend image gallery	Blend	https://www.blendimages.com/
Bubbl.us website	Bubbl.us	https://bubbl.us/
Canva infographic tool	Canva	https://www.canva.com/create/infographics/
Canvas Guide—How Do I Record a Conference?	Instructure	https://guides.instructure.com/m/4152/l/117864-how-do-i-record-a-conference
The Community College Consortium for Open Educational Resources website	The Community College Consortium for Open Educational Resources	https://www.cccoer.org/
Copyright Basics	University of San Diego	https://www.sandiego.edu/legal/resources/copyright.php
Copyright Clearance Center website	Copyright Clearance Center	https://www.copyright.com/
Coursera website	Coursera	https://www.coursera.org/

Creative Commons Licensing Types	Creative Commons	https://creativecommons.org/share-your-work/licensing-types-examples/
Creative Commons Search	Creative Commons	https://search.creative commons.org
Download Adobe Reader	Adobe	https://get.adobe.com/reader/
Echo360 website	Echo 360	https://echo360.com/
EdX website	EdX	https://www.edx.org/
Guide to Copyright and Fair Use	Education World	https://www.educationworld.com/a_curr/curr280.shtml
Ilos website	Ilos	https://www.ilosvideos.com/
Infogram website	Infogram	http://infogr.am/
Khan Academy website	Khan Academy	https://khanacademy.org
Lean In image gallery	Getty Images	http://leanin.org/getty/
LinkedIn Learning (formerly Lynda.com)	LinkedIn	https://www.linkedin.com/learning
Loom—Education Use Cases	Loom	https://www.useloom.com/use-cases#education
Loom website	Loom	https://www.useloom.com/
MERLOT website	MERLOT	https://www.merlot.org
MindMeister website	MindMeister	https://www.mindmeister.com/
Mindmup website	Mindmup	https://www.mindmup.com/
OER Commons website	OER Commons	https://www.oercommons.org/
Open Culture website	Open Culture	https://www.openculture.com/
Open Textbook Initiative	American Institute of Mathematics	https://aimath.org/textbooks/
Open Textbook Library	University of Minnesota	https://open.umn.edu/opentextbooks/
Open Textbooks	Open SUNY	https://textbooks.opensuny.org/
Open Textbooks	Oregon State University	http://open.oregonstate.edu/textbooks/
Open Textbooks Hub	OER Commons	https://www.oercommons.org/hubs/open-textbooks
Panopto website	Panopto	https://www.panopto.com
Piktochart website	Piktochart	http://piktochart.com/
Pixabay website	Pixabay	https://pixabay.com
Prezi website	Prezi	https://prezi.com

Representation Matters image gallery	Representation Matters	http://representationmatters.me/
Rhode Island Open Textbook Initiative	State of Rhode Island	http://www.innovate.ri.gov/opentextbook
Screencast-o-matic website	Screencast-o-matic	https://screencast-o-matic.com/
Skills Commons website	Skills Commons	https://www.skillscommons.org/
Softchalk website	Softchalk	https://softchalk.com
The TEACH Act	Copyright Clearance Center	https:// www.copyright.com/wp-content/uploads/2015/04/CR-Teach-Act.pdf
Teach With Wikipedia program	Wiki Education	https://wikiedu.org/teach-with-wikipedia/
TechSmith Camtasia video editor	TechSmith	https://www.techsmith.com/video-editor.html
TechSmith Relay lecture capture	TechSmith	https://www.techsmith.com/lecture-capture.html
UDL Principle—Multiple Means of Representation	Center for Applied Special Technology (CAST)	http://udlguidelines.cast.org/representation
UDL Universe—Visually Enhanced Syllabi	UDL Universe	https://enact.sonoma.edu/c.php?g=789377&p=5650618
Unsplash website	Unsplash	https://unsplash.com
Venngage website	Venngage	https://venngage.com/
VoiceThread website	VoiceThread	https://voicethread.com
YouTube—Automatic Captioning	YouTube	https://support.google.com/youtube/answer/6373554
Zoom website	Zoom	https://zoom.us/

Links From Chapter 1.5

No links

Links From Chapter 1.6

Link	Link Source	Link URL
30 Tools to Test Higher Education Website Accessibility	UX Design	https://uxdesign.cc/28-tools-to-test-higher-education-website-accessibility-a59be955b398
Access by Design: Accessible Instructional Materials Checklist for Faculty	Cal Poly San Luis Obispo	https://accessibility.calpoly.edu/content/instmaterials/fac_checklist
Accessible Digital Materials	Northern Illinois University	https://www.niu.edu/ethics-compliance/technology-accessibility/course-materials/index.shtml
Adobe Acrobat Accessibility Checker (PDF)	Adobe	https://www.adobe.com/content/dam/acom/en/accessibility/products/acrobat/pdfs/acrobat-xi-accessibility-checker.pdf
Adobe Touch Up Reading Order tool	Adobe	https://helpx.adobe.com/acrobat/using/touch-reading-order-tool-pdfs.html
Ally Accessibility tool	Blackboard	https://ally.ac
Article—ADA Compliance for Online Course Design	Educause Review	https://er.educause.edu/articles/2017/1/ada-compliance-for-online-course-design
Canvas Guide—How Do I Embed an Image in a Discussion Reply as a Student?	Instructure	https://community.canvaslms.com/docs/DOC-10700-4212190965
Canvas Guide—Once I Publish a Quiz, How Can I Give My Students Extra Attempts?	Instructure	https://community.canvaslms.com/docs/DOC-13076-415250753
Canvas Guide—Once I Publish a Timed Quiz, How Can I Give My Students Extra Time?	Instructure	https://community.canvaslms.com/docs/DOC-13053-4152276279
Canvas Guide—Rich Content Editor	Instructure	https://community.canvaslms.com/docs/DOC-12855-415241511
Canvas Tools Accessibility	California Virtual Campus—Online Education Initiative	https://ccconlineed.instructure.com/courses/297/pages/canvas-tools-accessibility
Characteristics of Effective Online Assignments	Brown University	https://www.brown.edu/sheridan/teaching-learning-resources/teaching-resources/course-design/enhancing-student-learning-technology/effective-online-assignments

Color Contrast Checker tool	WebAIM	https://webaim.org/resources/contrastchecker/
Create and verify PDF accessibility	Adobe	https://helpx.adobe.com/acrobat/using/create-verify-pdf-accessibility.html
Creating Accessible PDF Documents	San Francisco State University	http://its.sfsu.edu/guides/creating-accessible-pdf-documents-word-2013#use
Designating Table Headers in Microsoft Word	Penn State University	http://accessibility.psu.edu/microsoftoffice/microsofttableheaders/
FlipGrid and Accessibility	FlipGrid	https://help.flipgrid.com/hc/en-us/articles/115004848574-Flipgrid-and-Accessibility
Grackle accessibility checker for Google Suite tools	Grackle	https://www.grackledocs.com/
Guidelines for Adopting Publisher Content	Portland Community College	https://www.pcc.edu/instructional-support/accessibility/publishercontent/
Microsoft article—How to Use the Accessibility Checker	Microsoft	https://support.office.com/en-us/article/use-the-accessibility-checker-on-your-windows-desktop-to-find-accessibility-issues-a16f6de0-2f39-4a2b-8bd8-5ad801426c7f
Microsoft article—Add a Heading	Microsoft	https://support.office.com/en-us/article/add-a-heading-3eb8b917-56dc-4a17-891a-a026b2c790f2
Microsoft article—Add Alternative Text to a Shape, Picture, Chart, Table, SmartArt Graphic or Other Object	Microsoft	https://support.office.com/en-us/article/Add-alternative-text-to-a-shape-picture-chart-table-SmartArt-graphic-or-other-object-44989b2a-903c-4d9a-b742-6a75b451c669
Microsoft article—Create a Bulleted or Numbered List	Microsoft	https://support.office.com/en-us/article/Create-a-bulleted-or-numbered-list-9FF81241-58A8-4D88-8D8C-ACAB3006A23E
Microsoft article—Make Your Excel Spreadsheets Accessible	Microsoft	https://support.office.com/en-us/article/Make-your-Excel-spreadsheets-accessible-6cc05fc5-1314-48b5-8eb3-683e49b3e593

Microsoft article—Make your PowerPoint Presentations Accessible	Microsoft	https://support.office.com/en-us/article/Make-your-PowerPoint-presentations-accessible-6f7772b2-2f33-4bd2-8ca7-dae3b2b3ef25
Microsoft article—Make Your Word Documents Accessible	Microsoft	https://support.office.com/en-us/article/Make-your-Word-documents-accessible-d9bf3683-87ac-47ea-b91a-78dcacb3c66d
Microsoft article—Set the Reading Order on Each PowerPoint Slide	Microsoft	https://support.office.com/en-us/article/Make-your-Power-Point-presentations-accessible-6f7772b2-2f33-4bd2-8ca7-dae3b2b3ef25
National Center on Accessible Educational Materials	Center for Applied Special Technology (CAST)	http://aem.cast.org/
PDF Accessibility Checker tool (PAC 3)	Access for All	http://www.access-for-all.ch/en/pdf-lab/pdf-accessibility-checker-pac.html
Purdue Online Writing Lab—APA Formatting and Style Guide	Purdue University	https://owl.purdue.edu/owl/research_and_citation/apa_style/apa_formatting_and_style_guide/general_format.html
Section 508 Compliance Test Process for Microsoft Word Documents (PDF)	U.S. Department of Homeland Security	https://www.dhs.gov/sites/default/files/publications/DHS Section 508 MS Word Test Process.pdf
W3 Recommendation 1.4.3—Contrast (Minimum)	W3	https://www.w3.org/TR/2008/REC-WCAG20-20081211/#visual-audio-contrast-contrast
WebAIM Guide—Converting Documents to (Accessible) PDF	WebAIM	https://webaim.org/techniques/acrobat/converting
Writing descriptive links	Nielsen Norman Group	https://www.nngroup.com/articles/writing-links/
YouTube video—Adding an Image Into D2L	YouTube	https://www.youtube.com/watch?v=jPEUJ4SBWsE

Links From Chapter 2.1

Link	Link Source	Link URL
Article—How Do I Properly Cite Images in a Presentation or Publication?	University of Virginia	https://www.hsl.virginia.edu/services/howdoi/how-do-i-properly-cite-images-presentation-or-publication
Awareness Activities	Ed Change	http://www.edchange.org/multicultural/activityarch.html
Broward College—Online Library	Broward College	https://libguides.broward.edu/bconlinelibrary
Burst image gallery	Burst	https://burst.shopify.com
Canva website	Canva	https://canva.com
Coastline College—Online Library	Coastline College	https://www.coastline.edu/student-life/online-library/index.php
Developing and writing a diversity statement	Vanderbilt University Center for Teaching	https://cft.vanderbilt.edu/guides-sub-pages/developing-and-writing-a-diversity-statement/
Flickr image gallery—Women of Color in Tech	Women of Color in Tech	https://www.flickr.com/photos/wocintechchat/
How to Attribute Creative Commons Photos	Foter	http://foter.com/blog/how-to-attribute-creative-commons-photos/
Image Galleries That Address Image and Representation Bias (PDF)	Kevin Kelly	https://drive.google.com/open?id=123F5RnQ_vP_QD-NzoJAV-E0BlwadTvhWK
Lake Superior College Online Course Netiquette Guidelines	Lake Superior College	http://blogs.lsc.edu/expectations/netiquette-guidelines/
List of time management strategies	Western Governors University	https://www.wgu.edu/blog/time-management-strategies-online-college-students1810.html
Nappy image gallery	Nappy	https://www.nappy.co
Penn State—Online Learning Readiness survey	Penn State University	https://pennstate.qualtrics.com/jfe/form/SV_7QCNUPsyH9f012B
Pixabay website	Pixabay	https://pixabay.com
Purdue Online Writing Lab (OWL)—APA Style and Formatting Guide	Purdue University	https://owl.english.purdue.edu/owl/resource/560/10/
Rasmussen College—Online Library	Rasmussen College	https://guides.rasmussen.edu/library

Rochester Institute of Technology—Wallace Library—APA Citation Format	Rochester Institute of Technology	http://lgdata.s3-website-us-east-1.amazonaws.com/docs/1366/837696/apa6.pdf
Skyline College—Library Online Services	Skyline College	https://skylinecollege.edu/library/libraryinfo/onlineservices.php
Tri-County Community College—Library Resources for Online Students	Tri-County Community College	https://tricountycc.libguides.com/c.php?g=74586&p=1115199
Tutorial about online study skills and managing time	California Community College system	https://apps.3cmediasolutions.org/oei/modules/study-time/story/
Universal Design for Instruction Online Project	University of Connecticut	http://www.udi.uconn.edu/index.php?q=content/examples-udi-online-and-blended-courses
Unsplash website	Unsplash	https://unsplash.com
Wichita State University—Online Learning Readiness survey	Wichita State University	https://www.wichita.edu/services/mrc/elearning/online_orientation/online_self_assessment.php

Links From Chapter 2.2

Link	Link Source	Link URL
Coach's Eye website	TechSmith	https://coachseye.com
EdPuzzle	EdPuzzle	https://edpuzzle.com
Humanizing Online Learning	Michelle Pacansky-Brock	https://brocansky.com/humanizing
Jing website	TechSmith	https://www.techsmith.com/jing-tool.html
Pronto website	Pronto	http://pronto.io/education
Screencast-o-matic website	Screencast-o-matic	https://screencast-o-matic.com/
VoiceThread website	VoiceThread	https://voicethread.com
Words to time calculator	Edge Studio	http://www.edgestudio.com/production/words-to-time-calculator
YouTube video—A Vision of Students Today	Michael Wesch	https://www.youtube.com/watch?v=dGCJ46vyR9o

Links From Chapter 2.3

Link	Link Source	Link URL
ABCDE Method (for evaluating websites)	University of Hawaii – Hilo	https://hilo.hawaii.edu/library/evaluating-sources/abcde
Civil Politics website	Civil Politics	https://civilpolitics.org
Lake Superior College Online Course Netiquette Guidelines	Lake Superior College	http://blogs.lsc.edu/expectations/netiquette-guidelines/
List of fake news websites	Wikipedia	https://en.wikipedia.org/wiki/List_of_fake_news_websites

Links From Chapter 2.4

No links

Links From Chapter 3.1

Link	Link Source	Link URL
Online Equity Rubric	Peralta Community College District	https://web.peralta.edu/de/equity-initiative/equity/
Online Equity Training (Canvas course template)	Peralta Community College District	https://lor.instructure.com/resources/f35cd7a09da64112aff13a98b7ddf0cd
Qualtrics website	Qualtrics	https://www.qualtrics.com/
SurveyMonkey website	SurveyMonkey	http://surveymonkey.com
TooFast website	Mount Royal College	http://toofast.ca

Links From Chapter 3.2

Link	Link Source	Link URL
Digication	Digication	https://digication.com
The Education Alliance—Teaching Diverse Learners	Brown University	https://www.brown.edu/academics/education-alliance/teaching-diverse-learners/question-iv-0
Pathbrite	Pathbrite	https://pathbrite.com
VALUE Rubrics	Association of American Colleges & Universities	https://www.aacu.org/value-rubrics

REFERENCES

AbuSeileek, A. F. (2012). The effect of computer-assisted cooperative learning methods and group size on the EFL learners' achievement in communication skills. *Computers & Education, 58*(1), 231–239. https://doi.org/10.1016/j.compedu.2011.07.011

Accrediting Commission for Community and Junior Colleges. (2013, June). *Guide to evaluating distance education and correspondence education.* Author. https://accjc.org/wp-content/uploads/Guide-to-Evaluating-DE-and-CE_2013.pdf

Adobe. (n.d.). *Create and verify PDF accessibility.* helpx.adobe.com/acrobat/using/create-verify-pdf-accessibility.html

Adobe. (2012). *Using the Acrobat XI Pro accessibility checker.* www.adobe.com/content/dam/acom/en/accessibility/products/acrobat/pdfs/acrobat-xi-accessibility-checker.pdf

Adobe. (2020). *Reading order tool for PDFs (Acrobat Pro).* https://helpx.adobe.com/acrobat/using/touch-reading-order-tool-pdfs.html

Allen, I. E., & Seaman, J. (2011, November). *Going the distance: Online education in the United States 2011.* Babson Survey Research Group.

American Institute of Mathematics. (n.d.). *Open textbook initiative.* https://aimath.org/textbooks/

anak Marcus, V. B., Atan, N. A., Jumaat, N. F., Junaidi, J., & Said, M. N. H. M. (2018). Improving students' learning outcomes through e-service learning based on authentic learning strategy. *Innovative Teaching and Learning Journal, 2*(1), 8–16. http://161.139.21.34/itlj/index.php/itlj/article/view/13

Angelo, T. A., & Cross, K. P. (1993). *Classroom assessment techniques: A handbook for college teachers* (2nd ed.). Jossey-Bass.

Anglin, L., Anglin, K., Schumann, P. L., & Kaliski, J. A. (2008, January). Improving the efficiency and effectiveness of grading through the use of computer-assisted grading rubrics. *Decision Sciences Journal of Innovative Education, 6*(1), 51–73. http://dx.doi.org/10.1111/j.1540-4609.2007.00153.x

Association of American Colleges & Universities. (n.d.). *Value rubrics.* www.aacu.org/value-rubrics

Baker, R., Dee, T., Evans, B., & John, J. (2018). *Bias in online classes: Evidence from a field experiment* (CEPA Working Paper No. 18-03). http://cepa.stanford.edu/wp18-03

Barkley, E. F., & Major, C. H. (2016). *Learning assessment techniques: A handbook for college faculty.* Jossey-Bass.

Barnes, E., & LeDuc, E. (2018, May 9). Food scarcity on campus affects learning in the classroom. *The Scholarly Teacher*. https://www.scholarlyteacher.com/post/food-scarcity-affects-learning

Bavitz, C. (2020, March 27). *Clinical teaching and practice: Working from home* [Presentation slides]. https://hls.harvard.edu/content/uploads/2020/03/Work-from-Home-Clinics-03-27-2020-Bavitz.pdf

Bawa, P. (2016, January–March). Retention in online courses: Exploring issues and solutions—A literature review. *SAGE Open, 6*(1). https://doi.org/10.1177/2158244015621777

Beck, S. L. (2018). *Developing and writing a diversity statement.* Vanderbilt University Center for Teaching. https://cft.vanderbilt.edu/developing-and-writing-a-diversity-statement

Bender, T. (2005). Role playing in online education: A teaching tool to enhance student engagement and sustained learning. *Innovate, 1*(4). https://www.learntechlib.org/p/107276/

Benfield, G. (2002). *Designing and managing effective online discussions* [Briefing Papers Series]. Oxford University.

Bharath, D. (2020). Using eservice-learning to practice technical writing skills for emerging nonprofit professionals. *Journal of Nonprofit Education and Leadership, 10*(1), 62–81. https://js.sagamorepub.com/jnel/article/view/9420

Bill, C. (n.d.). *Christopher Bill guide to remote music education.* https://docs.google.com/document/d/1SoERjaLMA1Tro1FTf5i8iLckaLo3bL8Xuugr7el77Iw/

Blackboard. (n.d.). *Blackboard collaborate.* www.blackboard.com/online-collaborative-learning/blackboard-collaborate.html

Bloom, B. S. (1956).Taxonomy of educational objectives. *Handbook: The cognitive domain.* David McKay.

Bozarth, J., Chapman, D. D., & LaMonica, L. (2004). Preparing for distance learning: Designing an online student orientation course. *Journal of Educational Technology & Society, 7*(1), 87–106. www.jstor.org/stable/jeductechsoci.7.1.87

Brandon, A., & Nemeroff, A. (2016, October 26). *Creating inclusive courses with universal design.* https://sites.dartmouth.edu/edtech/2016/10/26/creating-inclusive-courses-with-universal-design/

Bregman, P. (2012, May 8). A super-efficient email process. *Harvard Business Review.* https://hbr.org/2012/05/a-super-efficient-email-proces.html

Brown University. (2020). *Characteristics of effective online assignments.* www.brown.edu/sheridan/teaching-learning-resources/teaching-resources/course-design/enhancing-student-learning-technology/effective-online-assignments

Brown University Education Alliance. (2020). *Question 4.* www.brown.edu/academics/education-alliance/teaching-diverse-learners/question-iv-0

Byrd-McDevitt, L. (2020, March 14). *The ultimate guide to virtual museum resources, e-learning, and online collections.* https://mcn.edu/a-guide-to-virtual-museum-resources/

Caldwell, B., Cooper, M., Reid, L. G., & Vanderheiden, G. (2008, December 11). *Web content accessibility guidelines (WCAG) 2.0.* https://www.w3.org/TR/2008/REC-WCAG20-20081211/#visual-audio-contrast-contrast

California Community Colleges. (n.d.). *Online study skills and managing time.* http://apps.3cmediasolutions.org/oei/modules/study-time/story/

California Community Colleges Chancellor's Office. (2013). *Distance education report (2013 Report).* Author.

California Community Colleges Chancellor's Office. (2018). *Distance education report (2017 Report).* https://www.cccco.edu/-/media/CCCCO-Website/About-Us/Reports/Files/2017-DE-Report-Final-ADA.pdf

California Virtual Campus—Online Education Initiative. (2019). *Improving online CTE Pathways Grant Program—grant summaries.* https://cvc.edu/pathwaysgrant/grant-summaries/

Camtasia. (n.d.). *Features.* https://www.techsmith.com/video-editor.html#Features

Cañas, A. J. (2003, July). *A summary of literature pertaining to the use of concept mapping techniques and technologies for education and performance support.* The Institute of Human and Machine Cognition. http://www.ihmc.us/users/acanas/Publications/ConceptMapLitReview/IHMC%20Literature%20Review%20on%20Concept%20Mapping.pdf

Canva. (2020). *Free infographic maker.* www.canva.com/create/infographics/

Canvas. (2020a). *How do I add and modify text in the Rich Content Editor as an instructor?* community.canvaslms.com/docs/DOC-12855-415241511

Canvas. (2020b). *How do I embed an image in a discussion reply as a student?* community.canvaslms.com/docs/DOC-10700-4212190965

Canvas Doc Team. (2020a, April 6). *Once I publish a timed quiz, how can I give my students extra time?* Canvas. https://community.canvaslms.com/docs/DOC-26214-4152276279

Canvas Doc Team. (2020b). *Once I publish a quiz, how can I give my students extra attempts?* Canvas. community.canvaslms.com/docs/DOC-13076-415250753

Canvas Guides. (n.d.). *How do I record a conference?* Canvas. https://guides.instructure.com/m/4152/l/117864-how-do-i-record-a-conference

Cardamone, C., & Lobel, L. (2016, March). Using citizen science to engage introductory students: From streams to the solar system. *Journal of Microbiology and Biology Education, 17*(1), 117–119. http://dx.doi.org/10.1128/jmbe.v17i1.1082

CAST. (n.d.a). *UDL and accessibility.* http://udloncampus.cast.org/page/udl_about#l1970371

CAST. (n.d.b). *About universal design for learning.* http://cast.org/our-work/about-udl.html

CAST. (2018a). *Universal design for learning guidelines version 2.2.* http://udlguidelines.cast.org/more/downloads

CAST. (2018b). *Build fluencies with graduated levels of support for practice and performance.* http://udlguidelines.cast.org/action-expression/expression-communication/fluencies-practice-performance

CAST. (2020). *The UDL guidelines.* udlguidelines.cast.org

CBS News. (2017, March 12). *CBS News poll: Majority of U.S. families touched by cancer.* https://www.cbsnews.com/news/cbs-news-poll-majority-of-us-families-touched-by-cancer/

Center for Urban Education. (n.d.). *Equity by design: Five principles.* University of Southern California. https://cue.usc.edu/equity-by-design-five-principles/

Chawla, K. (2015). *5 essential steps to building community for your online course.* EdSurge. https://www.edsurge.com/news/2015-06-24-5-essential-steps-to-building-community-for-your-online-course

Christie, B. (2019, July 30). *UDL-Universe home.* UDL-Universe. http://www.udluniverse.com

Cintrón, R., & Lang, J. R. (2012). Preparing students for online education: A case study of a readiness module. *Journal of Online Education.* http://www.nyu.edu/classes/keefer/waoe/cintronl.pdf

Claiborne, L., Morrell, J., Bandy, J., & Bruff, D. (n.d.). *Teaching outside the classroom.* Vanderbilt Center for Teaching. https://cft.vanderbilt.edu/guides-sub-pages/teaching-outside-the-classroom/

Clark, D. (2015). *Bloom's taxonomy of learning domains.* http://www.nwlink.com/~donclark/hrd/bloom.html#intro

Clemson University. (2016, July 18). *Creating an inclusive learning environment for all learners.* https://blogs.clemson.edu/online/2016/07/18/creating-an-inclusive-learning-environment-for-all-learners/

Colloquium Listings. (n.d.). *Home page.* https://musicscholarshipatadistance.com/

Community College Consortium for Open Education Resources. (n.d.). *About us.* https://www.cccoer.org/about/about-cccoer/

Conrad, F. G., Couper, M. P., Tourangeau, R., & Peytchev, A. (2010). The impact of progress indicators on task completion. *Interactive Computing, 22*(5), 417–427. https://doi.org/10.1016/j.intcom.2010.03.001

Copyright Clearance Center. (2011). *The TEACH Act.* https://www.copyright.com/wp-content/uploads/2015/04/CR-Teach-Act.pdf

Copyright Clearance Center. (2020). Home page. www.copyright.com

Costa, K. (2020). *99 Tips for creating simple and sustainable educational videos.* Stylus.

Creative Commons. (2020). *About CC licenses.* creativecommons.org/share-your-work/licensing-types-examples/

Crews, T. B., Wilkinson, K., & Neill, J. K. (2015, March). Principles for good practice in undergraduate education: Effective online course design to assist students' success. *MERLOT Journal of Online Learning and Teaching, 11*(1), 87–103. https://jolt.merlot.org/vol11no1/Crews_0315.pdf

Croft, N., Dalton, A., & Grant, M. (2010). Overcoming isolation in distance learning: Building a learning community through time and space. *Journal for Education in the Built Environment, 5*(1), 27–64. https://doi.org/10.11120/jebe.2010.05010027

Dance Studies Association. (2020, March 9). *Resources for moving dance-based pedagogy online.* https://dancestudiesassociation.org/news/2020/resources-for-moving-dance-based-pedagogy-online

Darabi, A., Arrastia, M. C., Nelson, D. W., Cornille, T., & Liang, X. (2010). Cognitive presence in asynchronous online learning: A comparison of four discussion strategies. *Journal of Computer Assisted Learning, 27*(3), 216–227. https:// doi.org/10.1111/j.1365-2729.2010.00392.x

DeAngelis, T. (2015). In search of cultural competence. *APA Monitor on Psychology, 46*(3). https://www.apa.org/monitor/2015/03/cultural-competence

Dennen, V. P. (2005, May). From message posting to learner dialogues: Factors affecting learner participation in asynchronous discussion. *Distance Education, 26*(1), 127–148. https://doi.org/10.1080/01587910500081376

Department of Homeland Security. (2015, May). *DHS section 508 compliance test process for applications.* https://www.dhs.gov/sites/default/files/publications/ DHS_Section_508_Compliance_Test_Process_for_Applications_0.pdf

Doran, G. T. (1981). There's a S.M.A.R.T. way to write management's goals and objectives. *Management Review, 70*(11), 35–36. https://community.mis.temple. edu/mis0855002fall2015/files/2015/10/S.M.A.R.T-Way-Management-Review.pdf

Doyle, T., & Zakrajsek, T. (2018). *The new science of learning* (2nd ed.). Stylus.

Dunlosky J., Rawson, K. A., Marsh, E. J., Nathan, M. J., Willingham, D. T. (2013). Improving students' learning with effective learning techniques: Promising directions from cognitive and educational psychology. *Psychological Science in the Public Interest, 14*(1), 4–58. https://doi.org/10.1177/1529100612453266

Dweck, C. S. (2017). *Mindset: Changing the way you think to fulfill your potential* (updated edition). Little, Brown.

Dweck, C. S., Walton, G. S., & Cohen, G. L. (2014). *Academic tenacity: Mindsets and skills that promote long-term learning.* Bill & Melinda Gates Foundation.

Echo360. (n.d.). *Recording and streaming.* https://echo360.com/platform/ recording-streaming/

Edge Studio. (n.d.). *Script timers.* www.edgestudio.com/production/words-to-time-calculator

Educator's World. (n.d.). *The educator's guide to copyright and fair use.* www .educationworld.com/a_curr/curr280.shtml

Eynon, B., & Gambino, L. (2017). *High-impact ePortfolio practice. A catalyst for student, faculty, and institutional learning.* Stylus.

Fink, L. D. (2003). *Creating significant learning experiences: An integrated approach to designing college courses.* Jossey-Bass.

Flipgrid. (n.d.). *Flipgrid and accessibility.* help.flipgrid.com/hc/en-us/articles/ 115004848574-Flipgrid-and-Accessibility

FoodFinder. (2020). *Home page.* foodfinder.us

Foter. (2015, March 4). *How to attribute creative commons photos.* Foter Blog. http://foter.com/blog/how-to-attribute-creative-commons-photos/

Freeman, S., Eddy, S. L., McDonough, M., Smith, M. K., Okoroafor, N., Jordt, H., & Wenderoth, M. P. (2014, May). Active learning increases student performance in science, engineering, and mathematics. *Proceedings of the National Academy of Sciences of the United States of America, 111*(23), 8410–8415. https:// doi.org/10.1073/pnas.1319030111

Gabelnick, F., MacGregor, J., Matthews, R., & Smith, B. L. (1990, Spring). *Learning communities: Creating connections among students, faculty, and disciplines* (New Directions for Teaching and Learning, no. 41). Jossey-Bass.

Garrison, D. R., Anderson, T., & Archer, W. (2000). Critical inquiry in a text-based environment: Computer conferencing in higher education. *Internet and Higher Education, 2*(2–3), 87–105. https://doi.org/10.1016/S1096-7516(00)00016-6

Geiger, L. A., Morris, D., Soboez, S. L., Shattuck, K., & Viterito, A. (2014, Spring). Effect of student readiness on student success in online courses. *Internet Learning, 3*(1), 73–84. https://doi.org/10.18278/il.3.1.7

Ginder, S. A., Kelly-Reid, J. E., & Mann, F. B. (2019, January). *Enrollment and employees in postsecondary institutions, fall 2017; and financial statistics and academic libraries, fiscal year 2017* (NCES report 2019-021rev). U.S. Department of Education. https://nces.ed.gov/pubs2019/2019021REV.pdf

Goldrick-Rab, S., Baker-Smith, C., Coca, V., Looker, E., & Williams, T. (2019, April). *College and university basic needs insecurity: A national #RealCollege survey report.* The Hope Center for College, Community, and Justice. https://hope4college.com/wp-content/uploads/2019/04/HOPE_realcollege_National_report_digital.pdf

Goldrick-Rab, S., Coca, V., Kienzl, G., Welton, C. R., Dahl, S., & Magnelia, S. (2020). *#RealCollege during the pandemic: New evidence on basic needs insecurity and student well-being.* The Hope Center for College, Community, and Justice. https://hope4college.com/wp-content/uploads/2020/06/Hopecenter_RealCollegeDuringthePandemic.pdf

Gorski, P. (n.d.). *Awareness activities.* Critical Multicultural Pavilion. www.edchange.org/multicultural/activityarch.html

Hart, C. (2012, Spring). Factors associated with student persistence in an online program of study: A review of the literature. *Journal of Interactive Online Learning, 1*(1). http://www.ncolr.org/jiol/issues/pdf/11.1.2.pdf

Hart, C., Friedmann, E., & Hill, M. (2015). Online course-taking and student outcomes in California community colleges. *Education Finance and Policy, 13*(1), 42–71. https://doi-org.libproxy.lib.unc.edu/10.1162/edfp_a_00218

Henderson, M., & Phillips, M. (2015). Video-based feedback on student assessment: Scarily personal. *Australasian Journal of Educational Technology, 31*(1), 51–66. http://newmediaresearch.educ.monash.edu.au/lnm/wp-content/uploads/2016/11/HendersonPhillips_2015_video_feedback_AJET.pdf

Hervani, A. A., Helms, M. M., Rutti, R. M., LaBonte, J., & Sarkarat, S. (2015). Service learning projects in online courses: Delivery strategies. *Journal of Learning in Higher Education, 11*(1), 35–41. https://files.eric.ed.gov/fulltext/EJ1141925.pdf

Hew, K. F., & Cheung, W. S. (2008). Attracting student participation in asynchronous online discussion: A case study of peer facilitation. *Computers & Education, 51*, 1111–1124. http://dx.doi.org/10.1016/j.compedu.2007.11.002

Horowitz, S. H., Rawe, J., & Whittaker, M. C. (2017). *The state of learning disabilities: Understanding the 1 in 5.* National Center for Learning Disabilities. https://ncld.org/stateofld

Hou, H. T. (2012). Analyzing the learning process of an online role-playing discussion activity. *Educational Technology & Society, 15*(1), 211–222. https://www.j-ets.net/collection/published-issues/15_1

Ideas for teaching clay online. (n.d.). https://docs.google.com/document/d/10L9zp1UlMItlUgWq5earU_UAML9-sYhMQwyobxfMCUI/

Ilosvideos. (n.d.). *Interactive video platform for education.* https://www.vidgrid
.com/use-cases/education/

INACSL Standards Committee. (2016). INACSL standards of best practice: Simulation SM debriefing. *Clinical Simulation in Nursing, 12*(S), S21–S25. http://
dx.doi.org/10.1016/j.ecns.2016.09.008

Jaggars, S. S. (2014). Democratization of education for whom? Online learning
and educational equity. *Diversity and Democracy, 17*(1). Association of American Colleges & Universities. https://www.aacu.org/diversitydemocracy/2014/
winter/jaggars

Johnson, D., & Johnson, R. (1975). *Learning together and alone, cooperation, competition, and individualization.* Prentice-Hall.

Johnson, H., Cuellar-Mejia, M., & Cook, K. (2015, June). *Successful online courses
in California's community colleges.* Public Policy Institute of California.

Jones, M., & Sneed, O. (2016, January 12). Fostering an inclusive environment when
developing online courses. *TeachOnline.* https://teachonline.asu.edu/2016/01/
fostering-inclusive-environment-developing-online-courses/

Jones, Q., Ravid, G., & Rafaeli, S. (2004). Information overload and the message dynamics of online interaction spaces: A theoretical model and empiri-
cal exploration. *Information Systems Research, 15*(2), 194–210. https://doi
.org/10.1287/isre.1040.0023

Jorgenson, D. A., Farrell, L. C., Fudge, J. L., & Pritchard, A. (2018, January). College connectedness: The student perspective. *Journal of the Scholarship of
Teaching and Learning, 18*(1), 75–95. https://doi.org/10.14434/josotl.v18i1.22371

Jung, I., Choi, S., Lim, C., & Leem, J. (2002). Effects of different types of interaction on learning achievement, satisfaction, and participation in web-based
instruction. *Innovations in Education and Teaching International, 39*(2), 153–
162. http://dx.doi.org/10.1080/14703290252934603

Karpicke, J. D. (June, 2016). A powerful way to improve learning and memory:
Practicing retrieval enhances long-term, meaningful learning. *Psychological Science Agenda.* http://www.apa.org/science/about/psa/2016/06/learning-memory
.aspx

Kaupp, R. (2012). Online penalty: The impact of online instruction on the Latino-
White achievement gap. *Journal of Applied Research in the Community College, 19*(2), 8–16. https://www.learntechlib.org/p/113519/

Kay, M., Matuszek, C., & Munson, S. A. (2015, April 18–23). Unequal representation
and gender stereotypes in image search results for occupations. In B. Begole &
J. Kim (Chairs), *Proceedings from CHI'15: Human Factors in Computing Systems*
(pp. 3819-3828), Association for Computing Machinery 33rd Annual Conference, Seoul, Republic of Korea. http://dx.doi.org/10.1145/2702123.2702520

Keist, J. (Interviewer), & Wood, J. L. (Presenter). (2019, January 15). *Engaging
and supporting male students of color* [Podcast episode 26]. Office of Community College Research and Leadership. occrl.illinois.edu/docs/libraries
provider4/podcast/episode-26-jlw.pdf?sfvrsn=cd558289_4

Kelly, K. (n.d.). *Image galleries that address image and representation bias.* Google
Drive. drive.google.com/open?id=123F5RnQ_vP_QDNzoJAV-EoBlwadTvhWK

Kelly, K. (2008a). Evaluating and improving your online teaching effectiveness. In S. Hirtz, D. G. Harper, and S. Mackenzie (Eds.), *Education for a digital world: Advice, guidelines, and effective practice from around the globe* (pp. 365–377). BCcampus and Commonwealth of Learning.

Kelly, K. (2008b). *Writing objectives* [Creative Commons License-Attribution (CC BY)]. San Francisco State University.

Kelly, K. (2014, Fall). Fostering inclusion with universal design for learning. *Diversity & Democracy, 17*(4), 27–28. https://www.aacu.org/diversitydemocracy/2014/fall/kelly

Kelly, K. (2019a). *Exploring recent OER research and the need to address experiences, efficacy, and equity.* Phil on Ed Tech. https://philonedtech.com/exploring-recent-oer-research-and-the-need-to-address-experiences-efficacy-and-equity/

Kelly, K. (2019b). *Online course design rubrics, part 1: What are they?* eLiterate. https://eliterate.us/online-course-design-rubrics-part-1-what-are-they/

Kelly, K. (2020). *Design for learning equity framework.* Learning Equity. http://learningequity.org

Kelly, R. (2014, January 7). *Creating a sense of instructor presence in the online classroom.* Faculty Focus. https://www.facultyfocus.com/articles/online-education/creating-a-sense-of-instructor-presence-in-the-online-classroom/

Khan Academy. (2020). *Home page.* http://www.khanacademy.org

Kiewra, K. A. (2008). *Teaching how to learn: The teacher's guide to student success.* Corwin Press.

Kim, J. (2013). Influence of group size on students' participation in online discussion forums. *Computers & Education, 62*, 123–129. http://dx.doi.org/10.1016/j.compedu.2012.10.025

Kizilcec, R. F., Saltarelli, A. J., Reich, J., & Cohen, G. L. (2017, January 20). Closing global achievement gaps in MOOCs. *Science, 355*(6322), 251–252. https://doi.org/10.1126/science.aag2063

Kleinfeld, J. (1975). Effective teachers of Eskimo and Indian students. *School Review, 83*(2), 301–344. https://www.jstor.org/stable/1084645

Kridelbaugh, D. M. (2016, March). The use of online citizen-science projects to provide experiential learning opportunities for nonmajor science students. *Journal of Microbiology and Biology Education, 17*(1), 105–106. https://doi.org/10.1128/jmbe.v17i1.1022

Kruger, J., & Dunning, D. (1999). Unskilled and unaware of it: How difficulties in recognizing one's own incompetence lead to inflated self-assessments. *Journal of Personality and Social Psychology, 77*(6), 1121–1134. https://doi.org/10.1037//0022-3514.77.6.1121

Kundu, A. (2020). *The power of student agency: Looking beyond grit to close the opportunity.* Teachers College Press.

Ladson-Billings, G. (1995, Summer). But that's just good teaching! The case for culturally relevant pedagogy. *Theory Into Practice, 34*(3), 159–165. https://www.jstor.org/stable/1476635

Ladson-Billings, G. (2006, October). From the achievement gap to the education debt: Understanding achievement in U.S. schools. *Educational Researcher,* 35(7), 3–12. https://www.jstor.org/stable/3876731

Lake Superior College. (n.d.). *LSC online course netiquette guidelines.* http://blogs .lsc.edu/expectations/netiquette-guidelines/

Lee, K. (2013, December). *Your brain on dopamine: The science of motivation.* http:// blog.idonethis.com/the-science-of-motivation-your-brain-on-dopamine/

Light, R. J. (2004). *Making the most of college: Students speak their minds.* Harvard University Press.

LinkedIn Learning. (n.d.). *Keep learning in the moments that matter.* www .linkedin.com/learning

Lister, M. (2014, December). Trends in the design of e-learning and online learning. *MERLOT Journal of Online Learning and Teaching, 10*(4), 671–680. https:// jolt.merlot.org/vol10no4/Lister_1214.pdf

Liu, S. Y., Gomez, J., & Yen, C. (2009). Community college online course retention and final grades: Predictability of social presence. *Journal of Interactive Online Learning, 8*(2), 165–182. https://eric.ed.gov/?id=EJ938828

Lombard, R., & Biglan, B. (2011). Using role play and team teaching as strategies to add depth to online discussion. In F. Pozzi & D. Persico (Eds.), *Techniques for fostering collaboration in online learning communities: Theoretical and practical perspectives* (pp. 164–182). IGI Global.

Loom. (n.d.). *Use cases.* www.useloom.com /use-cases#education

Lorenzi, F., MacKeogh, K., & Fox, S. (2004). Preparing students for learning in an online world: An evaluation of the student passport to Elearning (SPEL) model. *European Journal of Open Distance and E-Learning.* http://dx.doi .org/10.1002/9781118557686.ch30

Lumadue, R., & Fish, W. (2010). A technologically based approach to providing quality feedback to students: A paradigm shift for the 21st century. *Academic Leadership, The Online Journal, 8*(1). https://scholars.fhsu.edu/alj/vol8/iss1/5/

Lynch, M. M. (2001, November/December). Effective student preparation for online learning. *The Technology Source.* http://ts.mivu.org/default .asp?show=article&id=1034

Mager, R. F. (1962). *Preparing objectives for programmed instruction.* Fearon Publishers.

Mager, R. F. (1997). *Preparing instructional objectives: A critical tool in the development of effective instruction.* Center for Effective Performance.

Major, C. H., Harris, M. S., & Zakrajsek, T. (2016). *Teaching for learning: 101 intentionally designed educational activities to put students on the path to success.* Routledge.

Malan, S. P. T. (2000). The "new paradigm" of outcomes-based education in perspective. *Journal of Family Ecology and Consumer Sciences/Tydskrif vir Gesinsekologie en Verbruikerswetenskappe, 28*(1). http://dx.doi.org/10.4314/jfecs .v28i1.52788

Mansbach, J. (2015, September 14). *Using technology to develop critical thinking skills.* Northwestern University School of Professional Studies. https://dl.sps .northwestern.edu/blog/2015/09/using-technology-to-develop-students-critical-thinking-skills/

Marsh, E. J., & Butler, A. C. (2014). Memory in educational settings. In D. Reisberg (Ed.), *Oxford handbook of cognitive psychology* (pp. 299–317). Oxford University Press.

Maslow, A. H. (1943). A theory of human motivation. *Psychological Review, 50*(4), 370–396. https://doi.org/10.1037%2Fh0054346

Mathisen, P. (2012). Video feedback in higher education—A contribution to improving the quality of written feedback. *Nordic Journal of Digital Literacy, 7*(2), 97–116. http://www.pmathisen.no/4file/filer/artikler/videofeedback%20 in%20higher%20education%20petter%20mathisen%202012.pdf

McAvoy, B. R. (1985). How to choose and use educational objectives. *Medical Teacher, 7*(1), 27–35. https://doi.org/10.3109/01421598509036788

McGee, P., & Reis, A. (2012). Blended course design: A synthesis of best practices. *Journal of Asynchronous Learning Networks, 16*(4), 7–22. https://files.eric .ed.gov/fulltext/EJ982678.pdf

McKenzie, L. (2018, August 16). Student spending on course materials plummets. *Inside Higher Ed.* https://www.insidehighered.com/news/2018/08/16/students-are-spending-less-ever-course-materials

McLaughlan, R. G. (2007). Instructional strategies to educate for sustainability in technology assessment. *International Journal of Engineering Education, 23*(2), 201–208. http://hdl.handle.net/10453/6158

MERLOT. (2020). *Home page.* www.merlot.org

Merriam-Webster. (n.d.). Equity [Def. 1]. In *Merriam-Webster online.* https:// www.merriam-webster.com/dictionary/equity

Meyer, A., Rose, D. H., & Gordon, D. (2014). *Universal design for learning: Theory and practice.* CAST.

Michaelsen, L. K., Watson, W. E., Cragin, J. P., & Fink, L. D. (1982). Team-based learning: A potential solution to the problems of large classes. *Exchange: The Organizational Behavior Teaching Journal, 7*(4), 18–33. http://dx.doi .org/10.1177/105256298200700103

Microsoft. (n.d.a). *Add a heading.* support.office.com/en-us/article/add-a-heading-3eb8b917-56dc-4a17-891a-a026b2c790f2

Microsoft. (n.d.b). *Create a bulleted or numbered list.* support.office.com/en-us/ article/Create-a-bulleted-or-numbered-list-9FF81241-58A8-4D88-8D8C-ACAB3006A23E

Microsoft. (n.d.c). *Add alternative text to a shape, picture, chart, table, SmartArt graphic, or other object.* support.office.com/en-us/article/Add-alternative-text-to-a-shape-picture-chart-table-SmartArt-graphic-or-other-object-44989b2a-903c-4d9a-b742-6a75b451c669

Microsoft (n.d.d). *Make your PowerPoint presentations accessible to people with disabilities.* https://support.microsoft.com/en-gb/office/make-your-powerpoint-presentations-accessible-to-people-with-disabilities-6f7772b2-2f33-4bd2-8ca7-dae3b2b3ef25?ui=en-us&rs=en-gb&ad=gb

Microsoft. (n.d.e). *Make your Word documents accessible to people with disabilities.* https://support.office.com/en-us/article/Make-your-Word-documents-accessible-d9bf3683-87ac-47ea-b91a-78dcacb3c66d

Microsoft. (2011). *Accessibility: A guide for educators.* http://download.microsoft.com/download/0/7/3/073c1245-78c9-4790-ba41-73132204e43e/accessibility%20guide%20for%20educators%20version3.doc

Microsoft. (2020a). *Improve accessibility with the Accessibility Checker.* https://support.microsoft.com/en-us/office/improve-accessibility-with-the-accessibility-checker-a16f6de0-2f39-4a2b-8bd8-5ad801426c7f

Microsoft. (2020b). *Make your Excel documents accessible to people with disabilities.* support.office.com/en-us/article/Make-your-Excel-spreadsheets-accessible-6cc05fc5-1314-48b5-8eb3-683e49b3e593

Milkman, K. L., Akinola, M., & Chugh, D. (2015). What happens before? A field experiment exploring how pay and representation differentially shape bias on the pathway into organizations. *Journal of Applied Psychology, 100*(6), 1678–1712. http://dx.doi.org/10.1037/apl0000022

Minnesota Campus Compact–Center for Digital Civic Engagement. (n.d.). *Service-learning in online courses.* https://cdce.wordpress.com/service-learning-in-online-courses/

Molenda, M. (2003, May–June). In search of the elusive ADDIE model. *Performance Improvement, 42*(5), 34–37. http://dx.doi.org/10.1002/pfi.4930420508

Montgomery College. (2020). *Nursing simulation scenario library.* https://www.montgomerycollege.edu/academics/departments/nursing-tpss/nursing-simulation-scenario-library.html

Morrison, G. R., Ross, S. M., & Kemp, J. E. (2001). *Designing effective instruction* (3rd ed.). John Wiley & Sons.

Mueller, J. (2016). What is authentic assessment? *Authentic Assessment Toolbox.* http://jfmueller.faculty.noctrl.edu/toolbox/whatisit.htm

Nabours, K., & Koh, M. H. (2019). Outcomes of incorporating the science of learning into mathematics curriculum. *Community College Journal of Research and Practice, 44*(6), 412–426. http://dx.doi.org/10.1080/10668926.2019.1610674

Nash, B. (2009, April). *Tips for improving retention of distance learning students.* Faculty Focus.

National Council on State Boards of Nursing. (2015, February). *Nursing regulation recommendations for distance education in prelicensure nursing programs.* https://www.ncsbn.org/15_DLC_White_Paper.pdf

Nemec, J. (2020, June 25). *NACS report: Student spending on course materials continues to decline.* National Association of College Stores. https://www.nacs.org/advocacynewsmedia/pressreleases/tabid/1579/ArticleID/939/NACS-Report-Student-Spending-on-Course-Materials-Continues-to-Decline.aspx

Nesbit, J. C., & Adesope, O. O. (2006, Fall). Learning with concept and knowledge maps: A meta-analysis. *Review of Educational Research, 76*(3), 413–448. http://dx.doi.org/10.3102/00346543076003413

Nielsen Norman Group. (2014, March 9). *Writing hyperlinks: Salient, descriptive, start with keyword.* https://www.nngroup.com/articles/writing-links/

Nilson, L. B. (2007). *The graphic syllabus and the outcomes map: Communicating your course.* Jossey-Bass.

Nilson, L. B. (2013). *Creating self-regulated learners: Strategies to strengthen students' self-awareness and learning skills.* Stylus.

Objectives, goals, and outcomes: What's the difference? (1999). *Home Healthcare Nurse, 17*(5), 284–286. https://www.ncbi.nlm.nih.gov/pubmed/10562000

OER Commons. (n.d.). *Home page.* www.oercommons.org/

Online Art & Design Studio Instruction in the Age of "Social Distancing." (2020, March 10). In Facebook [Group Page]. https://www.facebook.com/groups/2872732516116624

Online Physical Education Network. (n.d.). *Home page.* https://openphysed.org/

Online Resources for Science Laboratories. (n.d.). *Remote teaching: All resources.* https://docs.google.com/spreadsheets/d/18iVSIeOqKjj58xcR8dYJS5rYvzZ4X1UGLWhl3brRzCM/htmlview?usp=drive_web&ouid=109599745464921472575&sle=true&urp=gmail_link

Online Teaching Conference. (n.d.). *Rigor through empathy: Becoming a warm demander.* http://tinyurl.com/warm-demander

OPEN Online Physical Education Network. (n.d.). *About.* https://openphysed.org/about

Open Textbook Library. (n.d.). *Home page.* open.umn.edu/opentextbooks/

Open Textbooks Hub. (n.d.) *About this hub.* www.oercommons.org/hubs/open-textbooks

Orso, D., & Doolittle, J. (2012, November 2). Instructor characteristics that affect online student success. *Faculty Focus.* https://www.facultyfocus.com/articles/online-education/instructor-characteristics-that-affect-online-student-success/

Pacansky-Brock, M. (n.d.a). *Art 10: Art appreciation online* [sample syllabus]. https://mtsac.libguides.com/ld.php?content_id=27697465

Pacansky-Brock, M. (n.d.b). *Humanizing.* https://brocansky.com/humanizing

Pacansky-Brock, M. (2013a, January 29). *Roll out an online teaching welcome mat with Animoto.* https://brocansky.com/2013/01/roll-out-an-online-teaching-welcome-mat-with-animoto.html

Pacansky-Brock, M. (2013b, October 4). *Mainstreaming academic innovation with emerging technologies.* https://brocansky.com/2013/10/mainstreaming-academic-innovation-with-emerging-technologies.html

Pacansky-Brock, M., Sargent, A. & Torres, F. (2020, June 19). *Rigor through empathy: Becoming a warm demander* [Conference presentation]. 2020 Online Teaching Conference, virtual. onlineteachingconference.org/session/rigor-through-empathy-becoming-a-warm-demander/

Panopto. (n.d.). *How to create and access bookmarks.* https://support.panopto.com/s/article/How-to-Create-and-Access-Bookmarks

Pashler, H., McDaniel, M., Rohrer, D., & Bjork, R. (2008). Learning styles: Concepts and evidence. *Psychological Science in the Public Interest, 9*(3), 105–119. http://dx.doi.org/10.1111/j.1539-6053.2009.01038.x

Paul, R. (1993). *Critical thinking: What every student needs to survive in a rapidly changing world*. Foundation for Critical Thinking. http://www.criticalthinking.org/pages/a-model-for-the-national-assessment-of-higher-order-thinking/591

PE Central. (n.d.). *Index*. https://www.pecentral.org/index.html

The P.E. Geek. (n.d.). *Home page*. https://thepegeek.com/

Pennsylvania State University. (n.d.). *Designating table headers*. http://accessibility.psu.edu/microsoftoffice/microsofttableheaders/

Peralta Community College District. (2019). *Peralta Equity Rubric, version 2.0* [Creative Commons license: Attribution-Share Alike (CC BY-SA)]. https://web.peralta.edu/de/peralta-online-equity-initiative/equity/

Pitt Community College Library. (n.d.). *OER: Open Educational Resources*. https://libguides.pittcc.edu/oer/find

Prezi. (2020). *Pricing*. https://prezi.com/pricing/?click_source=logged_element&page_location=header&element_text=pricing

Proctor, J. (n.d.). *Resources for teaching production courses in case of emergency*. https://docs.google.com/document/d/115zQ_t-mS-iuhJj6GKiK9vHkteIwWo6yAw2Rh8SJm1c/edit?usp=sharing

Qiu, M., & McDougall, D. (2015). Influence of group configuration on online discourse reading. *Computers & Education, 87*, 151–165. https://doi.org/10.1016/j.compedu.2015.04.006

Rensselaer Polytechnic Institute. (n.d.). *Objectives vs. outcomes*. https://provost.rpi.edu/learning-assessment/learning-outcomes/objectives-vs-outcomes

Renton Technical College. (n.d.). *Goals, outcomes, and objectives defined*. https://rtc.instructure.com/courses/1152250/pages/goals-outcomes-and-objectives-defined

Robert, J. (2018, August 27). Fostering human connection for meaningful learning in technologically advanced learning spaces. *Educause Review, 53*(5). https://er.educause.edu/articles/2018/8/fostering-human-connection-for-meaningful-learning-in-technologically-advanced-learning-spaces

Roediger, III, H. L., & Butler, A. C. (2011). The critical role of retrieval practice in long-term retention. *Trends in Cognitive Sciences, 15*(1), 20–27. https://doi.org/10.1016/j.tics.2010.09.003

Rose, D. H., & Meyer, A. (2002). *Teaching every student in the digital age: Universal design for learning*. Center for Applied Special Technology. https://www.cast.org/publications/2002/universal-design-learning-udl-teaching-every-student-rose

Rosenberg, M. E. (2018). An outcomes-based approach across the medical education continuum. *Transactions of the American Clinical and Climatological Association, 129*, 325–340. https://www.ncbi.nlm.nih.gov/pmc/articles/PMC6116626/

Rovai, A. P. (2007). Facilitating online discussions effectively. *Internet and Higher Education, 10*(1), 77–88. http://dx.doi.org/10.1016/j.iheduc.2006.10.001

Rovai, A. P., & Wighting, M. J. (2005). Feelings of alienation and community among higher education students in a virtual classroom. *The Internet and Higher Education, 8*, 97–110. https://doi.org/10.1016/j.iheduc.2005.03.001

Royal Academy of Music, Denmark. (2020, March 16). *Zoom in music mode* [Video file]. https://www.youtube.com/watch?v=5oNoWIiYECA

Sadera, W. A., Robertson, J., Song, L., & Midon, M. N. (2009). The role of community in online learning success. *MERLOT Journal of Online Learning & Teaching, 5*(2), 277–284. https://jolt.merlot.org/vol5no2/sadera_0609.pdf

Salisbury, O. (2016, March 8). The psychology of progress bars. *Spindogs.* https://www.spindogs.co.uk/blog/2016/03/08/the-psychology-of-progress-bars/

Samuel Merritt University. (2009). *Universal design for learning.* UDL QuickStart Guide Fall2019. https://docs.google.com/document/d/1TzLR4uwfUAxssK1Elx2ggD6yrS2we9SPpmHkTTybcyk/edit

San Francisco State University. (n.d.). *Creating accessible PDF documents with Word Guide (PC+Mac).* http://its.sfsu.edu//guides/creating-accessible-pdf-documents-word-2013#use

San Francisco State University. (2017). *Did you know that 75% of students reported that the cost of materials causes them stress?* https://affordablelearning.sfsu.edu/student-perspective

Saunders, S., & Kardia, D. (1997). *Creating inclusive college classrooms.* University of Michigan–Center for Research in Teaching and Learning. http://www.crlt.umich.edu/gsis/p3_1

Savery, J. R. (2005, Fall). BE VOCAL: Characteristics of successful online instructors. *Journal of Interactive Online Learning, 4*(2), 141–152. http://www.ncolr.org/jiol/issues/pdf/4.2.6.pdf

Schwartz, H. (2020, April 2). *Authentic teaching and connected learning in the age of COVID-19.* The Scholarly Teacher. https://www.scholarlyteacher.com/post/authentic-teaching-and-connected-learning-in-the-age-of-covid-19

Screencast-O-Matic. (n.d.). *Compare plan features.* https://screencast-o-matic.com/plans

Seaman, J. E., & Seaman, J. (2018). *Freeing the textbook: Educational resources in U.S. higher education, 2018.* Babson Research Group. https://www.onlinelearningsurvey.com/reports/freeingthetextbook2018.pdf

Senack, E. (2014, January). *Fixing the broken textbook market: How students respond to high textbook costs and demand alternatives.* U.S. Public Interest Research Group Education Fund & the Student Public Interest Research Groups. https://uspirg.org/sites/pirg/files/reports/NATIONAL%20Fixing%20Broken%20Textbooks%20Report1.pdf

SHAPE America: Society of Health and Physical Educators. (n.d.). *About SHAPE AMERICA.* https://www.shapeamerica.org/about/default.aspx

Shay, J., & Rees, M. (2004). Understanding why students select online courses and criteria they use in making that selection. *International Journal of Instructional Technology and Distance Learning, 1*(5). http://itdl.org/Journal/May_04/article03.htm

Shelton, K. (2011, Spring). A review of paradigms for evaluating the quality of online education programs. *Online Journal of Distance Learning Administration, 14*(1). https://eric.ed.gov/?id=EJ921847

Sheridan, K., & Kelly, M. (2010). The indicators of instructor presence that are important to students in online courses. *MERLOT Journal of Online Learning and Teaching, 6*(4). https://jolt.merlot.org/vol6no4/sheridan_1210.pdf

The Skeptical Educator. (2015, August 26). *Adding an image to D2L*. YouTube. https://www.youtube.com/watch?v=jPEUJ4SBWsE

Skills Commons. (n.d.). *Q: Are there guidelines to help assure the quality of the instructional design of materials?* https://support.skillscommons.org/faqs/q-are-there-guidelines-to-help-us-assure-the-quality-of-the-instructional-design-of-the-materials-we-created-for-the-taaccct-grant/

Society of Health and Physical Educators. (n.d.). *Home page*. www.shapeamerica.org

SoftChalk. (2020). *Home page*. https://softchalk.com/

Sorensen, T. (1965). *Kennedy: The classic biography*. HarperCollins.

Southeastern Oklahoma State University. (2020). *General information—Definition of credit hours*. http://www.se.edu/registrar/general-information/

Stannard, R. (2007). Using screen capture software in student feedback. *HEA English subject centre commissioned case studies*. http://www.english.heacademy.ac.uk/explore/publications/casestudies/technology/camtasia.php

Stannard, R. (2008). A new direction in feedback. *Humanizing Language Teaching, 10*(6). https://westminsterresearch.westminster.ac.uk/item/91ozo/a-new-direction-in-feedback

Stark, I. (2019). *Online equity training-template-fall 2019*. Canvas Commons. lor.instructure.com/resources/f35cd7a09da64112aff13a98b7ddf0cd

Stevens, D. D., & Levi, A. J. (2012). *Introduction to rubrics: An assessment tool to save grading time, convey effective feedback, and promote student learning*. Stylus.

Stromberg, J. (2013, December). It's a myth: There's no evidence that coffee stunts kids' growth. *Smithsonian Magazine*. https://www.smithsonianmag.com/science-nature/its-a-myth-theres-no-evidence-that-coffee-stunts-kids-growth-180948068/

Sun, A. (2014, September 16). *Equality is not enough: What the classroom has taught me about justice*. Everyday Feminism. https://everydayfeminism.com/2014/09/equality-is-not-enough/

Tanner, K. (2013, Fall). Structure matters: Twenty-one teaching strategies to promote student engagement and cultivate classroom equity. *CBE Life Sciences Education, 12*(3), 322–331. https://doi.org/10.1187/cbe.13-06-0115

TechSmith Relay. (n.d.). *Overview: Features designed for engaged learning*. https://www.techsmith.com/knowmia-education.html

Texas Tech University School of Music. (2020). *Teaching music courses & lessons*. Teaching, Learning, and Professional Development Center. https://www.depts.ttu.edu/tlpdc/Teaching_Music_Courses_Lessons.php

Thomas, L., Herbert, J., & Teras, M. (2014). A sense of belonging to enhance participation, success, and retention in online programs. *The International Journal of the First Year in Higher Education, 5*(2), 69–80. https://doi.org/10.5204/intjfyhe.v5i2.233

Tinto, V. (2003). Learning better together: The impact of learning communities on student success. *Higher Education Monograph Series, 2003–1*. Syracuse University–School of Education.

Tobin, T. (2017). *The copyright ninja: Rise of the ninja*. St. Aubin Comics.

Tobin, T. J., & Behling, K. T. (2018). *Reach everyone, teach everyone: Universal design for learning in higher education*. West Virginia University Press.

Trinity University. (n.d.). *Specific approaches & disciplines: Strategies for moving online*. https://sites.google.com/trinity.edu/keepteaching/teaching-guide/specific-approachesdisciplines

UCLA Health. (2016). *Course planning tip sheet*. https://www.uclahealth.org/nursing/workfiles/Education%20Courses/ContinuingEducation/ce-LearningOutcome-v-LearningObjective-052016.pdf

UDI Online Project. (2009). *Examples of UDI in online and blended courses*. Center on Postsecondary Education and Disability, University of Connecticut. https://cped.uconn.edu/udi/

UDL Guidelines. (n.d.). *Principle: Provide multiple means of representation*. CAST. udlguidelines.cast.org/representation.

University of North Carolina–Art & Art History. (n.d.). *Remote teaching resources for studio art and art history*. https://art.unc.edu/home/remote-teaching-resources-for-studio-art-and-art-history/

University of San Diego, Office of the General Counsel. (2020) *Copyright basics*. www.sandiego.edu/legal/resources/copyright.php

U.S. Department of Education. (2009). *Program integrity questions and answers—Credit hour*. https://www2.ed.gov/policy/highered/reg/hearulemaking/2009/credit.html

U.S. Department of Education, Information for Financial Aid Professionals. (2014, December 19). *Competency-based education programs–Questions and Answers* (GEN-14-23). Author. ifap.ed.gov/dear-colleague-letters/12-19-2014-gen-14-23-subject-competency-based-education-programs-questions

U.S. Department of Education, National Center for Education Statistics. (2015, November). *Distance education in postsecondary institutions. The condition of education*. Author. https://nces.ed.gov/programs/coe/indicator_sta.asp

U.S. Department of Education, National Center for Education Statistics. (2016). *Digest of education statistics, 2015* (NCES 2016-014). Author.

Vasquez, A. (2020, April 8). *Accessible tools for online collaboration and learning*. knowbility.org/blog/2020/accessible-online-tools/

Vesely, P., Bloom, L., & Sherlock, J. (2007, September). Key elements of building online community: Comparing faculty and student perceptions. *MERLOT Journal of Online Learning and Teaching, 3*(3), 234–246. http://jolt.merlot.org/vol3no3/vesely.pdf

VoiceThread. (2020). *Features.* https://voicethread.com/about/features/

Waesche, J. (2017). Use role play to increase student engagement in online discussions. In B. Chen, A. deNoyelles, & K. Thompson (Eds.), *Teaching online pedagogical pepository.* University of Central Florida Center for Distributed Learning. https://topr.online.ucf.edu/use-role-play-increase-student-engagement-online-discussions/

Waldner, L., McGorry, S., & Widener, M. (2010, December). Extreme e-service learning (XE-SL): E-service learning in the 100% online course. *MERLOT Journal of Online Learning and Teaching, 6*(4), 839–851. https://jolt.merlot.org/vol6no4/waldner_1210.pdf

Waldner, L. S., McGorry, S. Y., & Widener, M. C. (2012). E-service-learning: The evolution of service-learning to engage a growing online population. *Journal of Higher Education Outreach and Engagement, 16*(2), 123–150. https://d3tb2mkdocc4em.cloudfront.net/oce/wp-content/uploads/sites/134/2014/08/E-Service-Learning-The-Evolution-of-Service-Learning-to-Engage-a-Growing-Online-Student-Population.pdf

WebAIM. (n.d.a). *Contrast checker.* webaim.org/resources/contrastchecker/

WebAIM. (n.d.b). *PDF accessibility: Converting documents to PDFs.* https://webaim.org/techniques/acrobat/converting

Wesch, M. (2007, October 12). *A vision of students today* [Video]. YouTube. www.youtube.com/watch?v=dGCJ46vyR9o

Western Governor's University. (2018). *Time management strategy for online college students.* https://www.wgu.edu/blog/time-management-strategies-online-college-students1810.html

Westlaw. (2017). *CCR 55204—Instructor contact. California Code of Regulations.* Thomson Reuters. https://govt.westlaw.com/calregs/Document/I30AFD0EF02B449E187E6485AB412054F

White, D., & Manton, M. (2011, July). *Open educational resources: The value of reuse in higher education* [OER Impact Study]. University of Oxford. https://www.oerknowledgecloud.org/record123

Whitford, E. (2018, July 26). *Textbook trade-offs.* Inside Higher Ed. https://www.insidehighered.com/news/2018/07/26/students-sacrifice-meals-and-trips-home-pay-textbooks

Wichita State University. (n.d.). *Online readiness assessment.* www.wichita.edu/services/mrc/elearning/online_orientation/online_self_assessment.php

Wiggins, G., & McTighe, J. (2005). *Understanding by design* (2nd ed.). Association for Supervision & Curriculum Development.

Wilson, L. O. (n.d.). *Three domains of learning—Cognitive, affective, psychomotor.* https://thesecondprinciple.com/instructional-design/threedomainsoflearning/

Winkelmes, M. (2013). *Transparent assignment template.* https://tilthighered.com/assets/pdffiles/Transparent%20Assignment%20Template.pdf

Winkelmes, M. (2014). *Transparency in learning and teaching project.* https://tilthighered.com/transparency

Winkelmes, M., Bernacki, M., Butler, J., Zochowski, M., Golanics, J., & Weavil, K. H. (2016, Winter/Spring). A teaching intervention that increases underserved college students' success. *Peer Review, 18*(1/2). https://www.aacu.org/peerreview/2016/winter-spring/Winkelmes

Wood, J. L. (2015). *Teaching men of color in the community college: A guidebook.* Montezuma Publishing.

World Health Organization. (2019, October 8). *Blindness and vision impairment.* https://www.who.int/news-room/fact-sheets/detail/blindness-and-visual-impairment

Xu, D., & Jaggars, S. S. (2011, March). *Online and hybrid course enrollment and performance in Washington State community and technical colleges* [Working Paper No. 31]. Community College Research Center–Columbia University. https://ccrc.tc.columbia.edu/publications/online-hybrid-courses-washington.html

Yale Center for Teaching and Learning. (n.d.). *Awareness of implicit biases.* https://ctl.yale.edu/ImplicitBiasAwareness

YouTube. (n.d.). *Use automatic captioning.* https://support.google.com/youtube/answer/6373554

Zhao, C.-M., & Kuh, G. D. (2004, March). Adding value: Learning communities and student engagement. *Research in Higher Education, 45*(2), 115–138. http://home.ubalt.edu/ub78l45/MyLibrary/storage/HV3TEDZ2/12231609.pdf

Zoom. (n.d.). *Zoom meeting plans for your business.* https://zoom.us/pricing

Kevin Kelly teaches online courses as a lecturer in the Department of Equity, Leadership Studies, and Instructional Technologies at San Francisco State University, where he has also led as online teaching and learning manager. He works with colleges and universities as a consultant to address distance education, educational technology, and organizational challenges. Kelly now works full time as a higher education consultant, specializing in both common and niche areas, like distance education, equity and inclusion, teaching and learning (with or without technology), academic technology adoption and implementation, strategic planning, professional and leadership development, and more. He has played leadership roles in education technology (ed tech) startups focused on faculty professional development, including the Association of College and University Educators (ACUE) and Wiley Learning Institute. He recently coauthored with Linder and Tobin another Stylus book, *Going Alt-Ac: A Guide to Alternative Academic Careers* (2020). He also publishes online courses for the Education channel at LinkedIn Learning/Lynda.com. Follow and connect with Kelly on Twitter (@KevinKellyo) and LinkedIn.

Todd Zakrajsek is an associate professor in the Department of Family Medicine at the University of North Carolina (UNC) at Chapel Hill and an adjunct associate professor for faculty development in the Department of Clinical Sciences at North Carolina State University. Zakrajsek was a tenured associate professor of psychology and built faculty development efforts at three universities before joining UNC. At UNC, Zakrajsek provides resources for faculty on various topics related to teaching/learning, leadership, and scholarly activity. In addition to his university work, Zakrajsek directs multiple Lilly Teaching Conferences throughout the United States, is president of the International Teaching Learning Cooperative, and has served on many educationally related boards and work groups including *The Journal of Excellence in College Teaching, International Journal for the Scholarship of Teaching and Learning, College Teaching,* and *Education in the Health Professions*. Zakrajsek has consulted with organizations such as The American Council on Education (ACE), Lenovo Computer, Microsoft, and the Bill and Melinda Gates Foundation. He has

delivered keynote addresses and campus workshops at over 300 conferences and university campuses. Zakrajsek's recently coauthored books
include *The New Science of Learning* (2nd ed.) (Stylus Publishing, 2019),
*Dynamic Lecturing: Research-Based Strategies to Enhance Lecture Effective-
ness* (Stylus Publishing, 2017); and *Teaching for Learning: 101 Intentionally Designed Educational Activities to Put Students on the Path to Success*
(Routledge, 2015). Follow and connect with Zakrajsek on Twitter (@tod-
dzakrajsek) and LinkedIn.

Page numbers referring to figures are in *italics*.
Page numbers referring to tables are in **bold.**

heading styles
High-Impact ePortfolio Practice, 193
higher-order thinking, 191, *See also*
    assessment
human connectedness
    as focus for online teaching, 2
    as predictor of student success, 15
human connection, *See* human
    connectedness
humanizing, *See* online courses,
    humanizing

icebreaker activity, *See* activities
Illinois Online Network, course design
    rubric by, 14, 32, 176
ilos (screencast tool), 60
image gallery, 112, 120
inclusion
    strategies to foster, 112–113, 142–144
infographics, 61
instructional time, calculating, 43–44
instructor presence
    establishing (before course start
    date), 124–126
    maintaining, 129–130
    supporting students with, 126–128
interaction, regular and substantive,
    137–139, *See also* bias, interaction
interactive presentation tools, 60–61

Kennedy, J. F., 7
Khan Academy, 54, 55
Kundu, A., 173

Ladson-Billings, G., 18, 66, 142
Lean In (stock photo gallery), 63
learning community, *See* community
learning equity, *See* equity
learning management system (LMS)
    content editor tools in, 42, 43, 87,
    88
learning outcomes, *See* outcomes
lecture capture tools, 59
levels of thinking and achievement,
    See taxonomy

LinkedIn Learning, 56
LMS, *See* learning management
    systems
Loom (screencast tool), 60
Lynda.com, *See* LinkedIn Learning

MERLOT (Multimedia Educational
    Resources for Learning and
    Online Teaching), 54, 55
midsemester feedback, 177–178
MindMeister (concept map tool), 62
MindMup (concept map tool), 62
misconception/preconception check,
    See activities
Module Builder (online authoring
    tool), 61

netiquette, guidelines for online
    behavior, 16, 121
New Science of Learning, The, 40

objectives, *See* outcomes
OER, *See* open educational resources
OER Commons, 54
One-Minute Paper, 177, 193
One-Minute Thread, *See* activities
online authoring tools for rich media,
    61
online courses, *See also* distance
    education, online teaching
    humanizing, 47–49, 124
    setting up an organizational
    framework for, 38–41
    sites that aggregate, 56
    structure of
        page-level chunking, 41
        strategies for clarifying, 44–45
        topic-level chunking, 40
        transparent, 47
online education, *See* distance
    education, *See also* online
    teaching
Online Education Initiative (OEI),
    course design rubric by, 14, 32,
    105–106, 176, 179

Also in the Excellent Teacher series

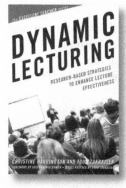

Dynamic Lecturing
Research-Based Strategies to Enhance Lecture Effectiveness

Christine Harrington and Todd Zakrajsek

Foreword by José Antonio Bowen

"Against the prevailing tide in higher education, Christine Harrington and Todd Zakrajsek argue that lectures, when prepared well and incorporated appropriately, are one of the most effective ways to enhance learning. The first part of their book is focused on making this case and on delineating the different forms a lecture can take. The second part of the book focuses on ways to make lectures more effective for learners. The third part provides tools and resources for preparing and evaluating lectures. These final two chapters give helpful rubrics, charts, and questionnaires that can easily be adapted for one's own lectures or for evaluating others' lectures. This book would be a useful addition to an individual professor's library and, most especially, to a center for teaching and learning library."—*Reflective Teaching (Wabash Center)*

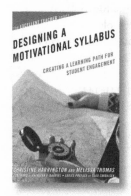

Designing a Motivational Syllabus
Creating a Learning Path for Student Engagement

Christine Harrington and Melissa Thomas

Foreword by Kathleen F. Gabriel

"Harrington and Thomas insightfully apply principles from the motivation research literature to demonstrate how course syllabi can be powerful tools for stimulating students' enthusiasm and motivation to actively engage in course activities. While the book is an invaluable resource for designing a syllabus that maps out a path for student success, it also provides information on course design, assessment, and teaching approaches. It is a must-read for all faculty who want to construct a syllabus that is sure to increase student engagement and learning!"—*Saundra McGuire, (Ret) Assistant Vice Chancellor & Professor of Chemistry, Director Emerita, Center for Academic Success; Louisiana State University*

22883 Quicksilver Drive
Sterling, VA 20166-2019 Subscribe to our e-mail alerts: www.Styluspub.com